Globalization and Popular Sovereignty

We are living in a time of global transformation in which new political arrangements are being formed and old political arrangements now seem insufficient. In this context, alternative forms of authority are gaining strength, putting pressure on the normative currency of democratic politics; the central categories of democratic theory need to be reexamined or they risk becoming coopted and diminished. Indeed, we must ask, how can the rule of the people be maintained in a transnational age?

This volume analyzes the impact of globalization on the concept of popular sovereignty and rethinks it for the transnational domain. It explores how popular sovereignty has historically determined the form of democratic citizenship and how democratic citizenship and legitimacy can be conceived in the transnational sphere in the absence of a global sovereign order. By inquiring into the new global context of popular sovereignty the book seeks to better understand the emerging structures of global governance and their potential for democratic legitimacy. Lupel argues that:

- The challenges of globalization necessitate a rethinking of the concept of popular sovereignty beyond the domain of the nation-state
- Such a rethinking reveals a tension between the particularism of democratic legitimacy and the universalism of cosmopolitan politics
- Thus critical attention to the constitutive processes of global governance must become an integral part of democratic theory in the context of globalization, and a principle of transnational popular sovereignty provides the best resources for this purpose.

This book will be of interest to students and scholars of globalization, democratic theory and international relations theory.

Adam Lupel is Editor at the International Peace Institute in New York. His work has appeared previously in *Constellations, Critical Sociology, Globalizations,* and *Polity.* Most recently he coedited "Peace Operations and Organized Crime," a special issue of *International Peacekeeping* (also published by Routledge).

Rethinking Globalizations

Edited by Barry Gills
University of Newcastle, UK

This series is designed to break new ground in the literature on globalization and its academic and popular understanding. Rather than perpetuating or simply reacting to the economic understanding of globalization, this series seeks to capture the term and broaden its meaning to encompass a wide range of issues and disciplines and convey a sense of alternative possibilities for the future.

1. Whither Globalization?
The Vortex of Knowledge and Globalization
James H. Mittelman

2. Globalization and Global History
Edited by Barry K. Gills and William R. Thompson

3. Rethinking Civilization
Communication and terror in the global village
Majid Tehranian

4. Globalization and Contestation
The New Great Counter-Movement
Ronaldo Munck

5. Global Activism
Ruth Reitan

6. Globalization, the City and Civil Society in Pacific Asia
Edited by Mike Douglass, K.C. Ho and Giok Ling Ooi

7. Challenging Euro-America's Politics of Identity
The Return of the Native
Jorge Luis Andrade Fernandes

8. The Global Politics of Globalization
"Empire" vs "Cosmopolis"
Edited by Barry K. Gills

9. The Globalization of Environmental Crisis
Edited by Jan Oosthoek and Barry K. Gills

10. Globalization as Evolutionary Process
Modeling Global Change
Edited by George Modelski, Tessaleno Devezas and William R. Thompson

11. The Political Economy of Global Security
War, Future Crises and Changes in Global Governance
Heikki Patomäki

12. Cultures of Globalization
Coherence, Hybridity, Contestation
Edited by Kevin Archer, M. Martin Bosman, M. Mark Amen and Ella Schmidt

13. Globalization and the Global Politics of Justice
Edited by Barry K. Gills

14. Global Economy Contested
Power and Conflict across the International Division of Labor
Edited by Marcus Taylor

15. Rethinking Insecurity, War and Violence
Beyond Savage Globalization?
Edited by Damian Grenfell and Paul James

16. Recognition and Redistribution
Beyond International Development
Edited by Heloise Weber and Mark T. Berger

17. The Social Economy
Working Alternatives in a Globalizing Era
Edited by Hasmet M. Uluorta

18. The Global Governance of Food
Edited by Sara R. Curran, April Linton, Abigail Cooke and Andrew Schrank

19. Global Poverty, Ethics and Human Rights
The Role of Multilateral Organisations
Edited by Desmond McNeill and Asunción Lera St. Clair

20. Globalization and Popular Sovereignty
Democracy's Transnational Dilemma
Adam Lupel

Globalization and Popular Sovereignty
Democracy's transnational dilemma

Adam Lupel

LONDON AND NEW YORK

First published 2009 by Routledge
2 Park Square, Milton Park, Abingdon, Oxon. OX14 4RN

Simultaneously published in the USA and Canada
by Routledge
711 Third Avenue, New York, NY 10017

Routledge is an imprint of the Taylor & Francis Group

First issued in paperback 2011

© 2009 Adam Lupel

Typeset in Times New Roman
by Taylor & Francis Books Ltd

All rights reserved. No part of this book may be reprinted or reproduced or utilised in any form or by any electronic, mechanical, or other means, now known or hereafter invented, including photocopying and recording, or in any information storage and retrieval system, without permission in writing from the publishers.

British Library Cataloguing in Publication Data
A catalogue record for this book is available from the British Library

Library of Congress Cataloging in Publication Data
Lupel, Adam.
Globalization and popular sovereignty: democracy's transnational dilemma/ Adam Lupel.
p. cm. – (Rethinking globilzations; 20)
Includes bibliographical references and index
1. Sovereignty. 2. Globalization–Political aspects. 3. Representative government and representation.
I. Title
JC327.L86 2009
320.1'5–dc22
2008053054

ISBN13: 978-0-415-77744-5 (hbk)
ISBN13: 978-0-415-67042-5 (pbk)
ISBN13: 978-0-203-87605-3 (ebk)

For Renata, my *certain rebirth*

Contents

	Preface	x
1	Introduction: Popular sovereignty and globalization	1
2	Trajectories of popular sovereignty	9
3	The liberal model of popular sovereignty: John Locke	23
4	The republican model of popular sovereignty: Jean-Jacques Rousseau	43
5	The deliberative model of popular sovereignty: Jürgen Habermas	67
6	Responses to globalization (I) Habermas's postnational constellation	94
7	Responses to globalization (II) David Held's cosmopolitan democracy and global civil society	111
8	Conclusion: Toward a transnational politics of popular sovereignty	128
	Notes	142
	Bibliography	170
	Index	181

Preface

The origins of this project lie in the energetic days of the late 1990s. At the turn of the millennium the idea of globalization was unavoidable, capturing the sense that the world was on the cusp of a revolutionary moment. The rapid expansion of the internet promised to make the barriers of distance meaningless, and a bullish consensus among key policy-makers on the merits of free trade and deregulated markets led to declarations that a unified global economy was at last in the offing – and the world would be all the better for it. On the now classic Cisco Systems ad, starry-eyed children from all over the world asked, "Are you ready?"

Well, turns out, not everyone was. By the end of 1999 protesters had paralyzed the World Trade Organization meeting in Seattle, sounding an altogether different bell about globalization, one that rang a tone of warning, not celebration. For the protesters, globalization represented gross inequality and the dominance of multinational corporations: unhindered capitalism run amuck. The "Battle of Seattle," and the capacity of civil society to pressure an international institution like the World Trade Organization, promised to breathe new life into progressive, anti-system movements at a time when many were declaring them dead and defeated at the end of "history," "ideology," and "utopia."

And then the attacks of September 11, 2001, shook everything and everyone, and terrorism became a dominant concern. For a time, debate shifted away from globalization toward discussions of empire, as the US and the Bush administration ramped up their military response to the attacks, from the mountains of Afghanistan to the sands and cities of Iraq, to Guantánamo Bay and "undisclosed locations" without number. For some, the vision of a world united under a comprehensive form of global governance and economies without borders entailed an only slightly veiled form of neo-imperialism.

Since then, with the extended fight in Iraq, the stubborn conflict in Afghanistan, and a weakening US economy, the debate has shifted further: from globalization through empire to multipolarity and the emergence of new powers, punctuated by the events of 08/08/08, as a lame duck US President watched the official "arrival" of China and Russia – watching, literally, as a spectator at the opening ceremony of the Beijing Olympics, and figuratively, as a hamstrung bystander, while Russia invaded Georgia, a US ally. At the same time, events have proven just how important globalization remains. An enormous financial crisis with roots in the US housing market rippled across the world in 2008, precipitating an international credit crunch that threatened to cause a global recession. As a result, Western leaders planned openly for a globally coordinated response.

Meanwhile, the debate over globalization has moved from one between global optimists and global skeptics to one over the character of globalization itself. The political struggle is not between globalists and antiglobalists, but among competing visions of alternative forms of globalization. That is, the key question is no longer, whether or not globalization, but, rather, which globalization?

In pursuing answers to this question I have long felt that globalization presents a fundamental dilemma: Democracy has become more widely accepted than ever, yet, confronted by global challenges, nationally based democratic institutions appear increasingly insufficient. As a result, new transnational structures are emerging, threatening to leave behind the traditional mechanisms of democratic accountability. Does this mean we need to choose between global governance and democratic governance? We must ask, how can the rule of the people be maintained in a transnational age? This is the most basic question that has driven this project from the beginning. And I argue that answering this question requires a fundamental rethinking of the categories of democratic theory, starting with the concept of popular sovereignty.

This book analyzes the impact of globalization on the concept of popular sovereignty and rethinks it for the transnational domain. It explores how popular sovereignty has historically determined the form of democratic citizenship and how democratic citizenship and legitimacy can be conceived in the transnational sphere. It argues that attempts to provide a democratic response to the challenges of globalization encounter a tension between the particularity of democratic legitimacy and the universalism of cosmopolitan politics. Learning to navigate that tension is the task of critical democratic theory today.

I will have much more to say about the specificities of my argument in the introduction that follows, but now is the time for some thanks. This project began as my Ph.D. dissertation at the New School for Social Research in New York. Thus thanks are very much due to my committee: Andrew Arato, Nancy Fraser, and Andreas Kalyvas. Andrew Arato's work on constitutionalism, Nancy Fraser's work on globalization, and Andreas Kalyvas's work on the constituent power all clearly left indelible marks on this project. In addition, Sankar Muthu had an early influence on the project, especially with respect to its treatment of the social contract tradition. Thanks are also due to William Scheuerman, James Bohman, and Max Pensky for their comments on conference papers and articles that became essential parts of the manuscript. Parts of Chapter 6 were originally published in *Polity* 36:2

(January 2004). And parts of Chapter 7 were originally published in *Globalizations* 2:1 (May 2005).

Much of the work done on this project occurred while I was Managing Editor of *Constellations: An International Journal of Critical and Democratic Theory*. The editors and staff provided an ideal intellectual environment to pursue these issues. Special thanks to Alfredo Perez, Brian Milstein, Erin O'Connor, Ernesto Verdeja, James Ingram, Kyra Holland, and Luca Follis, I completed the manuscript during my time as Editor at the International Peace Institute (IPI). Thanks are due to everyone at IPI for their collegiality and support, especially Terje Rød-Larsen, Adam Smith, Alison Gurin, David Witt, Ed Luck, Elizabeth Cousens, Ellie Hearne, Francesco Mancini, James Cockayne, Jeremy Dell, John Hirsch, Mashood Issaka and Warren Hoge.

Finally, I owe a profound debt of gratitude to my family: to my parents, Warren and Sally Lupel, without whom none of this would have been possible; their support has been instrumental and inspiring; and above all to Renata and Miranda, constant reminders of how beautiful life can be. "Oh brave new world that has such people in't."

A.L.
New York, October 2008

1 Introduction
Popular sovereignty and globalization

"It was the dilemma of an age when government could – some would say: must – be 'of the people' and 'for the people,' but could not in any operational sense be 'by the people.'"
    Eric Hobsbawm, *The Age of Extremes: A history of the World, 1914–1991* (Vintage, 1996).

And the idea that one part of a democratic society is capable of a reflexive intervention into society as a whole has, until now, been realized only in the context of nation-states. Today developments summarized under the term "globalization" have put this entire constellation into question.
    Jürgen Habermas, *The Postnational Constellation: Political Essays* (Polity/MIT Press, 2000)

We live in an age of extraordinary transformation, opportunity, and risk. On the one hand, in the wake of decolonization and democratization's "third wave" we now live at a time when it is widely accepted that the people ought to have political power. The question is not whether the people are the source of political legitimacy but rather what form of government can best express their authority. From the liberal democracies of Europe and North America, to the populist movements of South America, and the nominally communist states of East Asia, the people are named as the source of legitimate political power. Even the Grand Ayatollah Ali al-Sistani took to speaking the language of popular sovereignty in arguing for greater Shi'ite influence over the interim constitution in Iraq.[1]

However, on the other hand, we are also living at a time when "globalization" calls into question the democratization of power. To many, democracy today seems impractical and inefficient. According to a UNDP report on democracy in Latin America, democratization and market liberalization have occasioned only a negligible rise in per capita income. As a result, in 2004 only 43 percent of Latin Americans considered themselves "fully supportive of democracy." And over 54 percent indicated that they would "support an 'authoritarian' regime over a 'democratic' government" if it could provide the answer to their economic and social woes.[2] Yet in the context of globalization few governments if any seem to have such an answer.

2   *Globalization and Popular Sovereignty*

As the financial crisis of 2008 grew into the global economic recession of 2009, governments all over the world turned toward a more robust fiscal policy in response, even as the effects of each new banking crisis rippled across international markets, beyond their grasp, with no end in sight. Governing the integration of the world's economies and responding to the globalized threats of terrorism, financial collapse, or environmental devastation extend beyond the reach of even the most powerful states, challenging the capacity of national institutions – long associated with democratic governance – to respond to the exigencies of the times.

And at the same time, the institutions that may be in a position to respond to such demands are all but closed to the input of the vast majority of the world's population. The democratic deficit of regional organizations such as the European Union or international institutions like the World Bank or the World Trade Organization has been widely noted.[3] To the extent that national governments have a diminished capacity to determine their own fate, and that policy decisions of vital concern are being made by regional, international, or transnational bodies beyond the reach of democratic representation, "[p]olitical power is being reconfigured."[4]

While the expansion and acceleration of cultural, political, and economic activities cutting across national and regional borders is not inherently incompatible with democratic practice, such processes do present a significant challenge to the nation-state as democracy's dominant institutional form. As the nation-state experiences a diminished capacity for independent action and the stable reproduction of collective identities, its status as the preeminent site of democratic government comes into question. Of course, the state itself remains resilient: states continue to be the principal actors in international affairs; indeed, there is no sign of their imminent demise.

On the contrary, early twenty-first century developments suggest a strengthening of state-centered capitalism through sovereign wealth funds and state-owned business enterprises and energy companies, such as the China Investment Corporation or Gazprom, the Russian energy giant.[5] And the partial nationalization of banks in the US, UK, and continental Europe in the wake of the 2008 credit crisis suggests that liberal democracies are also heading in the direction of increased state intervention in the economy. However much of the early debate about globalization centered on its effects on *state* sovereignty, while, this book is concerned with its effect on *popular* sovereignty. How does globalization challenge the democratic rule of the people?

Globalization puts pressure on the traditional forms of democratic practice. In order for the processes of globalization to continue without resulting in a corresponding loss of the collective capacity to make legitimately binding decisions many of the central categories of democratic theory need to be reexamined. This book contributes to this project by rethinking the concept of *popular sovereignty*: What is the impact of globalization on the concept of popular sovereignty as a central category of democratic theory? How has popular sovereignty historically determined the form of democratic citizenship? And how can one conceive of democratic citizenship and legitimation in the transnational sphere in the absence of a global sovereign order? By inquiring into the new global context of popular sovereignty, I seek to better understand the emerging structures of global governance and their potential for democratic legitimation.

I argue (1) the challenges of globalization necessitate a rethinking of the concept of popular sovereignty beyond the domain of the nation-state; (2) that such a rethinking reveals a tension between the particularism of democratic legitimacy and the universalism of cosmopolitan politics – a tension I call *the problem of cosmopolitan founding*; therefore (3) critical attention to the constitutive processes of global governance must become an integral part of cosmopolitan theorizing and, I argue, the principle of *transnational* popular sovereignty provides the best resources for this purpose.

Definition of terms: nation-state, globalization, popular sovereignty

Since the 1990's a large literature surrounding the topic of "globalization" has called into question the capacity of the nation-state to fulfill its role as the primary container of democratic practice. The concept of popular sovereignty developed within the context of the consolidation of the modern state, and many of the current challenges to popular sovereignty, with respect to globalization, stem from the corresponding transformations in the nation-state form. Much of the debate concerning globalization has centered on the question of state sovereignty. State sovereignty refers to the status of a territorial administrative system that is not subject to any higher authority either from within its borders or from abroad. Popular sovereignty, more specifically, refers to a people's capacity for self-determination by constituting such an administrative system, or by assisting to steer or transform it once established.

Current processes of globalization undermine the democratic authority of nation-states, and inhibit their capacity to provide services, without providing for an alternative coherent administrative structure with avenues for popular participation or influence. In the absence of effective institutional structures for the purposes of collective self-determination in the transnational sphere, how can the people be understood to provide their consent to processes that originate beyond the scope of the nation-state? How could transnational power be thought of as accountable to the people?

The debate over state sovereignty in the late 1990s was often depicted to be between those who claimed the demise of the sovereign state was near and those who claimed that the sovereign state was as strong as ever.[6] The origins of contemporary notions of state sovereignty are generally traced back to the Peace of Westphalia of 1648. As understood since, state sovereignty is a reciprocal agreement among national governments giving independent states the right to pursue policy within their own territory free from external interference.[7] While the history of international relations suggests that the Westphalian ideal has never been fully realized, the principle of state sovereignty remains the cornerstone of international relations today.[8] Challenges to state sovereignty may be grouped under at least two headings: (1) challenges to state *authority* and (2) challenges to state *capacity*.

According to the Westphalian model, states are sovereign in that they recognize no superior authority beyond their own borders. However, in the context of globalization, this formulation has become increasingly harder to maintain. Beyond the borders of the nation-state, transnational institutional authorities have emerged increasingly salient. External authorities and powers have a growing influence over the internal affairs of states, to the extent that traditional understandings of state sovereignty are increasingly called into question by the growth of international systems of economic decision-making, law and security.[9] The proliferation of international decision-making bodies tends to extend the sphere of authority beyond the nation-state. The consolidation of the WTO, for example, signifies the appearance of an international institution that claims the authority to overrule national governments.

Whereas once international law was understood to lie between states, over the course of the twentieth century and into the twenty-first, it has aspired to rise above them. In recent years, international human rights law has represented a code to which individuals might appeal over and above the laws of their own country. Such appeals are often tragically ineffective; but when political forces favorably align, international human rights law may provide a powerful resource for the protection of individuals or minority groups from authoritarian or chauvinistic states.

In addition to challenging the nation-state's status as the final *authority* within its territorial boundaries, processes of globalization have put pressure on the state's *capacity* to provide effective government. This is particularly true regarding the relationship between international finance capital and domestic social welfare programs. As new information technology and neoliberal trade policy make far-flung markets more interconnected, national economies become increasingly interdependent. In the 1990s the acceleration of such connections, augmented by the decline of capital controls, and promoted by international institutions, contributed to an international atmosphere that put strong fiscal pressure on nation-states to practice extreme monetary austerity, avoiding capital flight, but diminishing state resources for the effective administration of services.[10] Furthermore, the proliferation and increased effectiveness of international terrorism and crime has made it increasingly difficult for states to provide their most basic service – the maintenance of order and security – without international cooperation. Such cooperation is often made contingent upon participation in international treaties that may restrict future state action.

In contemporary parlance, "globalization" often refers simply to the expansion of free trade and the growing integration of national economies the world over.[11] However, this represents a limited understanding of a multilayered phenomenon that encompasses political, cultural, military, and environmental factors as well as the specifically macroeconomic. The spread of AIDS and the threat of Avian Flu, international terrorism and drug trafficking, rising food prices, and the financial ripple effects of the subprime mortgage crisis, as well as global warming and the depletion of the world's rain forests are all elements in the globalization equation.

The term "globalization" summarizes a variety of processes that together increase the scale, speed, and effectiveness of social interactions across political, economic, cultural, and geographic borders.[12] The result is that activities and events in one region of the globe may have transcontinental effects, potentially reaching the far corners of the earth. This is a process with a long history that has accelerated in the last twenty years due in part to the end of the Cold War and the revolution in information technologies, including the rise of satellite communications and the world wide web. Yet the concept of globalization should not be understood as inherently implying the inevitable integration of the planet into a single world society. And globalization should not be understood as a simple zero-sum game for state sovereignty.[13] Often the challenge to the concept of state sovereignty comes not from restricting state power or overruling state authority, but by eliding the very distinction between the foreign and the domestic.

Globalization is not a force attacking the state from abroad, but rather a multilayered process that entails state participation. For example, domestic governments take part in the international harmonization of securities laws, and national central banks cooperate in the regulation of international financial markets. Thus government agencies can be simultaneously of the domestic order and part of the emerging system of global governance.[14] Globalization is an uneven process, benefiting some more than others and creating divisions as sure as it makes connections. Globalization is a fundamentally contested concept; its ultimate character and direction is a matter of dispute.

Anthony Giddens described the essential element of globalization as the intensification of *time–space distanciation*: the distance between linked localities is increasingly stretched, so that events and decisions in far-off places may have profound effects across the globe, and the actions of previously isolated locales may carry reverberations far beyond their own known horizons.[15] In this sense, globalization is defined by the stretching, intensifying, and accelerating of social, political, and economic connections across borders, regions, and between continents, creating networks of interaction that crisscross the planet.[16] And contrary to the analysis of some at the time, this process only continued apace in the wake of the attacks of September 11, 2001.[17] The phenomenon of 9/11 and its aftermath indeed did not announce the end of globalization but rather highlighted its reality as people around the globe watched the events unfold in real time, sharing a moment of history from half a world away. The attacks and the responses to them were part and parcel of globalization – not its antitheses.[18] Similarly, the apparent turn in the discourse toward a discussion of "empire" over "globalization," in the wake of the aggressive policies of the "Bush doctrine" and the war in Iraq, was not a displacement of considerations of globalization but rather a recognition of the complexity and political character of the phenomenon.[19]

David Held and Anthony McGrew have depicted debates over globalization as divided among three general positions: the hyperglobalist, the skeptic, and the transformationalist. From the *hyperglobalist* perspective, contemporary globalization heralds a new epoch of human history driven by the free movement of global capital and characterized by the inevitable rise of a world civilization that will result in the end of the nation-state. For the *skeptic*, however, this understanding of globalization is greatly exaggerated. Focusing on economic factors, the skeptic argues there is nothing unprecedented about current levels of national interdependence, and that nation-states continue to be and will remain the primary political and economic actors in international affairs for the foreseeable future. In contrast, the *transformationalist* sees the current epoch as one of unprecedented change. But, unlike the hyperglobalist, the transformationalist argues that the direction of this process remains uncertain and in contest.

The transformationalist disputes the claim that the sovereign state is a thing of the past, but also challenges the claim that states remain as strong as ever, arguing rather that globalization transforms the *relationship* between states, markets, sovereignty, and the transnational sphere. It challenges the governing and legitimation capacities of old political arrangements, domestically and internationally. And it thus adds new incentives to the search for political innovation.[20] This is the perspective from which I approach globalization in what follows: Globalization does not make popular sovereignty obsolete or impossible; rather, it *transforms* the constellation of its integral elements, and necessitates its reconsideration in altered contexts.

Popular sovereignty remains an integral principle of modern political thought and democratic practice. It signifies the general principle that "the people," broadly defined, play a central role in constituting steering and occasional transforming of the laws and institutions that govern their lives. And that the controlling reason for the foundation of law and government is the protection of individuals and groups from the abuses of power common to conditions of lawlessness. For some, this may necessitate active participation on the part of a rigorously defined citizenry; for others, it simply requires the establishment of a body of legal rights and procedures meant to set the boundaries of private and public autonomy. Either way, the normative principle of popular sovereignty signifies that the legitimacy of law and government rests upon the good of the people.

From the end of the Cold War through the first decade of the twenty-first century, appeals to democracy and the right to self-determination have enjoyed unprecedented normative purchase. But, ironically at the exact moment when the banner of democracy is at its historical height, the principal components of modern democratic practice are increasingly under pressure. The current historical context presents challenges to both sides of the term *popular sovereignty*. The notion of the *popular*, or the "people" as the democratic subject *par excellence*, and the concept of *sovereignty* as a necessary structure of final authority, are both undergoing radical transformation in the context of an incomplete process of globalization.

For example, on one side, new waves of immigration create increasingly diverse citizen-bodies, calling into question the very idea of a unified national "people;" at the same time, the transnational spread of a common materialist consumer culture elicits strong reactions from people sensing their national traditions under siege. And from the other side, state sovereignty remains the currency of international status but it is under increasing pressure: "International regimes" such as free trade agreements, military alliances, and transnational financial institutions, broaden the sphere of authority beyond the nation-state. The WTO claims the power to overrule national legislatures on issues of trade, while the "international community" reserves the right to intervene in domestic affairs when national governments are unwilling or unable to fulfill their primary "responsibility to protect" their own people from genocide, war crimes, ethnic cleansing, and crimes against humanity.[21] Such developments suggest the need to reevaluate the concept of *popular sovereignty* for the current era.

What's to come

To begin, *Chapter 2* will further introduce the project by exploring the origins of the concept of popular sovereignty, tracing its development along the path of two major trajectories. It will be important to understand how the concept of popular sovereignty has changed in the past in order to understand how it may continue to change in the future. The body of the book will follow by revisiting the classic liberal and republican models of popular sovereignty. *Chapter 3* on John Locke and *Chapter 4* on Jean-Jacques Rousseau will identify the core elements of the theory of popular sovereignty and articulate the problems posed by globalization for the concept as historically construed. The chapters will address how globalization affects the notion of the people and the concept of sovereignty with respect to the liberal and republican political traditions. *Chapter 5* will examine Jürgen Habermas's deliberative model as a direct response to the liberal and republican concepts of popular sovereignty, and it will examine the special challenges presented by globalization for the Habermasian theory of "popular sovereignty as procedure."[22]

Next, having analyzed the challenges posed by globalization to the liberal, republican and deliberative models of popular sovereignty, I will turn to a consideration of the possible responses. Specifically, I will examine two models of transnational politics that seek to respond to the challenges of globalization by resituating democratic practice beyond the confines of the nation-state: namely, *Chapter 6* will examine Habermas's theory of the "postnational constellation," and *Chapter 7*, David Held's theory of cosmopolitan democracy and the role of global civil society.[23]

Habermas's work on the "postnational constellation" represents an attempt to articulate a model of democratic practice capable of bridging the distance between globalizing present and cosmopolitan future. Habermas argues that democratic regional polities may offer the best practical stepping-stones to the democratic governance of global affairs, providing institutional structures capable for the first time of responding to the challenges of globalization. However, Habermas runs into trouble when attempting to conceptualize the constitutive authority of democratic global governance in such terms.

David Held claims that a commitment to democratic autonomy embedded in a cosmopolitan legal structure is a necessary condition of popular sovereignty in the context of globalization. If we choose democracy in the context of globalization, he suggests, we must choose some form of "cosmopolitan democracy." However, I argue that Held does not confront the significant problem of founding; that is, he does not articulate the process, identity or form of a constitutive authority capable of founding cosmopolitan democracy. He does not explain what it would mean to legitimately constitute such an order, given the fact many would not freely choose it. That is to say, the constitution of cosmopolitan democracy remains subject to a legitimation gap.

Given the emergence of de facto structures of transnational governance, the question *vis-à-vis* popular sovereignty becomes how to instill this process with democratic legitimacy. Globalization places increasing pressure on the state as the exclusive domain of democratic political practice. Thus the concept of popular sovereignty must be rethought beyond the scope of the nation-state if it is to retain any relevance as a principle of democratic authority. However, any theory of global governance consistent with the concept of popular sovereignty must take into account processes of collective self-determination at the local and national levels. Currently emerging structures of transnational governance exclude the constitutive authority of the people and thus lack the legitimacy and motivation to adequately address some of the most pressing issues of our times.

I argue that while both Habermas and Held attempt to provide cosmopolitan responses to the challenges of globalization they each encounter a tension between the particular contexts of democratic legitimacy and the universalism demanded of a global political culture capable of constituting a worldwide system of democratic governance. This tension represents a significant conceptual obstacle to the legitimate constitution of a cosmopolitan order that remains under-theorized. I call it *the problem of cosmopolitan founding*. Thus, I argue, such constitutive processes must become central to the project of cosmopolitan theorizing, and I conclude by offering a notion of transnational popular sovereignty as a conceptual tool for theorizing the politics of constituting democratic global governance – *transnational popular sovereignty*, the constitutive politics between globalizing present and cosmopolitan future.

I will explain.

2 Trajectories of popular sovereignty

To rethink the concept of popular sovereignty beyond the nation-state appears to entail a contradiction in terms. It is to make use of a concept beyond the context of its origin and application. Certainly, one can not simply transpose or expand the concept straight from nation-state to globe. The history of modern "sovereignty" as such is closely tied to the development and consolidation of the modern state. And any notion of popular sovereignty must in turn confront the questions inherent in this history. As F.H. Hinsley wrote in his now classic study, " ... the rise of state forms is a necessary condition of the notion of sovereignty, of the idea that there is a final and absolute political authority in the community. In a stateless society this idea is irrelevant."[1] Clearly this raises serious questions for any project considering the notion of sovereignty – popular or otherwise – beyond the nation-state. However, it will be argued, a globalizing society is not a stateless society, but rather a society where the relationship between *state* and *sovereignty* is transformed, where popular sovereignty is exercised within and between states.

To begin, it will be important to get some sense of the origins of the concept and how it has developed before going into detail on the liberal, republican, and deliberative models in subsequent chapters. It is necessary to understand the contingent character of the concept of popular sovereignty: to trace its past trajectories in order to understand how it may move beyond its current limits; to see how it has changed in the past, in order to understand how it is changing in the present, and how it may change further in the future. Arguments against the utility of the concept of popular sovereignty tend to equate its form with the unified command authority of an absolute monarch.[2] Understanding how the concept may be interpreted as following a trajectory away from this starting point will help to broaden the domain in which it may maintain its coherence. And it will help to prepare the way for unpacking its meaning in the context of globalization, a condition characterized by decentered structures of authority and the pluralization of political identities, a condition, as we will see, at odds with the concept of popular sovereignty as originally understood.

In discussing the concept of sovereignty a distinction may be made between domestic sovereignty and international legal sovereignty.[3] For now I will focus on the original, domestic meaning of the concept and how its development led to the notion of popular sovereignty. I will argue that in the conceptual history of the theory of popular sovereignty two broad movements may be discerned: first, from the concept of command authority to that of constitutive authority, and second, from a will-based model to a procedure-based model – from, what I call, *imperium* to *populus*, and from *voluntas* to *ratio*. And I will examine how the relationship between the origins of political power and legal validity transforms as a result of this movement.

In this context I understand political power in the Arendtian sense as the capacity for collective action, "the human ability, not just to act, but to act in concert."[4] For Arendt, power is a matter of immediate fact; it comes into being "when men join themselves together for the purpose of action," and it dissipates when they come apart.[5] It arises out of the grass roots of people acting together, and it remains necessarily connected to the continuity of public participation. Legal validity, on the other hand, has a less contingent quality; for Arendt, law must not be limited to the immediacy of power, but must be more durable. It must have validity for "the majorities and the minorities, the present and future generations."[6] It must hold currency across diverse perspectives, over time and defined space.

The history of popular sovereignty develops out of the complex relation between the effervescent power of the people – the grassroots pluralism of individuals acting together in political society – and the challenge of establishing secure, authoritative, legal structures that enable power to be exercised freely and productively. The course of this relationship takes on new significance as forms of governance come to transverse the globe and transnational legal structures emerge. As processes of globalization continue to develop we enter a new chapter of this complex history. In this context, understanding how governing structures may continue to be subject to popular political input becomes a question of utmost importance. I will suggest that the conceptual movement away from the command authority model opens up the possibility for considering the concept of popular sovereignty beyond the limits of the nation-state in the context of globalization.

From *imperium* to *populus*

While the notion of sovereignty could not become fully manifest until the centralization of administrative power in the territorial state, traces of the concept can be found much earlier. They may be uncovered in the idea of a supreme authority operative in the polity articulated in Aristotle's *Politics*,[7] or in the category of *imperium* found in the laws of Republican Rome.[8] But the concept's first steps toward maturity came not in Ancient Greece or in the Roman Republic but during the expansion of the great Empire. As the Roman Emperor consolidated his power over an increasingly extended territory, and maneuvered against the lingering elements of Republican authority, he and his allies asserted the case for imperial power through judicial doctrine. This resulted in the first legal tradition of a form of sovereignty stemming from the Roman notion of *imperium*, originally signifying supreme executive command, and only later taking on the meaning of centralized imperial authority.[9]

Nevertheless, the concept did not become fully formulated until the consolidation of the modern state form in the sixteenth century. Like in ancient Rome, the sixteenth century revision of the concept of sovereignty was a response to disorder and a product of the drive to legitimize the centralization of power.[10] While the word "sovereignty" had gained popularity by the beginning of the sixteenth century, it was not until 1576, in the midst of the French Wars of Religion, that Jean Bodin first provided a systematic theory of the concept, in part, as a reaction against the Huguenot claims for a right to resist the Crown. Based upon his study of a wide range of governing structures from ancient Persia, Greece, and Rome to modern Spain, England, and Turkey, Bodin argued the principle of sovereignty was found in all true states.[11] Established by contract between ruler and people, "sovereignty," he explained, "is the absolute and perpetual power of a commonwealth ... " or the "supreme and absolute power over citizens and subjects."[12]

Sovereignty according to Bodin could not be limited by a specific time period or term, nor could it be restricted by the bounds of positive law. And critical for Bodin, sovereignty could not be shared or divided; a mixed constitution for Bodin was a logical impossibility. The concept of sovereign power could avoid contradiction only if it remained indivisible, inalienable, and beyond regulation. The figure of the sovereign, for Bodin, embodied the source of all political power and legal authority.

Bodin did, however, distinguish between absolute sovereignty and mere absolutism. All modern theories of sovereignty contain a contractual element. They are characterized by a moment of agreement or compact between parties. The sovereign rose above the restrictions of positive law, yet remained within the confines of the historical political community, and thus he remained within its traditional boundaries of power and custom. In contrast to earlier notions of ruler contract, for Bodin the integration of ruler and ruled into a single political community was integral to the theory of sovereignty. And thus the sovereign could not claim to inhabit space beyond the long-time political customs of the commonwealth.[13] The Ruler was above the law but he remained a part of the political community. In order to avoid disorder, the people agreed to be subject to absolute sovereign authority. And this was the key: absolute power, it was claimed, was necessary for security, to maintain integration, to avoid chaos. This idea would of course find further elaboration in Hobbes's *Leviathan*, first appearing some seventy-five years later, and continues to resonate in today's arguments justifying the restriction of rights before the threat of terror.[14]

Bodin, however, was the first to elaborate coherently the principal elements of the modern theory of sovereignty: Within a defined territory there must be a supreme political authority, neither internally divided nor externally superseded. Sovereign power could not be shared between Church and State nor overruled by Pope or Emperor. The sovereign embodied both the seat of political power – of agency within the legal system – and the origin of the law itself. He was above the law, because no law could bind him, and no law could be binding without the force of his command.

These elements remain central to the theory of sovereignty as further developed by Hobbes. However, whereas for Bodin the sovereign contract was established between ruler and subjects, for Hobbes it was established between equal individuals. Whereas for Bodin the sovereign contracts with the people in the context of an extant and continuing political community, for Hobbes the constitution of the sovereign is itself the origin of the political community. According to Hobbes, sovereignty stems from a social contract between all men within a delimited territory. Subsequently, all modern theories of popular sovereignty developed in relation to this tradition; and thus the move from ruler contract in Bodin to social contract in Hobbes may be said to presage the move from monarchical command authority to popular constitutive authority, from *imperium* to *populus*.

As is well known, philosophers in the social contract tradition posit that, prior to the constitution of civil society, individuals lived in a state of nature characterized by radical freedom and basic equality. Over time, however, the radical individualism of this state inevitably resulted in an endless cycle of conflict. For Hobbes the state of nature was particularly brutal. It was characterized by a state of war between all men, rendering human life, in his famous words, "nasty, brutish and short."[15] It is toward the goal of rising out of a state of war that human beings enter into civil society. For Hobbes, civil society provides a common authority that may arbitrate the inevitable conflicts that arise between free and equal men. He argues, the only way to institute a common power with the authority to institute peace is for people "to conferre all their power and strength upon one Man, or upon one Assembly of men, that they may reduce all their Wills, by plurality of voices, unto one Will."[16]

Thus Hobbes argues that the rule of an absolute sovereign is the only legitimate form of government. Based upon human nature, it is the only form of government that can guarantee security. "The Peace of the Subjects," writes Hobbes, is "[t]he End of the institution of Sovereignty,"[17] and the form of sovereignty that Hobbes applies to accomplish this end is absolute. Out of the common interest of exiting the state of war individuals must come together to form a Commonwealth.[18]

The power of Hobbes's absolute sovereign is based in an original consensual arrangement, because the rights of the sovereign are founded in the covenant that each individual, out of the interest of security, makes with everyone else upon entering civil society. It is an agreement between equal individuals to form together a common polity and to be subject to its laws. Hobbes writes, "The Mutual transferring of right is what men call Contract."[19] Hobbes's theory is one of radical individualism; prior to the moment of contract no society can be said to exist, only a collection of individuals with a common interest in self-protection. In forming a common polity, according to Hobbes, they empower a sovereign to give body to the community as a whole. And it is only in the person of the sovereign that the people as a political community becomes manifest. The sovereign is thus absolute in that he cannot breach the covenant with the commonwealth because he *is* in fact the person of the commonwealth itself; and one cannot breach a covenant with oneself.[20] Thus for Hobbes, like Bodin, all political power and legal authority were unified in the figure of the absolute sovereign.

Yet, moving beyond Bodin, Hobbes's shift from ruler contract to social contract had broad implications. While it consolidated the theory of absolute sovereignty articulated by Bodin, it simultaneously helped to prepare the groundwork for the theory of popular sovereignty used to challenge monarchical absolutism in the late seventeenth and eighteenth centuries.[21] The idea that sovereignty depended upon an original moment of compact among free and equal persons placed the people at the center of the constitution of legitimate government. The result is that authority becomes less about the unity of command and more specifically about the origins of the "*author*ship" of law and government. This did not directly translate into a challenge to absolutism in Hobbes, because in the *Leviathan* the people as a community have no reality outside of the person of the sovereign. The moment of social contract for Hobbes simultaneously constitutes the structure of rule; the political unity of the people is meaningless outside the person of the Commonwealth, the Sovereign, the "Mortall God."[22] But some forty years later a strong challenge to absolutism would develop out of the social contract approach in the thought of John Locke who would provide a strong contrast to Hobbes on this point.

For Locke the social contract establishes the principle of political community independent of any structure of rule. Exiting the state of nature and constituting legitimate government thus entails a two-stage process. Hypothetically, individuals first come together, each agreeing upon the necessity to establish a political community. Once the principle of commonwealth has been established a majority of the community may then rightfully constitute a particular form of government. The implication of this two-stage process is that, whereas for Hobbes the dissolution of government necessarily means the return to chaos, for Locke it signifies the invocation of the constitutive authority of the people. For Hobbes, if a government fails or is successfully divided by competing authorities, the community is at immediate risk of descending back into the violent state of nature; without the person of the sovereign the commonwealth has no reality. In contrast, the dissolution of government for Locke does not at all signify the dissolution of political society.[23] Rather it invokes the constituent authority of the people to reconstitute legitimate government. Thus, while for Hobbes sovereignty is located in the ruling body of the state personifying the political community, for Locke it remains in the political community itself – the People. From Hobbes to Locke we have as such moved from absolute ruler sovereignty to liberal popular sovereignty, from *imperium* to *populus*.

While representing a big advance over the absolutist political philosophy of Hobbes, Locke's theory of popular sovereignty is certainly not democratic in the participatory or representative sense of the term. It is liberal and anti-absolutist, but it would be more than seventy years before the theory of popular sovereignty would take a more radically participatory democratic turn in the philosophy of Jean-Jacques Rousseau. For Locke, popular sovereignty is a principle of right: the people are sovereign in that government is instituted to protect their interests. Once established, the people do not participate directly in government, but its legitimacy remains contingent upon their tacit or express consent. Government is entrusted with legislative authority with the understanding that it exists to protect the rights of the people. If that trust is violated and government comes to abuse or endanger the rights of the people, government in effect forfeits the power entrusted to them, and the people thus have the right to resist their oppressors and establish a new government among them. Popular sovereignty for Locke thus rests on the people's right to institute government for the purpose of protecting their interests, and to resist the government that violates that purpose. It is defined by the constitutive authority of the people rather than the command authority of the ruler. In the terms of A.V. Dicey, the people for Locke are in effect the "political" sovereign but not the "legal" sovereign.[24] Legitimate government rests on the consent of the people, but the people have no specific role in the process of lawmaking.

Rousseau, however, articulated a more directly participatory model of popular sovereignty – more radically democratic than Locke but simultaneously closer to Hobbes and Bodin in its absolutism. According to Rousseau, in so far as the people are sovereign, legitimate legislation must involve their direct participation in the legislative process. Any law not ratified by the people assembled remains illegitimate. For Rousseau, sovereignty could not be delegated; thus true laws can be made only by the people themselves. Similar to Hobbes and Locke, Rousseau's concept of sovereignty develops out of a theory of the state of nature. As with all contract theory, for Rousseau the exit from the state of nature into civil society entails a consensual abandonment of natural independence in exchange for the acquisition of civil freedom. To achieve this, according to Rousseau, each individual must without reservation surrender himself and his natural rights to the whole of the community. In the state of nature man has the natural right to follow his own instincts and desires; in civil society he must surrender that private will to the common good. Upon entering civil society each individual agrees to surrender all private sovereign authority to the *general will* of the people as a whole. Sovereignty for Rousseau is thus "nothing but the exercise of the general will."²⁵ The people are sovereign in that they are the *authors* of the law. As a member of the people, each individual is both subject and sovereign. As an individual with private concerns one is subject to the general will of the people; and as a public citizen invested in the common good one is a member of the sovereign authority. The people are thus both the "political" and the "legal" sovereign.

According to Rousseau, in the interest of the common good the sovereign will is absolute. Individual citizens must give themselves over completely to the sovereignty of the general will: " ... the social pact gives the body politic absolute power over all its members. ... "²⁶ The citizens' obligations to the social body are obligations to a whole of which each one is a part. The mandate of the general will is as such self-directed, and therefore can never be legitimately resisted by the citizen. As Rousseau comments in his famous formulation: " ... whoever refuses to obey the general will shall be constrained to do so by the entire body: which means nothing other than that he shall be forced to be free."²⁷ Thus whereas Locke's understanding of popular sovereignty as a principle of right limits the Hobbesian understanding of absolute sovereignty, Rousseau in effect transfers the place of absolute sovereignty from the person of the monarch or governing body to the general will of the people as a whole.

In this sense, Rousseau's *Social Contract* represents a radicalization of popular sovereignty that simultaneously advances the movement from *imperium* to *populus* and yet reinvigorates political absolutism. From Bodin to Rousseau the *subject* of sovereignty changes from ruler to people, but its *form* remains the same: absolute. The general will in effect takes the place of the king and claims the seat of all power and legal authority. The possibility that popular sovereignty and absolutism could thus combine gives impetus to the second conceptual movement under consideration here: the trajectory from *voluntas* to *ratio*.

From *voluntas* to *ratio*

The model of popular sovereignty developed as a criticism of absolutism. It served as a critical tool to limit the power of government, to prevent despotism, and to ensure that no one be subject to arbitrary law. In the social contract tradition, civil society is established to erect a common structure of rules to which no one may claim superiority. The idea that men would establish absolute monarchy for such a purpose, according to Locke, entailed a fundamental contradiction. "[It] is to think that Men are so foolish that they take care to avoid what Mischiefs may be done to them by *Pole-Cats*, or *Foxes*, but are content, nay think it Safety, to be devoured by *Lions*."²⁸ The conjunction of popular sovereignty and absolutism in Rousseau raises the specter of the Lions' return to the *polis* – tyranny in the name of the people.

Concern to avoid this result has led to the historical rationalization of popular sovereignty. It has come to be understood by many that the will of the people must be mediated by the constitution of procedures that establish the preconditions for the safe and stable expression of the people's liberty. Popular sovereignty in large, complex, diverse settings necessitates the conceptual movement from *voluntus* to *ratio*, from absolutist will to rationalized procedure, from the belief that legal authority follows directly from the political will of the sovereign to the understanding that it must possess independent normative validity.

Rousseau, however, argued against a mediated form of popular sovereignty, in part, to protect against the possibility that the people could be usurped. He rejected the principle of representation, arguing that no one individual or group could possibly claim to speak for the people as a whole. According to Rousseau, the people had to participate directly in the legislative process in order to produce true law. However, the image of the whole people assembled to exercise the legislative power is more suited to the classical *polis* than to the modern state. In order for this type of non-representative popular sovereignty to function, states would have to be very small and relatively homogenous. It would seem that Rousseau's theory of popular sovereignty was immediately anachronistic.

Yet his thought had a profound influence upon the revolutionary times of the late eighteenth century. In making a strong and rhetorically powerful case that the normative implications of humanity's natural freedom was that government ought to be subordinated to the will of the people, Rousseau provided important inspiration at a time of popular revolt, especially in France. Nevertheless, his suspicion of representation also carried through to many of the generation of 1789; and in the context of a large country where direct democracy was impossible, this proved calamitous. A belief in both the absolute authority of the general will and the inherent impossibility of its representation easily became a source of tension and volatility in France, perpetually subjecting legislators to the claim that they had betrayed the will of the people and were thus illegitimate, challenging the unity of sovereignty and risking the descent into chaos.[29]

While in many respects inspiring the revolution, the Rousseauian concept of popular sovereignty would thus come back to haunt French republicanism. The history surrounding the role played by the Abbé Sieyés in the Revolution is emblematic of this problem and illustrates the move toward a more rationalized form of popular sovereignty. As one of the most influential architects of the French Revolution, Emmanuel-Joseph Sieyés adapted Rousseau's model of popular sovereignty, maintaining its popular absolutism but modifying it with a principle of representation. According to Sieyés, as soon as a group of isolated individuals in the state of nature wish to unite, as soon as they recognize their *common interest* in coming together, they constitute a nation.[30] Sieyés remained consistent with Rousseau in that he argued only such a people or nation could rightfully constitute government. According to Sieyés, the nation as the constituent power had the right to institute government anew without recourse to prior positive law or procedure.[31] The national will, for Sieyés, like the general will for Rousseau, was "the source of all legality."[32] And as such it could not be limited by law, "a nation is independent of any procedures; and no matter how it exercises its will, the mere fact of its doing so puts an end to positive law, because it is the source and supreme master of positive law."[33] And as such, in the constitution of law, according to Sieyés, the sovereignty of the nation is absolute. All political power and legal authority found their common origin in the nation.

However, Sieyés broke with Rousseau on the important issue of representation: "Since a large nation cannot physically assemble when extraordinary circumstances make this necessary, it must entrust extraordinary representatives with the necessary powers on such occasions."[34] Thus, whereas for Rousseau the general will of the people could not be expressed through representatives, for Sieyés representation formed a crucial part of the functioning of the constituent power in a large nation. In fact, during the constitutional debates of 1789, Sieyés argued that in a nation as populous as France the people could "speak or act only through its representatives."[35] Thus the constituent assembly assumed the absolute authority of the general will by claiming to represent the voice of the people, in so far as the people themselves could not speak. Sieyés thus argued that the representatives in the constituent National Assembly "are a substitute for the whole nation in the course of framing its constitution. They are as independent as the nation would be in that period."[36] That is to say, they were to occupy what Carl Schmitt would call the position of "sovereign or revolutionary dictatorship." According to Sieyés the representatives of the National Assembly wielded total authority to reconstitute the government of France without any connection to the previously constituted powers of the old regime. Unlike the Roman "commissarial dictatorship" – which held emergency powers but not legislative authority – the sovereign dictatorship holds total authority to establish a new constitution; it holds total political power and total legislative authority.[37]

Yet many at the time of the French Revolution remained highly suspicious of any elected institution's capacity to expressly represent the general will of the people. Rousseau's insistence on the unrepresentable character of the general will remained a truism to many in the National Assembly even after the dramatic events of June 1789.[38] And Sieyés was unable to completely convince them otherwise. The result was a tension-ridden constitution that instituted "competing claims to express the general will in the assembly, the king, and the people."[39] While the National Assembly reiterated the absolute sovereignty of the nation in its complete break with the *ancien régime*, the constitution of 1791 remained ultimately ambiguous about the location of effective national sovereignty, sowing the seeds of its own downfall.[40]

If sovereignty were to be directly expressed in the Assembly, stability would depend upon its own self-limitation. And this could not be reasonably expected, given the assembly would have a strong power interest in maintaining its position as sovereign dictator, producing an obvious tendency toward permanent revolution. However, if the king were to possess the power to limit the assembly the tendency would be the opposite, toward counter-revolution, augmenting the already heightened tensions in the nation. The alternative would be that the true sovereignty of the nation could not be represented and thus remained with the people at large. In the absence of legal procedures to channel the popular will, this meant the system of national sovereignty would have to rely upon the voice of the unorganized people in the streets, or the "corrective of popular insurrection"[41] – not a stable equation by any math.

In adopting a new constitution the National Assembly rejected any notion of reforming the old order. They claimed the authority to institute government *de novo* without any necessary connection to the *ancien régime* as an act of sovereign national will.[42] The *constituent power* of the Nation reserved total supremacy over the *constituted powers* of the state. And this formula necessarily would have to hold true in the new regime as well. While the power to make law in the new constitution was centered in a representative assembly, true sovereignty, it was believed by many, could not be represented; it remained in the general will of the Nation. As a result it was seen as necessary both to protect national sovereignty from the encroachment of the constituted powers of the state and to protect the constitution itself from a fickle public prone to frequent mobilization. Thus the constitution of 1791 permitted the king to suspend legislation for years at a time *in the name of the nation*, and it required long delays in the process of constitutional revision.[43]

As it became increasingly clear that this arrangement was a recipe for stagnation and counterrevolutionary obstruction, popular calls for action against the king, and for constitutional change in the name of the national will, escalated, culminating in the overthrow of the constitutional monarchy by August 1792. In the wake of this revolt, the French government became "radically provisional."[44] Constitutional limits on the people's ability to change government at will were deemed mere impediments to the true expression of national sovereignty, and in the subsequent chaos Terror in the name of revolution and "public safety" followed naturally.

By combining Sieyés's commitment to absolute national sovereignty with a Rousseauian suspicion of representation the National Assembly had made constitutional government nearly impossible, creating an environment of ungovernability, coupled with a radical democratic energy easily coopted by the forceful. By placing the nation in a state of nature with respect to prior institutions of government, and arguing that all manifestations of political power and law must originate in the national will, Sieyés based the revolution on a continually shifting ground and helped to set in motion a course of events that once begun had little chance of being brought under control.[45]

Sieyés spent much of the time after 1789 trying to restrain what he had helped to unleash. Ironically, he was, after all, a constitutionalist.[46] In the debates of 1794, following the Terror and the execution of Robespierre, Sieyés argued for the importance of limited government and the protection of individual liberty.[47] Sieyés, the architect of National Sovereignty, thus came to understand what became clear to many in the wake of the French Revolution. "As the principle of popular sovereignty has come to prevail against principles justifying ruler absolutism ... " according to F.H. Hinsley, "it has everywhere been found necessary, in time, to guard against its justification of popular tyranny and its culmination in anarchy by channeling it through the forms of the constitutional state."[48] Immanuel Kant, for example, followed Rousseau in arguing that "only the general united will of the people can be legislative."[49] But, he argued, this was possible only in the context of a state or a "civil condition" which provides the constitutional structure in which human freedom is possible, in which authority may be established to back up right.[50]

In fact, even before the experience of the French Revolution, the American Federalists understood this. As James Madison was aware, "it is impossible for the people spontaneously and universally to move toward their object."[51] In order for the people to serve as sovereign they must be mediated by a system of laws, including those that structure processes of representation. The constitution written in Philadelphia in 1787 was produced not by a sovereign assembly embodying the absolute power of the people, but rather by thirty-nine "patriots" who would later submit their work for ratification to legally constituted conventions in each of the thirteen states.[52] The new order would emerge out of a process of previously constituted self-governing bodies coming together to form "a more perfect union," and not out of a legal vacuum or "state of nature" as was supposed in Revolutionary France.

When the Federalists defended the idea that the people were the source of all legitimate power, they were not referring to the mobs, committees, and ad-hoc assemblies of the early 1770s. The *sovereign* people were "the organized multitude whose power was exerted in accordance with laws and limited by them."[53] For the American Federalists, while the people remained the sovereign source of all power, the source of law, after the founding, would become the Constitution itself.[54] In a large, complex society the practice of legitimate popular sovereignty depends upon the institution and protection of norm-guided legal procedures to discern the voice of the people from the chants of the crowd and the calls of the demagogue.

In large, complex societies, the people whose consent forms the basis of democratic legitimacy do not form a coherent whole with a single unmediated identifiable will. Theories of popular sovereignty that suggest otherwise open the door to the tyrannical appropriation of the people's mantle. The rise of the Terror is the paradigmatic example of this risk. In modern complex societies the pure will of the people is never self-evident; thus any claim to manifest it may be subject to contest. Modern theories of popular sovereignty must articulate potential mechanisms by which the legitimacy of competing democratic claims can be determined. In doing so they move away from the idea of an unmediated absolutist popular will toward a theory of norm-guided procedures, from pure *voluntas* to democratic *ratio*, often in the form of constitutionalism. While the locus of power may remain with the people, the origin of legal validity comes to rest with principles governing procedures that enable the capacity for collective self-government.

From national to transnational?

The theory of popular sovereignty develops out of a conception of unified command authority and may be interpreted as moving toward a more procedural, norm-guided model. In the absolutist notion of sovereignty the origins of political power and legal validity are unified. For Hobbes political power is possible only because the sovereign embodies the commonwealth. The will of the sovereign equals the will of the commonwealth, and possesses the authority of law. Outside of the body of the sovereign, the people as a whole have no reality; thus any challenge to the sovereign's authority risks the dissolution of the state, and may be legitimately repressed. The dangers inherent to this unlimited form of power and authority remain even when its agent shifts from monarch to people. In fact, as the French Terror would suggest, they may be even greater, lacking the temporary stability of a sound monarchy.

In the move from absolute *voluntas* to democratic *ratio* the sources of political power and legal validity separate, coming together only later in the practice of democratic politics. That is, the proceduralized notion of popular sovereignty seeks to keep the democratic content of the concept but to shed its absolutist form. It understands that legitimate political power can originate only in the collective action of the people, but holds that the normativity of legal authority must have alternative origins. There can be no immediate instantiation of the will of the people. To embody the power of popular sovereignty in a single subject is to corrupt it. This in many respects was the insight of the American separation of powers.

As we will see in Chapter 5, the procedural model of popular sovereignty has found its most recent and sophisticated expression in Jürgen Habermas's discourse theory of democracy. For Habermas, popular sovereignty no longer signifies the body of the people standing in for the deposed monarch. Rather it invokes the "formal conditions for the legal institutionalization of those discursive processes ... in which the sovereignty of the people assumes a binding character."[55] It identifies the general principles that structure the procedures by which the people can freely formulate opinions and express their will and it guides the institutionalization of the conditions in which democratic will-formation is made possible.

This conceptual development toward a norm-guided model of popular sovereignty does not represent a universal process or an inevitable history of progress. The voluntaristic model of popular sovereignty remained influential throughout the twentieth century, and continues so today. Carl Schmitt, for one, following Sieyés, argued that procedural norms or laws could never bind the unitary and indivisible constituent power of the people; for Schmitt, as soon as the popular political will was expressed it became logically superior to any formally constituted power.[56] And the history of populism in Latin America, for example, demonstrates the enduring presence of these ideas today: Hugo Chavez, for one, continues in the spirit of the assassinated Colombian leader Jorge Eliécer Gaitán, who famously once said, "No soy un hombre. Soy un pueblo,"[57] I am not a man. I am a people.

However, in what follows, it will become clear that popular sovereignty can no longer be understood through a simple voluntaristic model of command and obedience.[58] Such a vision depends too strongly on the structure of a solitary subject dictating a coercive social order. Nor can it be understood through the model of a great nation moving forward with a single voice. Given the pluralism of modern societies such an idea leaves open the door to almost certain abuse. I will argue that such conceptual incongruities become all the more apparent under conditions of globalization, characterized by the decentering of authority and the pluralization of political identities. This is a condition clearly at odds with the theory of popular sovereignty as originally understood.

Globalization challenges both sides of the concept of popular sovereignty. It challenges the very notion of sovereignty within a single nation-state, and it challenges the idea of the people as a coherent category capable of guiding national political practice. Can procedural models of popular sovereignty respond to these challenges? In Habermas's procedural model of deliberative democracy, the effectiveness of popular sovereignty is defined by the extent, quality, and accessibility of networks of communication where political opinions are debated and political wills are formed.[59] Given modern communication technology and mass media, Habermas argues, there are no insurmountable structural barriers to conceiving the functioning of such networks in a post-nation-state territory such as the European Union. Thus Habermas's procedural model may be able to adapt to expanded political contexts and in this sense it may have more resources to respond to the challenges of globalization than the traditional liberal and republican models.

However, as states and economies become increasingly interdependent more political decisions are made that have transnational and transcontinental effects, raising questions concerning the definition of relevant political constituencies. De facto structures of global governance come to transcend the procedural mechanisms capable of channeling popular political power on the national or even regional level, creating bodies of law, economic arrangements, and structures of regulation that have little or no receptivity to popular political input. This presents challenges for procedural models of popular sovereignty, as well as the more traditional liberal and republican models.

In such a context, can the concept of popular sovereignty remain operative as a principle of normative critique and political organization? If it cannot, can the governing structures of law and politics maintain their claims to legitimacy? Or, are we standing on the cusp of a third major trajectory in the history of popular sovereignty, *from national to transnational?*

In the interest of pursuing these questions, I set out in Chapters 3–5 to examine in detail three distinct models of popular sovereignty – the liberal, the republican, and the deliberative – in order to articulate the integral elements of a general theory of the concept, and to address how each model is specifically challenged by processes of globalization. Chapters 6–7 will then address possible responses to these challenges, in the interest of understanding how a form of democratic practice may take part in the constitution and legitimation of emerging forms of global governance.

3 The liberal model of popular sovereignty
John Locke

John Locke lived and wrote during a period of extraordinary conflict and transformation. Historians characterize the sixteenth and seventeenth centuries as the age of scientific revolution, mercantilism, and the consolidation of the modern state. In the arts it was the "golden age of drama," and the sensuous era of the Baroque. But it was also a destitute time of "famine, plague, poverty, slavery and belief in witchcraft." And perhaps above all it was a time of war: Between 1559 and 1715 Europe saw less than thirty years of international peace, and more than 100 years in which each of the region's major powers were simultaneously engaged in armed conflict.[1] For Locke, the religious and civil wars of the time were primarily political battles. Based in religious difference, to be sure, but ultimately, the wars were struggles over who should have political power. This was the "great Question" for Locke that in "all Ages" had posed a challenge to peace: "Not whether there be Power in the World, nor whence it came, but who should have it."[2] Locke's radical answer to this age-old question was a theory of popular sovereignty: he argued that each individual has a natural right to political power.

Until now, the pursuit of this right has been only approximately realizable within the confines of the nation-state. Over the next three chapters I will examine how the concept of popular sovereignty comes under increasing stress as globalization broadens the domains of law, politics, and governance beyond the nation-state's borders. Globalization, I argue, continues to develop in the post-9/11 world, even though many had expected that 9/11 and the War on Terror would precipitate a decline in global integration as a result of stricter border controls and fearful foreign investors. Yet the A.T. Kearney/ Foreign Policy Globalization Index shows a more highly integrated world at the end of 2002 than ever before.[3] And a sense of worldwide interconnection was undeniably on display on February 15, 2003, when up to 30 million people in more than 100 nations gathered simultaneously to protest the imminent attack on Iraq.[4] By 2009, *Foreign Policy* magazine concluded, despite financial collapse, gross inequality and serious limitations, globalization is "here to stay."[5]

Like the seventeenth century, the current age of globalization is similarly a time of extraordinary change and conflict when the question of political power must once again shift to the center of inquiry. We must ask, What happens to the concept of popular sovereignty in this reconfigured political context? How does its meaning transform? How may its practice develop?

In its most basic sense, the principle of popular sovereignty has always signified that the legitimacy of law and government rests upon public consent. Can this connection be maintained in a globalizing world? Every modern theory of sovereignty incorporates a theoretical moment of contract; the consent of the people has a role to play, albeit a limited one, even in the absolutist model of Thomas Hobbes. Yet it was not until John Locke's writings of the late seventeenth century that a fully elaborated social contract theory incorporated a notion of the people as the rightful bearers of sovereign power. In what follows, a consideration of Locke's thought will allow us to analyze some of the basic elements of the theory of popular sovereignty as it developed in the late seventeenth century, and to consider the challenges posed to it by processes of globalization.

Writing on the essential political issues of his time and directly advising major political players, Locke had a considerable impact on practical politics and the development of liberalism in England and America.[6] Theorizing individual rights, limited government, and private property, Locke's political thought is representative of the liberal model of popular sovereignty.[7] In order to articulate the basic elements of the theory of popular sovereignty and to examine how processes of globalization present a challenge to it, the concept needs to be broken down into its component parts. The next section will examine the status of "sovereignty" in Locke's account, and the section after it will examine the status of the "popular," or the notion of the people. Finally, the last section will examine the challenges posed by the processes of globalization to the Lockean model of popular sovereignty.

Lockean sovereignty

For Locke, as for Bodin or Hobbes, the principle of sovereignty pertains to the notion of final or supreme authority. The people for Locke are sovereign in three respects: (1) they are the constitutive authority behind the creation of government; (2) their consent determines the legitimacy of legal and political power within government; and (3) they have the authority to dissolve or alter government when it violates the ends for which it was constituted. These dimensions correspond to the sovereignty of the people *prior to*, *within*, and *independent of* government. I will argue that, while for Locke the sovereignty of the people is strong prior to and independent of government, it is weak within it.[8]

Sovereignty as constitutive authority

As all social contract theorists, Locke begins his discussion of the foundation of civil society with reflections on *the state of nature*. The state of nature does not describe an actual moment in human history prior to civil society, but rather it serves the analytic function of providing a universal background against which to understand the purposes and limits of government. It does not describe what is necessarily prior in time to civil society but rather prior in the chain of reasoning.[9] As such, twentieth-century social contract-inspired theories focus on hypothetical, not historical, states of nature: as in the case of Rawls's "original position," or Habermas's "ideal speech situation."[10] Unlike Hobbes, Locke did not consider the state of nature to be a lawless, moral vacuum. Rather he saw it as governed by *the Law of Nature*, which could be known by men through the power of reason. The law maintains, simply, that "being all equal and independent, no one ought to harm another in his Life, Health, Liberty, or Possessions."[11]

Whereas, for Hobbes, conflict and violence are inherent to the absence of civil society, Locke distinguished between the state of nature and the state of war. The freedom of the natural state is not one of absolute license. For Locke, reason demands certain rules are followed even in the absence of civil society. As long as people live by those rules, peace may reign. However, according to Locke, concomitant with the law of nature, human beings are endowed with two "natural powers." And, in the absence of a common authority to order society, these powers tend to provide sources of tension. First, everyone has the right to do whatever is deemed necessary for self-preservation; and second, everyone has the right to judge and punish those who violate the Law of Nature. By definition, there is no common authority to regulate people's actions in the state of nature, and, as a result, the free employment of the two natural powers tends toward a state of instability, insecurity and general violence, transforming the state of nature into a state of war. Conflict over scarce resources becomes inevitable when everyone is free to pursue self-interest without limit. And the probability of perpetual cycles of vengeance and retribution runs high when every individual is an independent judge and executor of the law.

Thus, for the sake of security, individuals must agree to form a community with common laws. In so doing each individual agrees to give up his two "natural powers" to the community as a whole. He surrenders both the right to use whatever means necessary to protect "life, liberty and estate," and the right to judge and punish those who violate natural law. These rights are first surrendered to the community, constituting political society based upon mutual consent, and then entrusted to a government based upon a principle of majority rule. Thus, as noted in Chapter 2, the constitution of government entails a two-stage process for Locke. First, isolated individuals in the state of nature come together, agreeing upon the need to form a society governed by common laws. And, second, after political-society-in-general is formed, the constitution of government-in-particular is established by majority rule. That is to say, first the people as a political community is formed, and then the people constitute their government.

For Locke a legitimate government may be democratic, oligarchic, monarchical or any mixture of the three; but, regardless of its form, the people remain the commonwealth's sovereign in that they are the *constitutive authority* behind the institution of government, and political legitimacy remains based upon their consent.[12] Government is made by the people to protect their property and secure their liberty. Thus if government were to turn against the interests of the people, it would betray its very *raison d'être*. For the pious Locke, in the same way that men are beholden to God, because God makes men, government is beholden to the people, because the people make government.[13] The people are sovereign in that they are the constituent authority behind the creation of government.

However, it is important to note that, unlike the constituent power of Sieyés or Schmitt, in the Lockean model the people do not found government from a position of groundlessness. Stemming from natural law, *right* limits even the constituent power of the sovereign people. The end of government is the protection of rights. Property – *individual* rights – is prior to both society and government, and its protection is the purpose for which both are established.[14] And while the "sole source of legitimate authority ... is the rational consent of individuals[,] [w]hat they can rationally consent to is limited by their own rights."[15]

Consent, right, and legitimacy

For Locke, popular sovereignty is thus a principle of right. The people are sovereign in that they institute government to protect their own interests, and to secure the freedom owed to them by the principles of natural right. Yet once government is established the sovereignty of the people is not expressed directly; for Locke, there is no positive right to political participation: rather, the people must trust the government to act in their interest. Thus we must ask: If sovereignty remains defined by the principle of final or supreme authority, how can the people be sovereign after the moment of founding if they do not have a right to participation? If government is somehow subject to the will of its maker, how is government subject to the people if the people do not directly influence the practice of governing? And, concomitantly, what obligates the people to obey the law if they are not involved in its legislation?

While the people may not participate in the legislation or execution of the law in the Lockean model, their consent does remain the key to its legitimacy. Locke's theory of consent in this sense provides the basis for understanding how government remains subject to the will of the people and how free and equal individuals may become rightfully obligated to obey positive law.[16] There are at least three stages of consent for Locke: the first based on consensus, the second based on majority will, and the third based on practice. The original foundation of civil society must be based on consensus; the constitution of government, however, may come about by majority will; and the legitimacy of an established legal order may be determined by the tacit consent implied by people living under its rules and partaking of its benefits.

According to Locke, given that all are originally free and equal, the foundation of civil society must be based upon a consensual agreement to leave the state of nature and join together to form a commonwealth: " ... no one can be put out of this Estate, and subjected to the Political Power of another, without his own Consent."[17] Every individual must agree to exit the state of nature and abandon his former independence. The decision to form a political community must be made by consensus. However, once political society is formed, subsequent decisions no longer require consensus because every individual has already agreed to submit to the majority will for the purpose of establishing a common authority to resolve conflict, protect property, and punish transgression. Thus, for Locke, the will of the majority is sufficient to establish the particular form of government for any single community.[18]

However, the necessity of consensus at the foundation of civil society, and the subsequent legitimacy of majority decision-making for the constitution of government, tell us little about sovereignty and political obligation after the original constitution of government. After government is established, how do the people communicate consent for any particular political order? Locke answers this question in part through the principle of *tacit consent*: " ... every Man, that hath any Possession, or Enjoyment, or any part of the Dominions of any Government, doth thereby give his *tacit Consent*, and is as far forth obliged to Obedience to the Laws of that Government, during such Enjoyment, as any one under it."[19] Even if consent is not directly expressed, it may be implied by an individual's willingness to partake in the benefits of society. According to this view, the possession and use of property protected by the law indicate a willingness to join civil society and thus obligate the owner to obey the law.

Tacit consent explains how naturally free and equal individuals can indirectly take part in the original moment of contract, consenting to the surrender of natural liberty for civil liberty. Locke, however, does specify that full membership in political society requires a fully expressed declaration of consent: tacit consent is insufficient.[20] A traveler passing through a foreign country making use of public land or roads tacitly consents to submit to the law of the land, not to change his citizenship.

Locke's theory of consent – tacit or otherwise – explains how political power may establish legitimate jurisdiction over individuals understood to be naturally free and equal. But how does that political power remain subject to the sovereignty of the people? According to Locke, whether the majority places it into the hands of a single individual, or a select few, or the entire community, the legislative power represents the highest authority in any single government. Yet the people have no positive right to participate directly in lawmaking; they surrender their natural powers to execute the law of nature to the community, which then entrusts it to the government, however structured. Nevertheless, according to Locke, to be legitimate the legislative power must remain loyal to the original ends of civil society; the legislative power may design laws "for no other end ultimately but *the good of the People.*"[21] And in this limited sense the legitimacy of the legislative power remains dependent upon the people.

Following A.V. Dicey, we can say that, within the Lockean commonwealth, the people remain the *political* sovereign, even when they are not the *legal* sovereign. According to Dicey, that body is legally sovereign that has "the power of lawmaking unrestricted by any legal limit." But "[t]hat body is 'politically' sovereign or supreme in a state the will of which is ultimately obeyed ... "[22] And these two forms of sovereignty are not by necessity contained within the same body. While the people do not directly participate in legislative affairs, they remain politically fundamental. The people do not make law, but government is established to protect their interests and consequently the legislative must follow their will in the broadest possible sense.

The question of how any particular government may determine the precise content of the will of the people, outside its direct articulation, however, Locke leaves unanswered. Obviously, in the liberal democratic tradition, this is in part the function of elections. But, for Locke's liberal-but-not-yet-democratic theory of popular sovereignty, the people must simply trust that the government will act in their interest and protect their fundamental rights. In the absence of strong mechanisms for the popular check on legislative and executive power, this is a rather weak form of political sovereignty, perhaps even merely symbolic, given the capacity of governments to manipulate perceptions concerning the public good.

However, in the Lockean model there is another way in which the people are politically sovereign in a stronger sense. The political sovereignty of the people within the commonwealth rests upon a normative claim of legitimacy: no government that goes against the interest of the people can rightfully claim to be legitimate. In the absence of popular participation the legitimacy of the law depends upon its conformity with right. The people set up government to secure their natural rights to "life, liberty, and estate." And if the government violates those rights the people are justified in opposing it.

Properly speaking, the legislative body is the highest power of government. Yet *sovereignty*, the final and supreme authority, remains with the people because they are the only power that may rightfully constitute, dissolve, or change the legislative power. While the legislative is the highest power in any particular government, " ... there remains still in the People a Supream Power to remove or alter the Legislative, when they find the Legislative act contrary to the trust reposed in them."[23] Famously, according to Locke, if government comes to wield arbitrary power, betraying the ends for which it was constituted, the people retain the right to rebel and institute a new order.[24]

As the constituent power, the people remain a sovereign force in the strong sense outside the parameters of the government, but not within it. In fact, as James Tully argues, " ... there is no sovereign in Locke's theory of government: both governed and governors are mutually subject to the law."[25] But when the governors go against that law, betraying the trust bestowed in them, their authority dissolves and sovereign power rightfully returns to the people.

The right to revolution

According to the earlier models of sovereignty represented by Bodin and Hobbes, the people agree to subject themselves completely to the sovereign power of the governing authority in the interests of security. The people *alienate* "all their power and strength upon one Man, or upon one Assembly of men," transferring even the right to make judgments concerning the legitimacy of their government.[26] In such case, the people give up any right to resist the sovereign, no matter how apparently oppressive. For, it is claimed, to assert the right to judge the sovereign would threaten the unity of civil society, and risk the descent into civil war, an end to be avoided at all costs.

In contrast to what may be called the *alienation* model, Locke articulates a model of *trust*. In this model the people "contract to conditionally entrust political power" to a monarch or other governing authorities. They consign the "two natural powers" – which had been freely exercised by individuals in the state of nature – to government on the condition it protects their "life, liberty and estate." And if an abusive government violates this trust the contract thereby dissolves and all political power rightfully returns to the people.[27]

Locke argues the complete alienation of all political power contradicts the original purpose of constituting political society. Giving an individual or group of individuals absolute control over all legislative and executive functions, and making resistance to tyranny illegitimate, endangers rather than secures liberty. Men enter into civil society in order to establish common laws between them; yet to absolutely transfer all political and legal power into a single body would place that body above the law and beyond reproach by anyone other than God. It would excise the possibility of standing rules to settle disputes between government and people. For Locke, by definition, such an arrangement would not satisfy the conditions for true political society: "For where-ever any two Men are, who have no standing Rule, and common Judge to Appeal to on Earth for the determination of Controversies of Right betwixt them, there they are still *in the state of Nature* ... "[28]

The alienation model claims that in order to guarantee stability and unity, the people must give up their right to resist sovereign power, even if it becomes abusive. In contrast, Locke's model of trust argues, given that the people establish government to protect their property,

> whenever the *Legislators endeavour to take away, and destroy the Property of the People* ... they put themselves into a state of War with the People ... By breach of this Trust they *forfeit the Power*, the People had put into their hands, for quite contrary ends, and it devolves to the People, who have a right to resume their original Liberty, and, by the

Establishment of a new Legislative ... provide for their own Safety and Security, which is the end for which they are in Society.[29]

The key difference here, as argued in Chapter 2, is that, in contrast to Hobbes, for Locke the exit from the state of nature entails a two-stage process. First, individuals come together to form political society; and then the political society comes to an agreement on how to constitute government. The significance being that, whereas for Hobbes the dissolution of government results in the chaotic return to the state of nature, for Locke it results in the reinvocation of the constituent power of the people.

In the Lockean model, governments dissolve whenever the legislative or executive "acts contrary to their Trust."[30] And it is the people's role to determine when this trust is violated, and in such case to alter or remove the offending power.[31] Carl Schmitt argued that the purest form of sovereignty is revealed at the moment of exception. According to this view, when the political community finds itself at a crossroads beyond the domain of established procedure and general norm he who has the power to take decisive action is sovereign.[32] In this sense, the people are sovereign according to Locke because, when governments fall, it is the people as a whole who retain the authority to reconstitute government as they see fit. They have the power of decision over the moment of exception.[33]

After the moment of founding, it is only in the right to rebellion that the people are sovereign in the strong sense. James Tully puts it this way: in Locke's theory of government, "[o]nly the activity of self-governing rebellion grounds freedom."[34] And "[t]he ultimate guardian is again said to be the ability of the people to judge if their governors are ruling in accordance with the public good and to be ready to remove them if they are not."[35] So in Locke the people are sovereign in the strong sense *prior to* the constitution of government and outside or *independent* of government, but only symbolically or latently sovereign *within* the domain of government. Thus, while Locke's theory of popular sovereignty is clearly less democratic then later notions of parliamentary sovereignty articulated, for example, by John Austin – which held open the door to popular sovereignty within the domain of government at the expense of the king – he is more radical in articulating the constituent power of the people prior to and independent of the state.[36]

The people are sovereign for Locke in that they are the *founding* authority, the constituent power that authorizes the institution of government, and for whose protection government is constituted. Thus, for Locke, sovereignty refers to the *constitutive authority* to institute government for the protection of natural right or to dissolve government when it violates the ends for which it was constituted. Yet to say that the people are sovereign raises the question Who are they? If the people have the power of decision over the moment of exception, who are the people? If the people constitute government, what constitutes the people?

The liberal people

Who are the people in Locke's theory of popular sovereignty? In common usage the concept of the people is frequently tied to the idea of nation or race; indeed, the two concepts are often used interchangeably.[37] However, this occludes an important distinction which Bernard Yack has succinctly expressed in the following terms: *the nation* may be understood as a "community over time" and *the people* as a "community over space."[38] Constitutive of national identity is the connection to a past, a shared history, or tradition. The people, on the other hand, refers to a collectivity defined by a particular territory.

At its most facile, the people for Locke are those individuals that entered into the social contract to form civil society and constitute government for the protection of property. Once civil society has been established the people are those that freely decide to enter or continue living in a society under the protection of government and the law. In this sense, the people for Locke constitutes a "community over space," necessarily tied to a territory subject to administrative power.

However, we recall that for Locke, in contrast to Hobbes, the constitution of civil society and "the people" pre-dates any specific administrative order. And thus we must consider whether even in the Lockean concept of the people there is an element of inherited collective identity or shared history. To what extent does "the people" in Locke also define a "community over time"? I will argue that in Locke "the people" is a political, not cultural, conception based upon the notions of consent and individual right; the collective people is formed out of individual interest, and its protection by administrative power remains its purpose. Mirroring the previous discussion of sovereignty it will be helpful in what follows to examine the character of the people as the constitutive authority prior to government (pp. 32–34), as the subject of consent within government (pp. 34–35), and as the agent of revolution independent of government (pp. 35–36).

The people as the constitutive authority

For Hobbes, the idea of political power in the state of nature is an oxymoron: the people exercise political power only in so far as they are represented by the institutions of the state. Outside the figure of the sovereign, according to Hobbes, the people, in effect, do not exist; they are only isolated individuals greedily pursuing their own self-interest. The political community is defined by the parameters of the state. This stands in contrast to the concept of the nation that understands the political community in terms of a particular cultural or ethnic identity that stands apart from and prior to the institutions of government. Locke shared the Hobbesian commitment to individualism but, unlike Hobbes, he also developed a theory of political power and community apart from the state.

Locke defines political power in civil society as the right to make laws "with Penalties of Death ... employing the force of the community in the Execution of such Laws, and in the defense of the Common-wealth from Foreign Injury ... "[39] According to this view, political power is an original attribute of the individual, and Locke's concept of the people follows directly from this starting point. The individual possesses political power in the state of nature in so far as he is (1) free to order his life and possessions as he wishes, (2) has the right to judge and punish anyone who violates the law of nature, and (3) has the right to use all force necessary to defend himself from attack. That is to say, the individual has political power in so far as he is a self-legislating being, upholding the law of nature with the right to make war on anyone who violates that law. Political power thus has three corresponding dimensions: the legislative, the executive, and the federative or warmaking dimensions.

From the Lockean perspective, the agreement to exit the state of nature and form a political community is made by independent individuals. The people constitute a collective, or a commonwealth, only in so far as each individual has a separate interest in the formation of political society. And it is based upon the original series of individual agreements that the majority will is then empowered to choose the particular form of government required to establish a common legal order to resolve any "controversies" that might arise.[40] The people for Locke are the constituent power in that they constitute government; and in so far as they do so, they hypothetically exist as a collective prior to its foundation. It is as a representative of the whole of the community that the majority decide upon its form of government; thus, for Locke, the collective people do stand apart from and prior to the institutions of government. But the collective identity of the commonwealth does not inherently refer back to some original or primordial ethno-national community. It is, rather, a function of the social contract that each individual makes with everyone else out of mutual self-interest.

According to James Tully, Locke's novelty is summed up in the idea that all " ... institutionalized forms of government are derived from and perpetually rest upon the prior freedom of the people to exercise political power themselves."[41] That is, the people are not wholly dependent upon institutionalized mechanisms to exercise political power, because political power was originally exercised by individuals. And so, in contrast to Hobbes, the people's independence from political structures prior to the constitution of government does not mean they lack the capacity for political agency. According to the natural freedom tradition of Hobbes – and Grotius and Pufendorf – political agency was possible in the people only as a corporate body manifest in legal institutions or recognized rulers.[42] In this tradition, the people as such never exercise political power themselves; they do so only indirectly by delegating or alienating their authority to representatives or monarchs respectively. Yet, if we follow Locke and understand political power as an original attribute of individual human practice in the state of nature, this equation must be transformed.

The people as constituent power are individuals coming together to exercise their natural political power in concert to erect the common authority necessary to protect their private property. And, in so far as this action constitutes a collective identity prior to state institutions, it is the *political* identity of individuals coming together out of independent self-interest, and not that of an ethno-cultural community engaged in collective self-determination.

The people as the subject of consent

If the people as constitutive authority come together to form civil society out of mutual self-interest, what defines the people within the commonwealth, once civil society and the state are established? Over time do the people for Locke come to develop a collective identity that is based upon more than mutual self-interest? Within civil society the people for Locke are those that are united under a single system of authoritative law. Thus within civil society the notion of the people is directly related to a juridical structure of property rights, conflict resolution, and retributive justice. Nothing requires this structure to be tied to a larger cultural identity. It remains instrumental for the protection of private "property" in the broadest sense of the word. Thus the concept of the people within the domain of established government remains political rather than ethno-cultural.

The people for Locke are defined as simply those who are united within a political system. And, he writes, " … it is easie to discern who are, and who are not, in *Political Society* together. Those who are united into one Body, and have a common establish'd Law and judicature to appeal to, with Authority to decide Controversies between them, and punish Offenders, *are in Civil Society* one with the other."[43] For Locke the only prerequisite for membership in the Commonwealth is express consent, the "positive Engagement, and express Promise and Compact."[44] As long as this consent is given, recognizing the benefits of civil society and pledging to abide by its rules, individuals within the commonwealth do not have to share the same ethnicity or religion.

Writing at a time of extraordinary religious turmoil, Locke sought the means to civil peace through the toleration of diversity. As John Gray and others have argued, the rise of the liberal state can be explained in part as a way of establishing a *modus vivendi* among the disputing parties of the European wars of religion.[45] Common political life does not require common religious belief. Government, according to Locke, cannot be responsible for the "care of souls."[46] There is no certainty that the religion of any single state is the true religion, and the speculative beliefs of free individuals may never be rightfully coerced.[47] Rather, for Locke, the role of the state is to protect the right of free and equal individuals to pursue their own faith. In the terms of contemporary political liberalism, it is to provide the basic structure within which people may freely pursue their own particular concepts of the *good* under the limitations of universal *right*.[48] The people united under the law are free to pursue diverse ways of life.

Speaking at a minimum, the people for Locke are those that consent to live under a common legal authority for the purpose of the protection of property and the flourishing of civil freedom. Within the commonwealth the people are that population that is framed by the protective capacity of the state: the Lockean people is therefore a heterogeneous *instrumental* collectivity for the protection of private property and civil freedom. And if the institutions that are set up for this purpose fail, or work toward opposite ends, the people have the right to annul them and reestablish them anew.

The people as the agent of revolution

Again, from the Lockean perspective, if government betrays the trust bestowed upon it, and seeks to enslave or exploit the people, jeopardizing the security of life, liberty, and material property, then the people have a right to rebel. When the legislative power betrays the people's trust in this manner, the people are no longer obligated to obey its law. Locke thought institutional answers to the problem of checking political power were incomplete. He argued that the ultimate check on the abuse of power was the potential for popular revolt. This was true for all types of government, no matter how ideal in form.[49] As James Tully states it, "the only guarantee against oppression is not a doctrine but the practice of revolution itself ... no form of government guarantees freedom and rights because every form can be abused."[50] For Locke, it is always just to resist oppression, and it must be up to the people themselves to determine when the threshold of rightful authority has been crossed, providing legitimate cause for rebellion. In such case the people are defined not as the founding authority, nor as the subject of consent, but rather they are defined in opposition to the state: the people as agent of revolution.

Others before Locke had argued in favor of a right to resistance. The monarchomach writers of the sixteenth and early seventeenth centuries, particularly Althusius, had argued for the right of the people to depose abusive power. The people as constituent power had a right to overthrow a tyrannical monarch because it was by their authority he had been crowned. However, in the monarchomach tradition the constituent authority of the people was generally located within representative institutions such as the Three Estates in France.[51] George Lawson, to whom Locke owed a great deal, argued on the other hand that "real majesty" or constituent authority could not be transferred to the representative bodies of the commonwealth. Rather, he argued that the constituent authority of the people stayed outside of the institutions of the commonwealth in the original political communities that had set up government in the first place.

Thus, like Locke, but unlike Hobbes, the dissolution of government for Lawson did not signify the destruction of political society.[52] However, unlike Locke, Lawson specified that in England, upon the dissolution of government, political community would be rightfully found in the "forty courts of the forty counties," that is, in the institutions of the local gentry.[53] Thus, for Lawson, the constituent power of the people could be found outside of the institutions of the commonwealth, but nevertheless, similar to the monarchomachs, he located it in representative bodies.

What is innovative about Locke in this regard is his focus on the individual, and the political power of the people themselves as individuals outside of established institutions.[54] Given the original freedom and equality of all humankind, the individual has a right to judge his or her government and dissent. This for Locke is political power in so far as it is a reappropriation of the original right to execute the law of nature. And in this sense, for Locke, rebelling against a tyrant is not just a matter of self-defense, but rather it is an act of political power.[55] Yet of course for resistance to rise to the rank of revolution, individual judgement must obviously "coincide with a similar judgement by many others."[56] This of course limits the frequency of revolution, enabling Locke to argue that popular sovereignty is not a recipe for great instability.[57]

What is important here is that for Locke, upon the dissolution of government brought upon by revolution or the betrayal of the people's trust, political power does not necessarily return to some previously constituted representative body, or original community. Rather it becomes expressed in a collectivity of individuals standing in judgment against an unjust government, and coming together in opposition to oppression. Thus we may define the people as the agent of revolution as a collection of individuals each with their own grievances forming a chain of equivalence in their opposition to the state.

The challenges of globalization I

We may sum up the Lockean theory of popular sovereignty as follows: Sovereignty refers to the authority to institute government for the protection of natural right and the authority to dissolve or alter government when its original ends are betrayed. The people for Locke are a political community formed for the instrumental purpose of protecting private property. The people are sovereign in that they are the *constitutive authority* behind all civil society; political legitimacy remains based upon their consent; and government is instituted to protect their interests. These elements remain integral to the liberal understanding of popular sovereignty and legitimate government today. Thus to ask how globalization affects this model is not a mere exercise in academic curiosity, but an active inquiry into the self-understanding of contemporary liberal democracy. Thus, in order to grapple with the challenges of contemporary democracy it will be helpful to ask, first, can the

Lockean theory of popular sovereignty maintain its coherence in the context of accelerating globalization?

The challenge to constitutive authority

For Locke the people are sovereign in so far as they are the constitutive authority behind the creation of government. Globalization challenges this equation in that it gives rise to a domain of governance that lies beyond the reach of the constitutive power of a single people. The emergence of the concept of sovereignty corresponded to the centralization of administrative power and authority within the territorial state. The emergence of the concept of globalization on the other hand corresponds to the opposite sense that authority is becoming increasingly decentralized under a complex system of "global governance."[58] Change is occurring on a global scale, and new structures of regulation and administration are developing in order to bring the process under some form of control to avoid the sense that we are living in a "runaway world."[59]

In order to regulate, navigate, mitigate, administer or survey the diverse phenomena of globalization, a variety of means have begun to develop. The term "global governance" summarizes the diversity and decentralized character of these processes. To speak of "governance" as opposed to "government" is to suggest that "the global system can enjoy the benefits of government without the existence of a formal governing structure."[60] At present, no single encompassing system is capable of administering the planet the way states administer defined national territories. Therefore independent agents and private networks, often with the cooperation of state institutions, have begun to take up the slack. As such, the sources of authority in world politics have broadened beyond the exclusive domain of states to include more and more private bodies of different kinds.[61] In this manner the constitution of global governance is gradually coming about by a decentered "evolutionary process," and much of it is occurring beyond the reach of public processes through which the people could exercise their constitutive authority.[62]

For example, A. Claire Cutler has shown how private international trade law, or the modern *lex mercatoria*, has come to constitute an effective system of non-state authority regulating international commerce autonomous from domestic or public international law:

> The law governs most aspects of international commercial relations, from the formation of contracts for the international sale of goods, transportation agreements, financing and insurance arrangements to the resolution of disputes through international commercial arbitration.[63]

Similarly, Gunther Teubner has pointed to the ways in which an autonomous *lex digitalis* is developing in the area of international internet law. Like the *lex mercatoria*, such law is based on private contractual relationships, not public processes of constitution-making, legislation, and judicial review. Thus as Teubner notes, "[p]olitical legitimacy is undoubtedly the Achilles heel of both autonomous legal systems. In principle, neither can claim to be linked into the usual legitimation chain of democratic will creation ... "[64]

This is not to argue that public institutions have become obsolete. In general, states remain the only institutions with the legitimacy to enforce compliance with the law. In fact, perhaps the oldest critique of the status of the *lex mercatoria* is its dependence on domestic courts to ensure compliance when market-based sanctions are not enough.[65] Similarly, when states do engage in international governance they are increasingly doing so in partnership with private organizations. Ngaire Woods notes that "[o]n the whole, private sector governance emerges where powerful states choose not to regulate, or indeed where states actively support private sectors in generating their own regime and then cooperate closely with that regime."[66] For example since 1998 the G-7 countries plus the IMF and the World Bank have recognized the authority of the privately based International Accounting Standards Committee to set and regulate accountancy standards worldwide. And the International Chamber of Commerce, setting rules for the conduct of international business, has had "consultative status" at the UN largely since its inception. Similar private "standard-setting" arrangements exist in other domains as well, including finance, chemical manufacturing, and the credit rating industry.[67]

While generated with the complicity of state institutions, such autonomous legal domains set up large areas of regulation and rulemaking that transcend the jurisdiction of national governments and maintain a certain degree of independence from them. Teubner describes it this way:

> Traditionally, the global legal order is divided into relatively autonomous national legal orders. Today, such distinctions have not become redundant, but have instead been overlaid by a different principle of differentiation: the law is also divided into autonomous transnational legal regimes, which define their jurisdiction along "issue-specific" rather than territorial lines, and which lay claim to global validity.[68]

This new principle of differentiation clearly poses a challenge to the Lockean concept of popular sovereignty. From the Lockean standpoint the people are sovereign because they are the constitutive authority behind government. Yet today a new layer of governance is emerging that has been removed from public processes of consent and majority decision-making. Global governance is being constituted beyond the domain of the people. Clearly, some elements of global governance are being constituted by the people's representatives in international organizations and intergovernmental networks.[69] Yet many others, like the modern *lex mercatoria*, are greatly private affairs. The Lockean constitutive authority is composed of individuals who come together in a defined territory to exercise their natural political power to erect a common authority – a *unified* legal order – to protect their rights to life, liberty and estate. Their purpose is to erect a universal structure for the common rule of law. The new autonomous legal orders, on the other hand, constitute a variety of rules of law – a *diversified* legal order – pertaining to specific issue areas.

The concern is that global governance thus becomes "distorted" away from the general interest of the people.[70] If for Locke government is beholden to the people because the people make government, to whose interest does global governance cater when constituted by influential members of the private sector? Do we go from government for the people to governance for the powerful? While setting rules with comprehensive influence over elements of international trade, for example, the modern *lex mercatoria*, Cutler argues, "is neither neutral in operation nor global in interest representation."[71] She contends, in fact, it is designed to defend the very particular commercial interests of an international merchant class that is predominantly based in the highly developed states of the West. Similarly, Robert Cox points to a vague constellation of interests behind the mechanisms of global economic governance that he calls "the *nébuleuse*," an informal elite network of financial, business, and political leaders that comes together to develop global economic policy at such gatherings as the World Economic Forum annual meeting.[72]

The extent to which the emerging system of global governance is indeed distorted toward the interests of the powerful – in effect reproducing inequality rather than ameliorating it – is a matter of debate. Yet even the World Economic Forum's *Global Governance Initiative* in its first annual report stated that "a global economic system designed by the wealthy is too often stacked against the poorest."[73] What is clear is that a complex, decentered, multilayered system of governance is emerging in the transnational domain. And to the extent that it does so outside of procedures of democratic accountability and transparency it clearly represents a challenge to the Lockean notion of the people as constitutive authority.

Globalizing consent, right and legitimacy?

According to Locke, after the original social contract establishes the principle of political society, the will of the majority is sufficient to constitute any society's particular form of government. We have seen that to the extent that the decentered, ad-hoc, and often private development of structures of global governance do not incorporate the will of the majority, their constitution violates the Lockean principle of the people as constituent authority. Similarly, processes of globalization complicate the practice of popular sovereignty at the local and national levels. Recall that for Locke direct participation in legislation is not necessary for the exercise of popular sovereignty; however, in order to conform to the principle of popular sovereignty government must (1) be based upon the consent of the people, and (2) protect the people's fundamental rights and interests.

If we understand the people in the liberal model as tied to a territory subject to administrative power, how can the notion of popular consent be operative in relation to economic and administrative powers that are not bound to a particular territory or regulated by a particular state? This question is significantly relevant in a world that is increasingly characterized by multilayered governance, where non-state authorities are increasingly important. As Susan Strange and others have shown, since the 1970s global politics has shifted away from an exclusive focus on the state toward a rising concern with the power of private actors – through regional markets, professional associations, transnational networks, etc.[74]

The increasing power of transnational economic actors and non-state authorities exclusively attached to no single bounded territory, and free from the limitations imposed by popular consent, calls into question the very relevance of the liberal notion of the people as a political category. Globalization is characterized by the predominance of "action at a distance" such that "[s]ome of the most fundamental forces and processes which determine the nature of life chances are now beyond the reach and control of individual nation-states."[75] For example, the trend toward greater and greater international corporate mergers and the multinationalization of production has led to the creation of "supranational economic spaces" extending beyond the reach of national policymakers and public planners.[76] In such a context, how could the people realistically express their consent or discontent? Often it is even difficult to know who or what is behind the forces that determine much of our lives.

As Norberto Bobbio once observed, while the meaning of democracy is subject to a wide variety of interpretations, the "transparency of power" must always be included among its defining characteristics.[77] The same can be said for the concept of popular sovereignty. If globalization results in the obfuscation of the centers of political power, the people have no recourse to ensure their interests are being represented and rights protected. In fact, much of economic global governance entails the removal of regulatory decisions from public control and oversight.[78]

For example, this is particularly true of the rise of international arbitration.[79] As private arbitration tribunals settle more and more international commercial disputes, domestic courts are deprived of the opportunity to review important matters that may have an effect on public policy. And thus conflicts of distinct public interest are resolved, and new commercial practices set, without the benefit of full public hearings. "The result is the removal of politically sensitive matters traditionally governed by mandatory national law, like competition, securities, tax regulation, intellectual property, and consumer protection, from public supervision and control."[80] When commercial disputes are settled through channels that bypass public processes, the interests of the people have no avenue of inclusion to influence decision-making. Thus it is all the more unlikely that their interests will be served. By diminishing the domain in which national courts exercise judicial review such developments restrict the ability of the state to protect the rights and interests of the people.[81] In so far as globalization expands the domain of governance beyond established mechanisms of consent and restricts the capacity of the state to protect the rights and serve the interest of the people it clearly poses challenges to the Lockean model of popular sovereignty.

Chapters 6 and 7 will address possible responses to globalization within the framework of the theory of popular sovereignty. But, for now, recall that while the legitimacy of government is based upon consent, for Locke the only true check upon the abuse of power is the potential for popular revolt. Ultimately, freedom is secured by the people's right to assert their constitutive authority. If government loses the capacity to secure the property of the people or it betrays their trust then it loses legitimacy and may be resisted. Thus, if globalization contributes to the loss of security and legitimacy, could popular sovereignty in the Lockean sense be reasserted through resistance?

Resistance and globalization

As argued on p. 31, the people are sovereign in the strong sense after the moment of founding only in so far as they reserve the right to revolt and set up a new order if their rights are abused and their interests go unprotected. How does the concept of globalization affect this component of Locke's model? Globalization as a term summarizes a collection of phenomena and processes. It does not name a uniform condition covering the entire globe, and some regions are more a part of these processes than are others. Indeed even where it has reached, it has done so unevenly.[82] Yet, conceptually, globalization envelops the whole planet. It is "all-encompassing."[83] It signifies the growing consciousness of interconnection – that events in one part of the world have an effect on all the others – that we do in fact live on a single planet. This is what Ulrich Beck calls "globality."[84] In such a context, no revolutionary or resistance movement may be understood in isolation from the broader global order; the people cannot go it alone, and this has positive and negative consequences for the project of resistance on both the domestic and international levels.

In the concrete, this is perhaps most evident in the economic sphere. For example, the contemporary globalization of finance greatly complicates the potential for radical change on the domestic level. The fall of the Soviet Union left the world without an alternative system to finance non-capitalist-driven development, abandoning socialist countries to stagnate in isolation unless they open their economies to market-driven investment, or, as in the exceptional case of Venezuela, have the luxury of vast oil reserves. Yet even more moderate left-leaning countries are restricted in the type of change they can institute. Due to the increased mobility of capital in a globalizing environment, today muscular Keynesian macroeconomic policies often prove too costly.[85] They risk stimulating the flight of investors who fear the potential of inflation and higher taxation. Thus, for example, the Brazilian labor leader

Luiz Inácio Lula da Silva surprised many by instituting strict fiscal discipline during his first year in office as President, cutting government spending and raising interest rates, despite his history of decrying such policies.

This is not to argue that globalization makes popular revolt in the face of corrupt or oppressive governments impossible. In fact, recent years have seen a number of such actions, from the mass mobilizations that overthrew Slobodan Milosovic in Serbia, or stimulated Shevardnadze's fall from grace in Georgia and the Orange Revolution in Ukraine, and on to the extended protests that led to the election of Evo Morales in Bolivia.[86] However, in the event of such revolts, the current structure of globalization constrains the freedom of the people to reconstitute society under a radically new structure. Earlier, I argued that the people are sovereign in that after the fall of government the people-as-a-whole retain the authority to reconstitute government according to the majority will. In so far as exogenous forces restrict the constitutive power of the people in the context of globalization, popular sovereignty thus becomes diminished from the Lockean point of view.

On the other hand, in many respects globalization has strengthened the hand of resistance movements, augmenting the power of the people as a political force outside of state institutions. The proliferation of international governmental and non-governmental organizations increases the number of potential mechanisms to be used by social movements, and expands the number of sites upon which pressure can be put. According to the Union of International Associations there are now over 25,500 international NGOs.[87] Such organizations can prove powerful allies to domestic movements protesting, for example, the systematic violation of human rights. Thus, in many respects, globalization stimulates contradictory tendencies for resistance movements.[88] While globalization diminishes state sovereignty, inhibiting governments' ability to respond to popular demands for radical change, it also expands opportunities for partnerships between domestic and international social movements, significantly amplifying the voice of protest or petition.

Margaret Keck and Kathryn Sikkink describe what they call the "boomerang pattern": when a social movement or NGO finds its own government unresponsive to its demands, and thus turns to the international community for help. Usually this takes the form of stimulating what Keck and Sikkink call "transnational advocacy networks," which then petition other states and third-party intergovernmental organizations to pressure the violating state to change. This has proven very effective in the past, for example in the case of the anti-apartheid movement.[89]

Globalization stimulates social, political and technological transformations that potentially bring people together across great distances. Thus it has the potential to facilitate the formation of solidarity networks of activists struggling against oppressive governments. Recall that on p. 36 we defined the Lockean agent of revolution as a collection of individuals forming a chain of equivalence in their opposition to an oppressive state. Thus we may say that, while globalization may restrict the constitutive authority of the people at the domestic level, it does provide the potential for a transnationalization of the people's subject-position as the agent of political resistance and change.

However, this does not mean that globalization is progressing toward the unification of the world's peoples into a single popular constitutive authority – far from it. Globalization entails contradictory tendencies, operating at various speeds, and at multiple levels of intensity, posing great challenges to any single system that would seek to encompass it. As globalization opens societies to the broader world, advancing cosmopolitan sensibilities, it also inspires reactions that reinforce local identities – the assertion of traditional practices in the face of modernizing influences from abroad. James Rosenau calls this "fragmegration" the simultaneous fragmentation and integration of social relations.[90]

Thus the Lockean notion of the people defined as individuals coming together to exercise their natural political power to erect a common authority to protect their private property extends to the global domain in only the most unequal, asymmetrical sense. While an emerging global civil society is beginning to have some success in influencing the course of global governance, "no new unity of humanity" has come to drive political action for the mass of the world's population.[91] The difficulties this poses for the articulation of a democratic response to the challenges of globalization and the notion of a global civil society will be discussed at length in Chapters 6 and 7.

For now, suffice it to say that globalization clearly presents a challenge to each of the fundamental dimensions of the Lockean model of popular sovereignty. It restricts the people's authority to constitute government, yet it expands the domain of law and governance beyond established mechanisms of consent or dissent. It challenges the capacity of the state to protect the rights and interests of the people, but it diminishes the people's capacity to respond by effecting radical change. Under these conditions can the concept of popular sovereignty maintain its coherence? If its fundamental components are substantially diminished in the context of a transforming world is the very concept pushed toward the breaking point? Or would it be possible to reformulate the theory of popular sovereignty in the context of globalization? Before we reach any conclusions on these points we must turn to two more models of popular sovereignty that illuminate other elements integral to the theory: the republican model of Jean-Jacques Rousseau and the deliberative model of Jürgen Habermas.

4 The republican model of popular sovereignty

Jean-Jacques Rousseau

Celebrated and vilified in his time, Jean-Jacques Rousseau was many things to many people: republican revolutionary, proto-totalitarian, social critic, classicist reactionary, virtuous citizen, and mad solitary. An eloquent advocate of republicanism in a time of monarchy, he no doubt contributed to the intellectual climate leading to the French Revolution. His critique of eighteenth-century society penetrated to its very core: society had "reduced" everything to "appearances," occluding reality and separating humanity from its true nature.[1] Naturally free, human beings lived as slaves; and Rousseau set out to discover the dimension of their chains and their potential for emancipation.

As is well known, Rousseau argued that human beings are naturally good, equal and free; left in their natural state they are docile, independent creatures that pay heed to their own instincts and desires and avoid contact with others. *Pace* Hobbes, the natural condition of the human being is thus not aggression and the state of war but, rather, solitary self-sufficiency. For Rousseau, human beings are by nature "peaceable and timorous," tending to flee at the slightest hint of danger.[2] It is society that corrupts humanity's natural goodness and sense of compassion; in fact, Rousseau argues, "it is by their institutions alone that men have become wicked."[3]

According to this Romantic view, human beings lived freely prior to civil society. They were independent, guided only by the inner compass of natural inclination. Now, assailed Rousseau, they live beholden to the opinions of others and subject to external authorities not of their own making.[4] Orginally, human beings were happily solitary and autonomous; in modern times they see themselves only through the eyes of others, conforming under the pressure of superficial social convention.[5] And, for Rousseau, this represents "the end of natural freedom" even when it is voluntary.[6] In modern times, human beings are internally divided and alienated from authority. They are selfish, vain, petty, and superficial. But according to Rousseau, " ... all these vices belong not so much to man, as to man badly governed."[7]

Rousseau's famous "Social Contract," then, is an attempt at imagining how things might have been different. It represents an alternative history. While it provided a touchstone for revolutionaries in the eighteenth, nineteenth and twentieth centuries, it is not a programmatic manifesto, nor a blueprint for the overthrow of any current corrupt order. In Jean Starobinski's words, it is "inaugural," not "revolutionary."[8] It constitutes a normative ideal from which to build a critique of present-day society. It seeks to understand on the conceptual level how the natural freedom, equality, and goodness of humanity can be reconciled with the submission to authority in society. Rousseau recognizes that there is no return to the state of innocence.[9] But the choice is not between a return to natural man and submission to bourgeois society; rather, Rousseau argues, the answer lies in the cultivation of republican citizens. And integral to this project is the institution of popular sovereignty. Such reflections remain all the more pertinent today.

Whereas the Lockean liberal model of popular sovereignty focused on the *protection* of *individual* right and interest, the Rousseauian republican model is concerned with the *collective self-determination* of society, and the pursuit of the common good of the people as a whole. It defines the authority by which a people freely determine the shape of their society and the conditions of their government. Today, a major component of the "anti" or "alternative" globalization movement represents a reaction to the sense that this is precisely the type of freedom being lost. This is evident in calls for the "self-determination of all peoples" at the World Social Forum.[10] Or, more concretely, it is expressed in the region-spanning resurgence of the left in Latin America, calling for a reconsolidation of national sovereignty in reaction to the failures of the neoliberal policies of the IMF and the World Bank.[11]

Similar to Chapter 3, this chapter will seek to understand the particular challenges of globalization to the Rousseauian model of popular sovereignty by breaking down the concept into its component parts. The next section will address the concept of sovereignty in Rousseau; the following section will analyze the distinctive role of the category of the people; and finally, the last section will address globalization's specific challenges to the model.

Sovereignty and the general will

I have argued that popular sovereignty may be understood as a central principle of democratic theory and practice. And thus in order to understand the state of democracy in the context of globalization a reconsideration of the concept of popular sovereignty is needed. Yet, ironically, while Rousseau advocated the direct participation of the people in the legislative process, his model of popular sovereignty exhibits potentially antidemocratic tendencies. In Chapter 2 I argued that Rousseau's concept of sovereignty is a direct descendant of Bodin's absolutism. It is important to consider the extent to which this makes it potentially antithetical to democratic practice and the free rule of the people.

As explained in Chapter 2, sovereignty for Rousseau is collective, participatory, and absolute. It is the exercise of the general will of society for the institution of the common good of all. In what follows I will examine the specific characteristics of this particular form of sovereignty and its relation to democratic practice. First, I will articulate the important distinction between sovereignty and government in Rousseau's writings. Next I will examine the concept of the general will, interrogating claims that it represents a proto-totalitarian category that sacrifices individual freedom in the name of the whole. And finally, I will analyze the social and institutional conditions for the successful exercise of popular sovereignty according to Rousseau. I will argue that Rousseauian sovereignty is in fact a democratic form of sovereignty, which, however, carries strict social and institutional requirements that, as we will see, make it difficult to sustain in the context of globalization. Nevertheless, I will argue its strong defense of the normative commitment to the collective self-determination of society makes it an enduring model of popular sovereignty that remains an integral component of any contemporary discussion of the topic.

The distinction between sovereignty and government

For Rousseau, sovereignty represents the source of legislative authority, the capacity to establish a body of laws which are "properly speaking, nothing but the conditions of the civil association."[12] The laws established by the sovereign represent the foundation of civil society, and as such are concerned exclusively with the relation of society as a whole to itself. That is, the people as sovereign legislate as a whole for the whole. No individual person, faction, or group may be singled out by the state; for Rousseau, such an act would contradict the principle of law. Popular sovereignty thus exists in the collective self-ordering of society, or in the people as a collectivity setting the conditions of its own self-determination.[13]

When considering the republican definition of sovereignty and the constitution of legitimate law it is important that a clear distinction be made between sovereignty and government. Sovereignty is the realization of the general will of the people; government is the "administration" of its laws. Whereas the sovereign makes the law, the government merely executes it. Sovereignty is the will that constitutes the order of society, and government is the force that implements its directives. Whereas sovereignty is general: it determines the course of the body politic as a whole; government is concerned with particulars: it affects the behavior of individuals, or parts of society, not its fundamental structure. Government is situated between the people as sovereign and individuals as subjects. It administers the laws of the former, to ensure the conformity of the latter.[14]

Sovereignty originates in the people, and only the people can wield it. Rousseauian sovereignty does not concern itself with the day-to-day workings of administration. Rather, the exercise of popular sovereignty for Rousseau is a process of *collective self-determination* by which a community actively constitutes the order in which it lives. It is in this sense a participatory, world-making concept of sovereignty.

Thus, while at times of normal day-to-day operation the government wields the force of state, sovereignty identifies a greater power independent of government. And for Rousseau this power is the people assembled as a collectivity. For Rousseau, as for Locke, the constitution of the people as a community precedes the constitution of government, and as such has legal priority over it. As soon as the sovereign people are assembled, the authority of government is suspended, and the people retain the right and power to alter the government as they see fit.[15] As we saw in Locke, the people remain the *constitutive authority* even after the establishment of government.

The sovereign will of the people is absolute, but this does not translate into absolute power for the administrative order. One can distinguish two separate levels of obligation in Rousseau: On the one hand, individual citizens give themselves over completely to the sovereignty of the general will. On the other hand, the institutions and agents of government cannot represent the sovereign will; they can only administer its directives.[16] In this sense, the government's power over individual citizens is limited.

For Rousseau, the participatory model of popular sovereignty serves to protect against tyranny. The regular assembly of the people provides a check on any executive power that would seek to rule at the expense of its subjects, in violation of the common good. The institutional tendency of government is to increasingly encroach upon the sovereign power of the people. Thus public participation in the legislative authority becomes vital for the maintenance of the people's sovereignty. For Rousseau, the necessity of direct participation in lawmaking is due not only to the unrepresentability of sovereignty discussed in Chapter 2 but also to the fact that regular assembly prevents the consolidation of power in the hands of a single magistrate or monarch. It limits the possibility that sovereignty may be usurped by an ambitious prince or a self-interested government.[17]

The maintenance of public freedom and the prevention of tyranny are integral components of Rousseau's model of popular sovereignty. Nevertheless, the absolute character of the sovereign general will has led some to suspect the opposite; namely, that a form of tyranny is in fact endemic to Rousseau's model. In Chapter 2 I argued that moving from Bodin to Rousseau the *subject* of sovereignty shifts from ruler to people while the *form* remains the same: absolute. This has left some critics to claim that Rousseau may be read as a proto-totalitarian, notwithstanding the distinction between government and sovereignty.[18]

To the extent that the general will carries the claim to be always "upright" and that no individual – nor any group – has the right to disobey or resist it, the sovereignty of the general will appears to require absolute subjugation. And yet the nurturing of freedom in society constitutes a central preoccupation of Rousseau's *oeuvre*. Thus in continuing to discuss the definition of sovereignty in Rousseau we must examine the character of its generality and the limits of its power. To what extent does the general will retain elements of an unlimited Hobbesian sovereignty, and thus anticipate later forms of totalitarian rule, and to what extent does it represent a more circumscribed "democratic" form of sovereignty?

Generality and the will: a democratic sovereignty?

In the *Social Contract*, upon exiting the state of nature and forming civil society each individual agrees to surrender his right to private judgment against the society as a whole, committing to bind himself absolutely to the directives of its general will. Rousseau seeks the society in which this represents freedom's development not its loss, in which the individual, by binding himself to all, subjects himself to no one, and gains the benefits of society while remaining as free as he was in the state of nature. However, it must be asked, to what extent is the freedom of the individual will compatible with the sovereignty of the general will?

The general will, in contrast to the individual will, tends toward equality and inclusion, rather than partiality and exclusion.[19] It is the will of "man in general" within a given community.[20] Or, more important, it is the will of society understood as a coherent whole; and it is thus a collective sense of will. This is to be distinguished from the will of the majority, which may represent a separate or particular interest in relation to smaller groupings within society. For Rousseau, "... what generalizes the will is not so much the number of voices, as it is the common interest which unites them."[21]

Patrick Riley argues that to speak of a "general will" is in fact a contradiction in terms: "the ideas of generality and will are mutually exclusive."[22] A will by definition is particular. It is the desire of a specific agent to do or to have some specific thing. The general will, he argues, is thus better understood as a metaphor which combines the modern foundation to political legitimacy – consent or contract – with the social unity of the ancient *res publica*. From this perspective what Rousseau describes is not a form of will at all, but rather a social ethic of the common good. What Rousseau admired most about the ancient republics was the image of the "perfectly socialized man," the citizen who felt completely integrated with society's needs and expectations. For such a man the execution of duty comes naturally.[23] For Riley, there remains an ambivalence or "vacillation" in Rousseau on whether the source of social integration is to be found in the "reconciliation of wills" or in the "absence of will" altogether.[24]

Yet the attempt to excise the concept of will entirely from the republican model of popular sovereignty surely encounters difficulties. The will is a necessary component of the modern sense of authorization or legitimacy, and Rousseau understood this. If political authority is not based on God or nature, and if human beings all start from a condition of freedom and equality, individual consent is the only way to found political authority. This is the fundamental innovation of the modern social contract tradition of which Rousseau is a part, following Hobbes and Locke.[25]

In addition there is a more procedural sense in which individual will is important for Rousseau. In order for deliberation in the popular assembly to result in an accurate determination of the general will, it is important that each individual express "only his own opinion," rather than a partisan interest of some group or faction within the state. It is only in assessing the common interests and desires of all *as individuals* that the common good of society as a collective will of equals can be determined.[26] Authoritative determinations of the general will are not based on a form of "group-think," which lends itself to uncritical following, but on the process of autonomous individuals actively coming together to deliberate upon their collective good. The general will is a "dynamic consensus" that depends upon the honest input of independent citizens, and in this sense it is a "thoroughly democratic" form of sovereignty.[27]

Furthermore, while at a conceptual level generality and will are mutually exclusive, practically, the general will clearly maintains an element of particularity. The general will is not "universal" – Rousseau rejected Diderot's belief in a "general will of humanity."[28] The general will is *generalized* with respect to the individual's relation to society but *particular* in relation to other communities. It is a particular will in so far as the agent doing the willing is a specific society distinguished from all others.[29]

The key for Rousseau is to discover the form of society that would produce citizens who would individually will the common good. He seeks a society in which the individual will and the general will are in harmony, where there is no need to forcibly restrict individual freedom, because individuals instinctively seek the good of the whole. In part, Riley understands this; what Rousseau sought, he writes, was "a political morality of the common good in which the individual is not suppressed but simply does not appear in contradistinction to ... society."[30]

Thus when Rousseau says the general will is always "upright" he is not suggesting that the majority or the state is always right no matter what the opinion of individuals. But rather that it is always just to seek the general good of society as a whole over the pursuit of strictly individualistic concerns.[31] In this sense, the sovereignty of the general will is absolute in that it must always be followed, but simultaneously it is in fact limited to the extent that it would be a contradiction in terms for it to will something that does not serve the public good.[32] It is structurally limited to determinations of the common good.

Tyranny – and what later came to be called totalitarianism – thus never develops from the filial devotion to the sovereign general will, but only from its misinterpretation, malappropriation, and institutional corruption. However, while in principle the general will is always right, it is not always easy to discover or to put into practice. It is always just to follow the path of the common good, but it is not always clear where the path is heading; seldom is it defined by a well marked trail. At times, particular interests claiming to represent the general good may potentially mislead the people, and thus corrupt the application of sovereign authority.[33] The result is that the pursuit of the general will requires not only republican virtue, but wisdom as well.

The risk of cooptation

Rousseau makes plain the distinction between general will, majority will, and the will of all. However, after the original moment of unanimous contract, the content of the general will for legislative purposes tends to be decided upon by the majority will of the people assembled. The original social contract is unanimous: each individual must agree to surrender the sovereignty of his private judgment to the direction of the general will. However after this original consensus – and the ratification of the constitution provided by the lawgiver[34] – the people's sovereign authority is exercised in legislative assemblies that must deliberate and decide upon the specific content of the general will for the purposes of lawmaking. And Rousseau cautions that while the general will is always right, in such a legislative context "it does not follow that the people's deliberations are always equally upright."[35] The people's declarations of the general will are not always accurate. The people may be misled and mistaken.

Nevertheless, under the proper conditions, according to Rousseau, the general will is nothing more than what the people assembled determines it to be. The general will cannot be a set standard of justice independent from public deliberation. To understand it in this way would be to sacrifice the republican commitment to collective self-determination.[36] Thus some argue the structure is inherently flawed and inevitably leads to the cooptation of sovereignty by partial, potentially tyrannical interests.[37] In a participatory system there is a patent risk that determinations of the general will could include particular interests in the guise of the general. There is always the chance that "a few skillful men" will succeed in giving their private interest the appearance of the public interest, convincing the people to back what is ultimately contrary to the common good.[38]

Rousseau was aware of this risk, and one can read his body of work as largely an attempt to articulate the form of society that would diminish it. For Rousseau, the key is not simply that the people assemble and legislate, but that they do so under the proper social and institutional conditions. Rousseau sought to articulate the conditions necessary for the flourishing of human freedom within society just as it had been in the state of nature. How can men commit themselves to the bounds of community while remaining under the direction of their own will alone?

The model of a supremely integrated society characterized by a high degree of social unity and equality was central to his response. An exact correspondence between common good and individual will arises spontaneously when society is small and homogeneous, and each man is like the others. Private interests then may develop in harmony with the common interest. However, the general will, we must remember, is not a mere collection of individual wills; and the entrance into society does imply a transformation. The social contract begins a socialization process that, according to Rousseau, can be a good thing, but only if it produces the kind of social solidarity or holistic community that Rousseau imagines existed in Sparta and early republican Rome.

Social unity and a virtuous commitment to the common good were all-important for Rousseau.[39] He despised factions of any kind within society, and argued that unanimity in deliberation was a clear sign of the presence of the general will. The people of the Rousseauian model of popular sovereignty are not just any collection of deliberating citizens. They are characterized by an extraordinary bond of solidarity. If the unified people are the source of sovereignty for Rousseau, then we must ask, what defines the character of the people? Who are they, and what creates the collective bond? Furthermore, while we have found that the freedom of individual wills is not completely absorbed by the sovereignty of the general will, the status of individual difference in such a unified homogeneous society remains to be considered. Therefore, before moving on to a consideration of the challenges of globalization, we must examine Rousseau's concept of the people to complete our investigation of his model of popular sovereignty.

The republican people

According to the *Social Contract*, the people are those who have unanimously consented to join together to form civil society. They come together to "defend and protect the person and goods of each associate with the full common force."[40] Once civil society is established, residence and participation in the polity represent consent for the original compact. In this sense, Rousseau's conception of the people, like Locke's, is a political conception. It has no necessary connection to a cultural identity apart from citizenship in the polity. However, the "univocal" structure of the sovereign people as manifest in the general will raises a fundamental political question: What can unite a variety of individuals behind a single will? Does the consolidation of will behind a notion of "the people" as a singular sovereign cultivate the need for a unifying national myth that in turn tends to transcend the strictly legal/political relation?[41] According to Lord Acton, "the idea of the sovereignty of the people, uncontrolled by the past, gave birth to the idea of nationality."[42] And in fact, at times, Rousseau does use the terms "people" and "nation" interchangeably.[43] I will argue that while Rousseau does come to depend upon a concept of national or patriotic identity, it is a cultivated, not essentialist, identity.

Equality and homogeneity

Certainly, much more so then in the liberal model, there is a strong need for a substantive form of homogeneity in Rousseau's republican model. To quote Lord Acton once more, "To have a collective will, unity is necessary[.]"[44] At one level, this unity may be understood as a component of the establishment of civil equality, nothing more. In order for the social contract to institute freedom, each individual must enter civil society by consent. As each associate without exception agrees to give up his natural independence in a unanimous surrender to the general will, the relationship of each individual to the whole is one of total equality. And thus according to Rousseau, it is one of total freedom because, "each, by giving himself to all, gives himself to no one."[45] In abandoning the state of natural equality, a relationship of civil equality is established. Each person as an individual is in an equal position *vis-à-vis* their rights against the group. The homogeneity of the republican *demos* is based on equality before the law independent of cultural or ethnic identity.

However, while the relationship of equality refers most directly to equality before the law, it does entail a more substantive component as well. In addition to legal equality, a well ordered society, according to Rousseau, is characterized by a requisite amount of material equality. Namely, civil freedom requires that "no citizen be so very rich that he can buy another, and none so poor that he is compelled to sell himself."[46] Republican freedom implies the freedom from domination.[47] The free society must discourage the accumulation of a preponderance of wealth in the hands of the few, for such imbalance translates into power differences that put the disadvantaged into positions of extreme vulnerability.

In addition, and perhaps more troubling for Rousseau, inequality creates divided interests within civil society. The presence of diverse interests renders the manifestation of the general will all the more difficult. The more diversity, the more differences of opinion are likely to be present, and thus the more space opens between individual wills and the general will. And as a result, more compromise is required, necessitating a greater application of force to ensure conformity to the law, and thus limiting the exercise of individual freedom.[48]

However, the opposite seems equally if not more plausible: individual freedom is *more* constrained in the absence of diverse interests. Rousseau's opposition to diversity in society is based on the conviction that a participatory model of popular sovereignty directed by a concept of the general will functions best – or is the most free – when self-interest and group interest do not conflict. Yet setting such an ideal into practice tends toward the systematic denial of real difference, resulting in oppression, not emancipation. Individual or minority dissent easily becomes characterized as antagonistic to the people's will and thus subject to suppression or persecution.

Rousseau seeks to reconstruct the freedom of the state of nature in society. In the state of nature human beings were at one with themselves and their environment. An obvious way to reconstruct the oneness of the state of nature in society is to imagine each individual as somehow as close to the same as possible. In this way, considering the individual interest of the other and the general interest of society would simply entail self-reflection, for the interests of all would be the same. However, in such a society, difference may easily come to represent the abject, the marginal, or forbidden.[49] In fact, there are two paths by which an isomorphism may develop between individual interest and general interest, and both entail social homogeneity. One is through original commonality – the pre-political nation – and the other through cultivation – the development of republican virtue, a heightened sense of "social spirit," or patriotism.

Nation and the lawgiver

It is not always clear to what extent the solidarity of individuals in society, for Rousseau, is based upon an original commonality and to what extent social processes are enough. On the one hand, the people for Rousseau are socialized as a people by the institutions of civil society and law. The people could not already have the virtues of citizens before the lawgiver institutes them as bound together under law, for this would mistake, Rousseau argues, "the effect for the cause."[50] The shift from individual man to citizen of the polity entails nothing less than a transformation of the human condition. The individual is transformed from perfection in solitude to dependence as a limited part of the whole.[51]

The people as a sovereign whole define the citizen as a member of the polity. Whereas man in the state of nature is self-satisfied and unconcerned with others, and the bourgeois man is preoccupied with his own comfort and self-preservation, the ideal republican citizen understands himself wholly in relation to the state. What is good for society as a whole is good for him as an individual; there is no disconnect between citizen and polity.[52] And yet while the republican people as a collective body of citizens are defined by their relationship to the institutions of the state, their existence as a people simultaneously must pre-date their constitution as a legally bounded community. The people must precede the lawgiver in order to function as the sovereign constitutive authority with the agency to ratify his work. Like Locke, there is a two-stage process at work: the people come together out of a mutual interest in exiting the state of nature and constituting a relation of civil association. And only then can they begin to establish a form of government.

A republic founded among a population of individuals with no previous connection or agreed common interest would be sure to fail. In order to be fit for "legislation" – fit for political founding – the people must already be "bound together by some union of origin, interest or convention...."[53] According to Rousseau, even if the collective character of the people is not fully developed before they have laws, a legal constitution must be rooted in some common bond in order to be effective. For Rousseau, this bond develops originally out of social proximity – people living in similar environments at close distances, sharing the same climate, eating the same food, and thus living similar lives. This he argues causes particular "Nations" to form, "united in morals and character" but "not by Rules and Laws."[54]

In a small homogeneous society, where everyone knows everyone else and everyone shares a basic form of life – e.g., pastoral, maritime, agricultural, etc. – a strong spirit of social solidarity could develop "spontaneously" out of the human being's natural sense of sympathy and self-love.[55] As, according to Rousseau, everyone has a natural sense of self-love (*amour soi-même*) and a corresponding repulsion at seeing like people suffer, a small homogeneous group of people living in close proximity could quite naturally develop a public culture of solidarity.[56] Does this then signify the existence of a pre-political or even essentialist national identity at the core of Rousseau's concept of the people? I suggest it does not.

In fact this form of nationhood is better understood as the most basic form of solidarity stemming from the original social contract – the consensual compact of a group of individuals living near each other to form a political community for the mutual benefit of exiting the state of nature. For Rousseau, the political nation is in fact not rooted in nature; rather it is a product of convention.[57] Nature does not establish in each people a Herderian "standard of perfection" that it must seek to develop over time.[58] Rather, for Rousseau it takes republican institutions to cultivate such a standard. The consolidation of solidarity and the cultivation of "social spirit" must come from the established institutions and public culture of the state. And it is thus in the process of founding a republic that the identity of a people truly comes to form, and not before.

Unlike Locke, the capacity to institute a proper government – which for Rousseau could establish the fundamental laws of republican society – necessitates wisdom beyond the capacity and instincts of individuals recently emerged from the state of nature. It requires the superior talents of a figure from outside of the community embodied in the extraordinary figure of the lawgiver. It requires a "superior intelligence" that could match the particular characteristics of a young nation to the institutions best suited to its development.[59] Prior to their establishment, human beings, according to Rousseau, simply do not have the sense of collective good necessary to envision society constituted according to the directives of the general will. And in this sense, Rousseau writes, "we do not properly begin to become men until after having been Citizens," and similarly the people do not properly begin to become a nation until after having become engaged in the practice of collective self-determination through law.[60]

Thus the lawgiver who drafts the constitution that establishes the basic framework of society, nevertheless, does not have the power to enact it as such. He has neither sovereign authority nor governing magistracy, according to Rousseau. He is the rare historical figure of the selfless statesman that presents the constitution to the people, only to recede from public view.[61] It is the people who must take up the sovereign responsibility of ratification and subsequent legislation.[62] The figure of the lawgiver remains, however, as the exemplar to the people of the type of extraordinary public virtue that is at the heart of what Rousseau defined as the "civil religion," constituted to cultivate the people's commitment to the common good and the solidarity of the nation. The people must in effect arrive at a moment of transformative recognition when the lawgiver shows them the way and they choose to follow it. While the people do have a common bond that forms them as a people prior to political founding, it takes the establishment of state institutions to enable the practical sovereignty of the general will and to cultivate the solidarity necessary to develop and maintain it. It is in fact after the founding that the true work of building social solidarity begins.

Patriotism and civil religion

"In the natural order of things" particular interest and the common good "exclude one another;" the purpose of political society, for Rousseau, is to bring them into harmony.[63] As such, national unity was vital for Rousseau, and as we have seen, its source could not be found in nature. It had to be cultivated, for "in the long run peoples are what government makes them be."[64] In order to constitute a society in which all the particular wills come to conform with the general will, the sovereign must find a way to "… make virtue reign," to make the pursuit of the common good over particular self-interests the norm.[65] In an idyllic, very small, homogeneous state this could theoretically arise spontaneously through the fusion of self-love and sympathy for the other-that-is-like-oneself.[66] However, in even the most moderately complex society, republican virtue must be cultivated, and institutions must be established for that express purpose.

In the *Social Contract*, a relatively open civil religion fulfills this role. Rousseau was in agreement with Hobbes that sovereignty could not be divided between political and religious authorities. However, a civil religion, he argued, must tolerate diverse religious practices, as long they do not interfere with the public duties of the citizen. A civil religion does not constitute a centralized national "church." Rather, Rousseau writes, it is "a purely civil profession of faith the articles of which it is up to the Sovereign to fix, not precisely as dogmas of Religion but as sentiments of sociability, without which it is impossible to be either a good Citizen or a loyal subject."[67] The civil religion represents the bare essentials necessary to ensure a propensity to respect the law and value the unity of the community. Most important is to avoid the division of society along theological lines.

Such civil articles of faith are in some sense the minimum requirement for Rousseau. The *Social Contract* remains at the level of abstract ideal. It is not until his *Considerations on the Government of Poland* that Rousseau provides a more complete indication of what the cultivation of social solidarity in a real existing society would look like. In his recommendations to Count Wielhorski he was clear: "It is education that must give souls the national form, and so direct their tastes and opinions that they will be patriotic by inclination, passion, necessity. Upon opening its eyes, a child should see the fatherland, and see only it until his dying day."[68] The great ancient lawgivers were all guided by the same purpose; namely, to find the particular set of practices and institutions that would "bond" citizens to each other and to their "fatherland."

Considerations on the Government of Poland describes a model of patriotism that emphasizes the cultivation of national distinction in the interest of inculcating a love of country in each member of society. While this serves the purpose of strongly encouraging the sacrifice of individual interest to the national or general interest, it also serves, for Rousseau, as a bulwark against foreign domination, whether military or cultural. For, if the people are instilled with a great love of country, no force can destroy the nation; it will live on in the people's hearts. Rousseau counsels that, with the proper cultivation of national spirit, even if, for example, Russia were to "swallow" Poland, it could never fully "digest" it. The key according to Rousseau was to cultivate not only a love of country but also a corresponding "natural revulsion to mingling with foreigners."[69]

It is in such passages that it becomes most clear that, for Rousseau, a commitment to patriotism and a commitment to cosmopolitan humanitarianism are mutually exclusive. The pursuit of the particular good of the nation and the pursuit of the goals of universal humanity cannot occupy the passions of the same heart.[70] For Rousseau, the freedom of the nation becomes dependent upon its identity as a separate entity with particular cultural characteristics distinguished from all others. The civil religion – or the religion of the citizen, as opposed to the religion of man or priest – sees everything outside the nation as "infidel, alien, [and] barbarous."[71] And thus the collective self-determination of a society constructed upon a principle of homogeneity and rigorous unity is dependent upon its remaining free from outside influence – a requirement that is incompatible with even the most minimally invasive idea of the effects of historical globalization.

What is more, if the collective self-determination of society means the freedom to develop as a nation without comparison to others, any alien influence upon the culture becomes a threat to its particular identity as a separate society engaged in its own particular form of self-rule. This necessitates not only a clear cultural separation, but also a structural suspicion of others or outsiders as always potentially corrupting forces. Thus Rousseau held up militaristic Sparta as a social ideal, and preferred the general Cato to the philosopher Socrates.[72] He admired the military society's solidarity producing capacity to organize social life around the pursuit of a collective goal. And this was reflected in the military character of his recommendations to Poland. Patriotic duty comes to resemble military duty in the expectation of selfless sacrifice, unthinking loyalty to the group, and the continuous preparation for conflict with a foreign force.

However, at the same time, Rousseau felt that war was itself unnatural and best to be avoided. A commitment to patriotism as a solidarity-producing virtue should not result in the development of warmongering as a *raison d'état*; he desired the solidarity of the militant nation without the bloodshed of war. "On the one hand," Judith Shklar observes, "he detested the cosmopolitanism of the intellectuals and admired the martial spirit of Sparta; on the other he hated war and conquest, which were, as he knew well, the instruments of despotism."[73] Yet the only way a state could remain perpetually on a war footing but simultaneously free from war would be to avoid contact with other states altogether. In relation to other states, the ideal polity would mimic man in the state of nature: it would remain totally independent, peaceable, and generally isolated from all others.[74] In the state of nature, while men may have come into conflict when their paths crossed, they seldom met, and so the world was at peace.[75] Such would be the ideal for nation-states as well.

If this seems completely unrealistic in the context of globalization today, it was not much less so in Rousseau's time, and he was aware of it. In fact, Rousseau was fully engaged with debates on international war and peace, particularly in his essays on Abbé Saint-Pierre's "Project for Perpetual Peace," which may be read as a forerunner of today's collective security models. And Rousseau was not at all optimistic. While the pursuit of international peace is "the most worthy occupation of man,"[76] Rousseau felt that the sovereign pursuit of self-interest by independent nation-states would make it inevitable that some state would eventually take advantage of any established peace for its own selfish gains.[77]

For Rousseau, popular sovereignty defines the participatory collective self-determination of society understood as a distinct group of people committed to the pursuit of their common good via the rule of the general will. Clearly, if this remains incompatible with the presence of internal difference and external interaction with foreign states, the model would experience serious difficulty in a time of increasingly permeable borders and transnational interdependence. It should be clear that we must now turn to a consideration of the challenges posed by globalization to Rousseau's model of popular sovereignty

Challenges of globalization II

Rousseau's model of popular sovereignty is concerned with the maintenance of natural freedom within the necessary confines of civil society. It seeks to define the ways in which individuals may participate in the collective self-institution of society, so that people may feel they have contributed to the formation of the world in which they live under laws of their own making. This becomes possible, for Rousseau, only when society is characterized by a high degree of economic equality and social homogeneity. Individual desires are more likely to correspond with the common good and the general will when society is small, unified, and homogeneous. This is a vision of society, however, that is increasingly anachronistic. In what follows I will analyze globalization's challenges to three elements of the Rousseauian model of popular sovereignty: the principles of collective self-determination, social homogeneity, and political participation.

The next subsection will argue that while globalization challenges the premise that collective self-determination requires isolation, this does not represent the demise of the principle but rather its transformation. The following one will argue that globalization precipitates the broadening of social heterogeneity and, as currently organized, economic inequality, presenting a clear incompatibility with the Rousseauian model as originally formulated. And finally, the subsection after that will explore the ways in which globalization challenges the republican ideal of participatory democracy, precipitating the need to incorporate new avenues for participation and representation into transnational political institutions and processes – which will be the subject of subsequent chapters. While globalization clearly challenges the fundamental components of the Rousseauian model, I will argue that his republican notions of collective self-determination and participation remain integral to any understanding of democracy today.

The challenge to collective self-determination

Clearly, a model of collective self-determination premised on isolation is incompatible with processes of globalization. Globalization signifies increased interconnections between peoples and states. It means more movements of populations, products, and information across international borders. The rise of illegal immigration, drug trafficking, and crossborder pollution highlights the inability of states to comprehensively control their territorial boundaries. And with the rise in electronic media it becomes increasingly difficult for governments to prevent their populations from becoming informed about events or perspectives from abroad. State capacity for large-scale censorship in the age of the world wide web, while certainly not a thing of the past – as the agreement in 2006 between Google and the People's Republic of China demonstrated – has clearly diminished substantially. Thomas Friedman optimistically calls this the "democratization of information."[78]

Globalization signifies increased interdependence; and any model that understands self-determination in terms of pure self-reliance disconnected from outside influence is destined to be anachronistic in a globalizing world. Yet is it necessary to define collective self-determination in such isolationist terms? Certainly, in the past, the principle of sovereignty represented the international assertion of state autonomy as domestic independence from external authority, originally represented by the Holy Roman Empire or the Roman Catholic Church.[79] But such sovereignty was in practice the privilege of only the few great European powers that could assert "effective" control over a consolidated territory. And when such powers sought to expand their influence by force, and assert control over other territories beyond Europe, there was nothing in the principles of classic international law that could forbid it. This was of course the legal context of nineteenth-century European imperialism.[80]

Today, however, sovereignty is the declared right of all states in the international system; and state autonomy refers both to the positive principle of self-determination and to the negative principle of non-intervention.[81] The right to the self-determination of all peoples and the norm of non-intervention in internal affairs have been inscribed in international law since the founding of the United Nations in 1945. Nevertheless, this has not come to mean that each people has the right to be left alone entirely. The criteria of "independence" sufficient to satisfy the principles of state autonomy or self-determination remain unclear; but certainly not all "peoples" can form their own independent states, and realistically, all states no matter their size depend upon their connections with others. Robert Keohane, arguing from a "neorealist" point of view, has rightly observed that the world is now determined by a condition of "complex interdependence."[82]

Under such conditions, Keohane argues, the meaning of state sovereignty has transformed; it no longer serves to imply supreme authority over all that occurs within state boundaries. As has been previously discussed, multinational corporations, foreign states, and international organizations all make decisions that have considerable impact on the economics, security, and environment of life within state borders. State sovereignty thus comes to signify not the total effective power over a territory but the very significant legal authority and institutional means to negotiate the transnational processes affecting the character of the domestic sphere under conditions of globalization. Keohane writes:

> What sovereignty does confer on states under conditions of complex interdependence is legal authority that can either be exercised to the detriment of other state's interests or be bargained away in return for influence over others' policies and therefore greater gains from exchange. Rather than connoting the exercise of supremacy within a given territory, sovereignty provides the state with a legal grip on an aspect of the transnational process, whether involving multinational investment, the world's ecology, or the movement of migrants, drug dealers, and terrorists.[83]

Transnational processes, especially in the economic sphere, are not overrunning or simply circumventing the state; rather, they are in large part being driven by state actors. Parliaments take down trade barriers, loosen capital controls, and establish the conditions for foreign investment and multinational production.[84]

This does not mean that states operate without constraint, but simply that they participate in the process, negotiating with international actors and other states with an eye toward maximizing national welfare. Thus to the extent that states are organized democratically, collective self-determination and globalization are not necessarily incompatible. Clearly a model of collective self-determination that incorporates the influence of exogenous forces challenges the ideal Rousseauian model. Yet if the republican spirit of popular sovereignty is to remain at all applicable in the contemporary environment, we must see that, *contra* Rousseau, self-determination in the context of globalization cannot require "the right to be left alone," but rather the right to participate in the larger community, and to be empowered to negotiate the terms of interaction and transnational association.[85] Thus globalization does not necessarily lead to the demise of the principle of collective self-determination, but rather to its transformation.

That said, the positive transformation of collective self-determination into a form of transnational interaction depends upon having the power to influence the forces of globalization. And clearly some communities have considerably more bargaining chips when negotiating the terms of their entry into the transnational economy than others. Globalization at present is structured in a highly stratified and exclusionary manner. And this too clearly presents a challenge to the Rousseauian model of popular sovereignty. The Rousseauian model depends upon a domestic context of egalitarian homogeneity, and globalization presents a constant challenge to the image of the domestic sphere as a domain of homogeneous solidarity.

Homogeneity, inequality, and the general will

Recall that integral to Rousseau's model of popular sovereignty is the correspondence between individual will and the common good, along with the idea that this correspondence arises most easily when society is small and each individual is similar to the rest. Inequality and heterogeneity increase the likelihood of a divergence between the general will and the wills of individuals. And it increases the likelihood of the formation of factions and sectarian interests in society, which, according to Rousseau, is antithetical to the proper articulation of the general will, and increases the need for the application of force to maintain social order, resulting in the reduction of freedom.[86]

Currently, processes of globalization put pressure on the image of a Rousseauian national homogeneity in two ways: by stimulating economic inequality and by precipitating a rise in domestic cultural diversity. The general will, Rousseau argues, tends toward equality. In contrast, as many have noted, globalization has occasioned a considerable rise in international *in*equality. The ratio of income between the top 20 percent and the bottom 20 percent of the world's population rose from 30:1 in 1960 to 74:1 in 1997.[87] And, as of 2001, the wealthiest 20 percent of the world's population earned a total of

82.7 percent of the world's income.[88] In 2006 Branko Milanovic, a leading World Bank economist on the topic of inequality, reported that "the ratio between the average income received by the richest 5 per cent and the poorest 5 per cent of people in the world is 165 to 1. The richest people earn in about 48 hours as much as the poorest people earn in a year."[89]

Such extreme inequality breeds dependence and translates into asymmetries of power incompatible with political autonomy and self-determination, and thus stands in opposition to the republican model of popular sovereignty articulated by Rousseau. Furthermore, the structure of international inequality challenges the principle of national unity that is so essential to the republican model, by calling into question the continued perception that interests are indeed structured along national lines. The wealthy in New York have arguably more interests in common with the wealthy in Paris or Mexico City than they do with the poor in their own country; and one could argue, as Jeff Faux has, that neoliberal economic policy is often a reflection of this political reality.[90] In this respect, transnational capital wields power in the defense of class interest, not national interest or the common good of the nation.

In addition to international inequality, by many measures domestic rates of inequality are also on the rise within both the global North and the global South.[91] However, it should be noted that, whether domestic inequality is a direct result of globalization writ large or rather the result of state policies acquiescing in a particular form of globalization – namely neoliberalism – is not clear at present. Taking into account the variety of results experienced by developing countries over the last forty years suggests a complex phenomenon is at work, one that cannot simply be described as globalization equals inequality. In the 1990s "extreme poverty" was cut by half in East Asia – thanks largely to the rapidly growing economy of China – but fell only slightly in sub-Saharan Africa – even getting worse in at least twenty countries.[92] Much of this may be explained as in part the result of corruption and violent conflict; thus domestic policy and governance certainly share the burden of responsibility for rising inequality in the context of globalization, although one should not underestimate historical causes rooted in the experience of colonial exploitation.

Considering the policies of neoliberal globalization, not all countries begin equally equipped to take advantage of the supposed benefits of market integration and foreign investment. Geoffrey Garrett has argued national development must cross a minimal threshold in both political and economic terms before neoliberal globalization could possibly result in positive benefits; and that, ironically, middle-income countries are the least well positioned to take advantage of globalization, because they can't compete in terms of cheap labour or high technology. Thus the imposition of market reforms and free trade has not proven to be the one-size-fits-all solution to economic growth as some originally thought.[93] The imposition of market reforms and free trade in underdeveloped countries has often had disastrous results. Yet, whatever its direct or indirect causes, current levels of inequality have given rise to significant levels of practical political exclusion and are thus again incompatible with the republican model of popular sovereignty. Extreme inequality leaves the poor in a position of dependence upon the wealthy. And, in the language of Amartya Sen, extreme poverty – found not only in sub-Saharan Africa or parts of Asia and Latin America, but also among marginalized communities in the rich countries of Europe and North America – deprives individuals of the "capabilities" necessary for effective political participation.[94]

It is not clear, however, that an alternative model of globalization could not have different results. For example, proposals coming out of the World Social Forum movements call not for a return to a nation-state-centered politics but for a form of regionalization and international democratization that would benefit the developing world's position *vis-à-vis* neoliberal versions of globalization.[95] Thus the choice is not between globalizing neoliberal inequality and a return to protectionist nationalism. Rather, progressive social movements are increasingly formulating strategies to achieve a more equitable alternative globalization.

While the economic benefits and liabilities of globalization will continue to be debated, the recent wave of population movements has clearly precipitated a rise in heterogeneity in much of the world, especially in the countries of the industrialized northern hemisphere. For example, in the late nineteenth century foreigners represented only a fraction of 1 percent of the total population in both Sweden and Germany. Between 1960 and 1990 the percentage of foreign population rose from 2.5 percent to 5.6 percent in Sweden and from 1.2 percent to 8.2 percent in Germany.[96] And this has only continued in the post-Cold War world. According to Eurostat, the statistical agency of the European Union, the foreign-born population of Germany had risen to 12.3 percent by 2005.[97] In both cases this rise has represented the presence of significant numbers of non-Europeans for the very first time.

Similarly, even a historically immigrant country like the United States has begun to experience levels of ethnic diversity never before seen. While the US foreign-born population reached its peak of 14 percent in 1910, it has experienced a sharp rise from its low of 5 percent in 1970 to an estimated 11.7 percent in 2003.[98] The difference between 1910 and 2003, however, is that US immigration in the late nineteenth and early twentieth centuries was predominantly European, while today we are witnessing large numbers of Asian and Hispanic immigrants.[99] Non-Hispanic whites are a minority in the metropolitan areas of Los Angeles, Miami, Houston, and San Francisco, and will be by 2010 in the multi-state New York metropolitan area.[100] Thus diversity is arguably even higher today in the United States than it was during the great population movements prior to World War I.

Recall that while Rousseau's concept of the people does not require strict ethnic homogeneity, it does require a tangible sense of national solidarity that unites the people against the perceived corrupting forces of outside influence. And it requires the cultivation of a general spirit of civic virtue such that self-interest does not come into conflict with the national common good. In the Rousseauian model anything that challenges "social unity" has no place in the republic. And thus, from this perspective, the immigration of distinct cultural groups with distinct histories and sustained connections to foreign lands clearly represents a serious challenge.[101]

Increased migration means increased communications and cultural exchange between societies, giving rise to diverse populations with multiple loyalties and "hyphenated" identities, challenging the established norms of a unified national culture.[102] And this is intensified when it is facilitated by the profound proliferation of electronic media. Today, the immigrant does not necessarily have to choose between assimilation and marginalization – either the loss of native identity or the withdrawal into an exile community functionally disconnected from home. With high-tech telecommunications immigrant communities can stay in regular touch with family left behind, read their local newspapers on the internet, and watch the national television of their native country live via satellite.

To the extent we can still describe the globe in terms of center–periphery relations, population movements do not travel simply in the direction of peripheries to centers, as is often imagined, but back from center to periphery, as well as within center and within periphery.[103] Thus we can speak of not just international migration but a broader phenomenon of transnational migration and general population movement that includes increased international tourism and business travel. Consequently, cultural flows are much less unidirectional, and are often difficult to describe according to a regular linear shape.[104]

The movement of people inevitably includes the crossing of ideas, beliefs, practices, arts, politics, etc. And it is never predictable what such interactions will produce. Discussions of immigration often revolve around the relationship between host country and immigrant communities, but migration also affects the countries of origin substantially. As emigrants become more capable of maintaining contact with their native countries, and travel back and forth is more accessible and time-efficient, the exchange of information and capital from one to another becomes greater. Currency remittances from emigrants back to Mexico from the United States or to Algeria from France have become extremely important parts of those countries' balance of payments. And as a result of such transactions, expatriate communities can become politically important constituencies courted by their national governments. Mexican politicians campaign in the southwestern United States, and Colombia has instituted seats in the legislature specifically elected by citizens living outside of the country – in the "exterior."

Furthermore, with the existence of large numbers of citizens abroad, national identities inevitably transform, often taking on new *trans*national qualities. Communication between emigrant communities and their home countries invites comparisons and contrasts; and local standards of living or levels of political freedom are measured by a new standard. From the perspective of distance, regional differences appear less significant or divisive. Immigrant communities of Indians and Pakistanis share "South Asian" neighborhoods; and Mexicans and Argentinians come to discover they share a common Latin American identity, giving rise to a new sense of "transnational community," again calling into question uniform models of national identity.

Consider how immigration's challenge to uniform models of national identity came into sharp relief in France in 2005. The French republican ideal of national unity has long resulted in an immigration policy that stressed assimilation and resistance to any recognition of national or ethnic difference. However, this has led to the emergence of a largely excluded, unrecognized sector of society that does not feel part of the majority, but remains unrecognized by the state as a distinct group in itself. The failure of the French model became apparent when young, mostly Muslim, youths rioted for days in October and November of 2005, burning cars outside Paris and around the country, set off by a comparatively minor incident with the police in the wake of inflammatory statements by then Interior Minister Nicholas Sarkozy.

The obvious alternative to the oppositional model of assimilation or exclusion is one of multiculturalism and the recognition of multiple group identities and privileges within a given national society. However, the very idea of multiculturalism has precipitated a backlash in many European countries, at times resulting in spikes of popularity for far-right parties such as Jean Marie Le Pen's French National Front, or the late Jörg Haider's Austrian Freedom Party, in turn further exacerbating national divisions.[105]

However, some form of multiculturalist pluralism seems the only alternative in a world where populations and cultures are on the move, and diverse peoples must share common public institutions and participate in their democratic legitimation. As processes of globalization continue to accelerate and consolidate through technological advances in transportation and communication, and the global economy continues to make demands for mobile labor and flexible capital, in the absence of a reactionary political/military catastrophe unleashing large scale destructive forces, it is difficult to imagine a reversal of the diversification of national populations currently under way. In such a context the Rousseauian model of national homogeneity becomes increasingly obsolete.

Transnational participation?

Seyla Benhabib has argued that the current constellation of issues surrounding transnational politics and questions of immigration, naturalization, and the plight of asylum seekers or refugees reveals the need to move beyond the model of "unitary citizenship" altogether.[106] She points to the development of an alternative model of citizenship compatible with transnationalism taking form within the European Union. In the context of the EU, she argues, one is already witnessing the emergence of a new form of "disaggregated" citizenship, where the social, political, and identity components of citizenship are not necessarily linked together. Voting rights, social entitlements, and national identity are not inextricably unified under a single category of citizenship. In some EU countries, designated foreign nationals may acquire local voting rights, while others may have the right to specific social entitlements but not to vote.[107] Thus in some sense as populations move and diversify so must forms of citizenship.

Yet this considerable advance in immigration policy reflects only a partial response to a set of phenomena with a concomitant problem: "We are facing the genuine risk," writes Benhabib, "that the worldwide movement of peoples and commodities, news and information will create a permanent flow of individuals without commitment, industries without liabilities, news without public conscience, and the dissemination of information without a sense of boundaries and discretion."[108] The possibility that many of the most influential forces of politics, economics, and information could operate from a domain void of public identity or awareness serves to alienate the people from the institutions that govern their lives. And in turn it undermines the development of the type of republican attachment – the sense of belonging to a well defined people with a common good capable of being articulated, or a general will capable of being expressed – that is integral to the Rousseauian model of popular sovereignty.

If the future of citizenship is a transnational model of flexibility and disaggregation, the added question becomes one of democratic participation. From the perspective of the republican model of popular sovereignty, what does this new context mean for political participation? And how can the people participate in the constitution of the institutions and laws of the new transnational domain of society and politics? Recall that, for Rousseau, direct citizen participation was necessary not only to satisfy the requirements of sovereign legislation but also as the primary prophylactic against the rise of tyrannical governments. The regular assembly of the people serves to limit executive authority, which has a natural tendency to accrue power at the expense of the sovereign people. Similarly, in a time in which global standards and transnational institutions are being constituted, some form of popular participation is necessary to check the excessive accrual of power by neo-imperial states or transnational corporate interests.

Integral to the concept of popular sovereignty, in all its forms, is the capacity to protect against tyranny, whether through the assertion of rights, the threat of revolution, or the regular participation of the people. Yet clearly the regular assembly of a global citizenry is not a possibility. This is a question both of scale and of jurisdiction. The transnational scale is simply too vast to imagine a form of Rousseauian direct participation, and too irregular to define a coherent body of republican citizens. But, even allowing for modern forms of political representation, it is not always clear what issues should be settled where. Political participation will continue to be important on the local and national levels, but issues of transnational concern are increasingly in need of legislation and regulation. Thus the issue becomes one of deciding what institutions are responsible for what domains; what issues belong to what political bodies; where should questions of controversy be decided; and what people have the right to participate in making such decisions. It becomes a matter of "framing" issues as local, national, or transnational, and of establishing mechanisms for the possibility of political participation beyond the nation-state form.[109]

In an age of complex interdependence, where many decisions are made beyond the nation-state that affect local populations, the incorporation of processes of democratic participation into the structures of transnational governance becomes decidedly important. We will analyze in detail two prominent attempts to satisfy this concern in Chapters 6 and 7: Habermas's model of postnational democracy, and David Held's cosmopolitan democracy. But for now suffice it to say that, with respect to the question of political participation, the context of globalization clearly represents a challenge to Rousseau's model of popular sovereignty.

While Rousseau's rebellious commitment to collective self-determination in the face of monarchical authority makes his work one of enduring vitality, the strict parameters of homogeneity and direct participation are clearly designed for another time and place. However, this is not an observation particular to the most recent stages of modern political development. The demand for direct participation in the practice of legislation has long ago been superseded in modern complex democracies. Modern democracy is representative democracy.[110] Thus direct democracy cannot be required for a contemporary model of popular sovereignty. If it is an acknowledged truth that the totality of the people cannot participate directly in lawmaking in any modern complex democracy, it is all the more true in the context of globalization. In any large-scale society the "whole people" from whom political legitimacy is derived is neither equal to those who participate in legislation, nor even equal to those who engage in less direct forms of political participation such as voting. When we expand the scale from the national to the transnational this disjuncture becomes all the more apparent.

Between those who actually participate in legislation and the abstract collectivity of the "whole people," liberal rights fill in to protect democratic autonomy. Rights serve to limit the encroachment of power upon individual freedom and property; and they serve to represent popular sovereignty's core claim: political power is legitimate only when individuals are recognized as members of the collective author of the law and not as its mere subjects. As Hauke Brunkhorst states, "The human-rights content of popular sovereignty demands that everyone, even citizens in *status negativus* (and that includes ... since the globalization of law and politics, *actually* every person), has the right to be treated as if they were members of the sovereign."[111]

To be clear, this is not to suggest that participation becomes superfluous for the majority with the development of modern rights, for, in the absence of a vigilant participatory public, rights claims become hollow, without effect. As we will see in the following chapter, rights remain dependent upon strong participatory processes for their practical substance. Thus Rousseau's clarion call for popular participation remains an important one, essential to any discussion of popular sovereignty and the pursuit of collective self-determination, even today. The key is to seek the proper combination of liberal and republican norms in a modern complex model of democratic practice. And it is with such an intention that we must now turn to Habermas and the deliberative model of popular sovereignty.

5 The deliberative model of popular sovereignty
Jürgen Habermas

As presented in the previous two chapters, the Lockean model of popular sovereignty is concerned with the constitutive authority of the people and the protection of individual rights, while the Rousseauian model is focused upon the collective self-determination of society according to the demands of the general will. Understood in this way, a dichotomy emerges between the two models of popular sovereignty: one is concerned with the protection of the *private* sphere of free and equal individuals; and the other, with the cultivation of a *public* sphere of citizens actively engaged in a collective process of self-rule. Habermas's deliberative model seeks to mediate between these two poles.

The deliberative model of popular sovereignty "invests the democratic process with normative connotations stronger than those of the liberal model but weaker than those of the republican model ... it takes elements from both sides and fits them together in a new way."[1] For Habermas, the republican model has the advantage that it preserves the radical democratic impulse behind the principle of popular sovereignty: it remains committed to the vision of society as self-organizing. Republican citizenship is characterized by a commitment to the *positive* liberties necessary to guarantee extensive participation in the common practice of collective self-determination.[2]

On the other hand, modern pluralism and social complexity transform the conditions of popular sovereignty, making the Rousseauian vision of a univocal, homogeneous society of virtuous citizens antiquated at best and, at worst, subject to oppressive distortion. Misappropriated in a diverse society, the principle of the general will's absolute sovereignty could subject minorities to a terrible fate.[3] With that in mind, liberalism has the advantage of protecting individuals and minorities from the possible abuse of an ideological majority wielding the administrative power of the state and its monopoly of legitimate violence. Liberal citizenship is committed to the establishment of *negative* liberties or civil rights that protect individual autonomy against the collective power of groups or institutions. Thus Habermas seeks to retain elements of the liberal model as well.

The novelty of Habermas's contribution to the theory of popular sovereignty lies in the claim that the seemingly opposed elements of liberalism and republicanism – private and public, individual and group, negative liberty and positive liberty – are in fact all necessarily interdependent parts of the practice of constitutional democracy in modern complex societies. One side does not make sense without the other.

However, in mediating between liberalism and republicanism Habermas presents a "desubstantialized" model of popular sovereignty as "subjectless," "anonymous," and "intersubjectively dissolved."[4] In so doing, critics have charged, he has drained all the strength from the concept.[5] Can the people be "dissolved" and yet remain self-determining? Can sovereignty be "dispersed" and yet continue to be a structure of final authority with sufficient protective capacity? In what follows I will pursue these questions and in so doing I will defend the deliberative model as a positive development in the theory of popular sovereignty. However, as before, I will argue that globalization raises serious questions for the model's long-term viability, absent creative innovation. Similar to the previous chapters, the discussion will be divided into three major sections: the next section will examine the deliberative model of sovereignty through the idea of popular sovereignty as procedure; the following one will discuss the categories of the people and the public in Habermas's model; and the last section will show how globalization presents challenges even for this the most flexible and decentered of models of popular sovereignty.

Popular sovereignty as procedure

By definition, the rule of the people must be mediated by a system of law in modern, complex, diverse societies. However, in order for the legal system to claim legitimacy it must be connected to a process by which the people may participate in its creation, reproduction, and periodic transformation. The rule of the people means the rule of law, but the rule of law must be established and sustained by a process that incorporates the participation of the people.[6] As such, Habermas discusses popular sovereignty as a form of democratic "procedure,"[7] which is not to say he excludes "substance" entirely in favor of an excessively formalistic politics – this is important to note from the very start. Rather, he writes, "In light of the fallibility of our knowledge ... neither form nor substance taken by itself, suffices."[8]

Procedure here is understood less in terms of an opposition to substance – as it is often positioned in North American debates – and more as a process of public reasoning based in both the institutionalized and the spontaneous give-and-take of arguments concerning political, social and economic affairs.[9] The idea of "popular sovereignty as procedure" stems from the simple conviction that it ought to be possible to establish a process to publicly justify laws and the political system as a whole with relevant communicable reasons. According to this view the practice of popular sovereignty becomes dispersed across society in a multilevel process of political communication, debate, and will formation: "Set communicatively aflow, sovereignty makes itself felt in the power of public discourses."[10]

In order to begin to unpack what Habermas means by this we must first look at its foundation in the concept of communicative action and the formal pragmatics of speech, pp. 70–73. I will then turn to his subsequent articulation of the discourse-theoretic democratic principle, pp. 73–75; its relation to the theory of the public sphere, pp. 75–78; and the co-originality of popular sovereignty and human rights, pp. 79–81. In so doing, I will argue that the deliberative model of popular sovereignty is a rigorously procedural model that at the same time does not abandon the radical, participatory spirit of Rousseau, but rather incorporates it into a flexible, complex, intersubjective model of political discourse and practice.

Communicative action and discourse theory

Habermas's theory of deliberative democracy stems from his previous work on communicative action, the formal pragmatics of speech and discourse ethics, in combination with his more recent reflections on the medium of law as such.[11] In mediating between the liberal and republican paradigms of law, Habermas seeks an alternative foundation to democratic practice that avoids both the metaphysics of the natural law tradition and the normative weakness of legal positivism.[12] His point of departure for developing the deliberative model of popular sovereignty is the pragmatic structure of communicative action. "The ideas of justice and solidarity," he argues, "are already *implicit* in the idealizing presuppositions of communicative action, above all in the reciprocal recognition of persons capable of orienting their actions to validity claims."[13] Whereas the Lockean and Rousseauian models of popular sovereignty begin with reflections upon freedom in the hypothetical state of nature, Habermas's project begins with an analysis of the ordinary day-to-day use of language. Habermas's project is "reconstructive": the principles of practical reason are to be found, not through the solitary reflections of the individual philosopher, but through a reconstruction of the intersubjective structures of communication oriented toward mutual understanding.

Communicative action is defined as the interaction of people seeking to come to a mutual understanding or agreement through ordinary language use with the purpose of social coordination;[14] and it is understood as the opposite of strategic action:

> Whereas in strategic action one actor seeks to *influence* the behavior of another by means of the threat of sanctions or the prospect of gratification in order to *cause* the interaction to continue as the first actor desires, in communicative action one actor seeks *rationally* to *motivate* another by relying on the illocutionary binding/bonding effect (*Bindungseffekt*) of the offer contained in his speech act.[15]

Put simply, communicative action occurs when one seeks to make another agree by providing convincing reasons. According to Habermas there is an inherent rationality to this process "inscribed in the linguistic *telos* of mutual understanding."[16]

When people communicate with the purpose of coordinating their action through mutual understanding, they make assertions. They speak to one another in ordinary language, making claims concerning the task at hand or the given context. And, according to Habermas, the success of communicative action depends upon what he calls the *validity basis of speech* – the implicit guarantee made by interlocutors that they could support their claims with reasons or consistent behavior.[17] Thus Habermas explains, "'validity' (*Gultigkeit*) must be understood epistemically as 'validity (*Geltung*) that is established for us'."[18] Whether a claim is legitimate depends upon whether it may be rationally defended against the challenges of others; a claim may be considered valid only when it can be established intersubjectively.

While communicative action in general describes all communication oriented toward mutual understanding, discourse ethics is specifically concerned with moments of rupture, when the basic background assumptions of social life come into question. It addresses the pragmatic structure of argumentation when, as Seyla Benhabib describes it, "both facts about what is the case and norms about what is right are challenged and no longer taken for granted."[19] It is concerned with calling into question previously accepted social norms either to reestablish their validity or to formulate new norms through a process of argumentative discourse with the ultimate goal of achieving a new "rationally motivated agreement."[20]

Given the impetus and goal of such discourses, a specific pragmatic structure emerges.[21] Habermas's argument concerning the resulting "formal pragmatics" of speech and argumentation is complex and technical, stemming from readings of Pierce, Austin, Searle, and Apel, among others.[22] My goal, however, is not a comprehensive assessment of Habermas's linguist turn, but to understand its relation to the later development of the deliberative model of popular sovereignty. With that in mind, the essential Habermasian point is this: The process of universalization is internal to the logic of argumentation based upon the necessary pragmatic presuppositions made by sincere interlocutors. Habermas writes:

> Every person who accepts the universal and necessary communicative presuppositions of argumentative speech and who know what it means to justify a norm of action implicitly presupposes as valid the principle of universalization ... [23]

The universalization principle, or (U), might also be called the consensus principle. It states that only social norms that may produce a consensus in rational argumentative discourse are valid:

(U) All affected can accept the consequences and the side effects [the norm's] *general* observance can be anticipated to have for the satisfaction of *everyone's* interests (and these consequences are preferred to those of known alternative possibilities for regulation).[24]

Social norms legitimated through discourses are universal in the sense that they are *generalized* for those affected by their observance. They may transcend the particular interests of those involved, but their universality is not defined by an unassailable timelessness. "Discourses take place in particular social contexts and are subject to the limitations of time and space."[25] Intersubjective validity is based on the practice of concrete discourses situated in particular places. While claims to truth or rightness may point beyond their immediate context, over time, as new knowledge becomes available, opinions are likely to change. Thus behavioral expectations must be continually open to reevaluation. Discursively validated moral norms are not foundationally universal, but fallibly so.[26]

If I assume (1) that a discourse is open to all affected by its consequences, (2) that the claims presented are tied to coherent intersubjectively recognizable reasons that support them, and that (3) the goal of the argument is to arrive at a rationally motivated consensus, then only certain types of norms could be considered valid without falling into a form of "performative contradiction" – i.e., those norms that satisfy (U). This, according to Habermas, is the case whether or not the assumptions are based upon fact. "[D]iscourse rules ... state only that participants in argumentation must assume these conditions to be approximately realized ..."[27]

Habermas had previously discussed such formal presuppositions in terms of an "ideal speech situation" in which we could understand communication as completely unobstructed, transparent, and purely based on the pursuit of mutual understanding and the cooperative search for truth.[28] However, he has long since moved away from this formulation, favoring the language of "idealizations." Whereas the concept of the *ideal speech situation* "suggests an end state that must be strived for," the concept of the *idealization* reflects the perspective of the interlocutor engaged in an open-ended process.[29] Rather than the suggestion of an ideal *telos*, it expresses what Michael Power calls the "vocabulary of the 'as if'."[30] Thus the force of the argument turns not on claims concerning the foundational nature of language as such, but rather on the pragmatic experience of how people understand themselves when they communicate.[31] For Habermas, in order to take part earnestly in argumentative discourse one must participate "as if" mutual understanding and the cooperative search for truth were the goal. To do otherwise is again to be engaged in a "performative contradiction."[32]

However, if Habermas argues that, as *participants* to discourse, people *must* presuppose that rational consensus is possible, Thomas McCarthy points out that as *observers* of modern society people must also recognize the likelihood of disagreement.[33] And this too must be reflected in the procedural model of popular sovereignty. Habermas is in fact well aware of this reality, and thus he is adamant that one may not simply expand the concept of discourse ethics into a theory of democracy. Political discourse is more complicated than moral discourse; it must incorporate a variety of concerns, including practical questions of policy application, and divisive questions of identity. If for no other reason, political discourse is distinct from moral discourse, due to its fundamental relationship to institutional government and the law. Thus "[a]n unmediated application of discourse ethics ... to the democratic process leads to muddled analyses ..."[34] To bridge discourse theory and the practice of popular sovereignty a consideration of positive law is essential.

Dissensus and the democratic principle

The relationship between popular sovereignty and discourse theory is best expressed through the relation between the legal form and Habermas's three rules of consensus: the discourse principle, the universalization principle, and the democratic principle. According to Habermas, the discourse principle (D) is inherent to the "conditions of communicative association in general."[35] It states, "just those action norms are valid to which all possibly affected persons could agree as participants in rational discourses."[36] And the principle of democracy for Habermas results from "the interpenetration of the discourse principle and the legal form," where (D) logically implies a general claim to political autonomy, and the legal medium alone presupposes a general claim to the right to personal liberty.[37] Although Habermas introduces the discourse principle (D) after he articulates the universalization principle (U), it should be understood as logically prior. It occupies a more abstract level. The discourse principle represents the general concept, prior to any distinction between morality and law; the universalization and democratic principles, in turn, represent its application to particular domains, namely morality and democratic legitimacy.[38]

Specifically, the democratic principle holds that "only those statutes may claim legitimacy that can meet with the assent (*Zustimmung*) of all citizens in a discursive process of legislation that in turn has been legally constituted."[39] This formulation, establishing universal assent as the standard for democratic legitimacy, has come under considerable criticism for setting the bar too high.[40] It seems to maintain the same rigorous requirement of consensus reserved for discourses over moral questions. Yet, as previously suggested, modern political discourse is distinct from moral discourse in that it concerns the institutionalization of legal relationships in complex societies. Whereas (U), the universalization principle, concerns a single form of argumentation – moral discourse – the democratic principle concerns the institutionalization of a variety of forms of argumentation, including the moral, the ethical, and the pragmatic, as part of a procedure of legitimate lawmaking.[41]

The goal of an ideal application of discourse ethics is to come to a consensus over the norms with which to regulate social interaction in the most general terms. In contrast, democratic law regulates social interaction in specific legal communities under specific historical and institutional conditions. Therefore, in addition to universalizable moral claims, particular pragmatic and ethical claims are inherently a part of democratic political discourse. Habermas writes: "As soon as rational collective will-formation aims at concrete legal programs, it must cross the boundaries of justice discourses and include problems of value ... and the balancing of interests."[42] Thus, in contrast to exclusively moral discourses, political discourses may entail processes that do not require or result in strict consensus, for example processes of compromise or bargaining.

Whereas, ideally, interlocutors arrive at a moral consensus in the same way – from the *force of the better argument* – parties to a compromise agree each for their own reasons. The goal is not mutual understanding, but the arrival at a merely acceptable conclusion to a dispute. In moral discourses the goal is to arrive at an uncoerced consensus. In processes of bargaining, on the other hand, the parties are oriented toward their own success, whatever the effect on the other. Threats, promises, and shows of force often arise as a part of political discourse in addition to rationalized exchanges.[43] However, in order for the results of bargaining and compromise to be considered fair they must be the result of a process that all can consider legitimate. Thus the discourse principle – oriented toward "uncoerced consensus" – still applies, "namely through procedures that *regulate* bargaining from the standpoint of fairness."[44]

The universalization principle does not apply to political discourse as a whole. Yet, in order to be legitimate, political decision-making must be conducted under a procedure that everyone could be reasonably expected to accept; and in this sense it too must satisfy a form of the consensus criteria. Habermas would agree with McCarthy that the absence of consensus is a normal part of modern politics, and as such political decisions must be made "despite ongoing dissensus."[45] But the crucial point for Habermas is that in order for such decisions to be considered legitimate they must be made according to a procedure that has been institutionalized according to a stricter application of the discourse principle. All affected should be able to agree that the decision-making process is fair. That is, legitimate non-consensual political discourses are carried out in the confines of a procedure laid out by what William Rehg calls a preliminary "metadiscourse."[46] Thus a procedural consensus lies at the core of legitimate democratic practice and unanimity does remain the stated ideal of the Habermasian democratic principle.

While James Bohman would allow that the standard for agreement in political discourse is more modest than it is for moral discourse, he nevertheless criticizes Habermas for setting unanimity among citizens as the ultimate "goal" of democratic politics. Bohman argues, it is too rigorous and counterfactual an ideal and should be replaced by a weaker one that emphasizes participatory access to a deliberative process of majority rule.[47] Habermas does, of course, hold participation as central to democratic legitimacy, and he accepts majority rule as "one of the more important" procedures of legislative decision-making. More important than universal assent for each piece of legislation, Habermas is concerned with a complex process of "legitimation through procedure."[48]

Nevertheless, Bohman suggests that, by setting unanimity as the ideal standard for democratic legitimacy, majority rule becomes a "mere expedient" for Habermas, a second best without inherent value. This is true to the extent that, for Habermas, "Democratic majority decisions are only caesura in a process of argumentation that has been (temporarily) interrupted under the pressure to decide."[49] The ideal of universal assent extended out to an undetermined future sets up a division between the ideal of democratic legitimacy and the real practice of democratic politics in modern complex societies. And according to Bohman this undermines popular sovereignty by creating a "strong separation of public opinion and formal decision-making."[50] While Habermas's model does indeed divide into "two tracks,"[51] and this becomes a crucial point of debates over his model, the division, he claims, serves to reinterpret and update the concept of popular sovereignty, not undermine it. I will explain.

Popular sovereignty and the public sphere

Habermas's deliberative model of popular sovereignty is indeed a dualistic, or two-track, model. And integral to any discussion of the two-track model of deliberative politics is the concept of the public sphere. The deliberative model of popular sovereignty divides between the "decision-oriented deliberations" of formal parliamentary bodies and the "informal processes of opinion formation" in the broader public sphere at large.[52] Habermas first discussed the concept of the public sphere in detail in his landmark study *The Stuctural Transformation of the Public Sphere*, which engendered a voluminous literature in response, most recently in the United States after its belated appearance in English translation in 1989. In *Structural Transformation* Habermas describes the seventeenth- and eighteenth-century emergence of a sphere of public discourse developing out of the world of letters into a space for articulating the needs of society and developing critiques of public authority to hold power accountable to the people.[53]

This early public sphere was a phenomenon of the bourgeoisie, a collection of private individuals outside the corridors of political power, brought together in discussion and debate over matters of common concern. It was, as Habermas described it, a sphere of "private people come together as a public."[54] However, my interest here is not in the historical arguments of *Structural Transformation* and their particular controversies, but rather in how the theory of the public sphere functions in Habermas's mature theory of popular sovereignty as procedure.[55]

In response to criticism, Habermas has admitted that his original formulation entailed many "empirical shortfalls."[56] In the years between *Structural*

Transformation and *Between Facts and Norms* Habermas updated the concept of the public sphere considerably. He now recognizes, for example, that from the start there existed competing public spheres of various forms, and that like all social spaces the public sphere is riven with conflict and power struggles. He thus, in my opinion, does provide a response to critics like Jodi Dean and Chantal Mouffe who critique the concept as oppressively unitary and naive to the intransigent reality of social conflict.[57]

There are in fact two ways to look at the structure of the public sphere and the two-track model of deliberative politics in *Between Facts and Norms.* And much depends upon which comes to the fore. Habermas wavers between the two models, and this results in a problematic tension. The distinction turns on the question of how to understand the circulation of power in a two-track model and thus the relation between the communicative power of the people and the decision-making power of the political administration.[58]

First, there is the model that follows from Nancy Fraser's influential critique of *Structural Transformation.* Here the two-track model is discussed in terms of "strong" publics and "weak" publics.[59] The "weak" public sphere is the informal network of discourses and spaces through which the exchange of ideas and opinions spreads through societies. Its structure is highly variable, comprised of "episodic" publics – momentary gatherings of discussion in the street or in bars or cafés – "occasional" publics – the periodic meetings of, for example, professional conferences, party conventions, or church gatherings – and "abstract" publics – the domain of newspaper, magazine, and blog readers, television viewers, or radio listeners connected by the media.[60] The weak public sphere represents the "vehicle of 'public' opinion"[61] where the needs of society are articulated and criticisms of the political administration are debated.

Weak publics entail processes of opinion formation but not decision-making. The concept of the "strong" public sphere, on the other hand, represents the public processes of institutions involved in discourse conducted under the pressure to decide. Parliamentary bodies are the quintessential example of a "strong" public – a deliberative body with decision-making power. In strong publics both opinion formation and will formation occur. A parliament in this sense, according to Fraser, represents "a public sphere *within* the state."[62] Both weak publics and strong publics are sites for the exercise of communicative power. They both feature the communicative power of people coming together to discuss issues of common concern and the policies marshaled in response. They operate according to the same medium of communication, and in this way the decision-making strong publics remain porous to input arising out of the multiple sites of the opinion-forming weak publics.

The second manner in which the two-track model appears in *Between Facts and Norms* is through Bernhard Peters's distinction between center and periphery.[63] The center pertains to the government, including the legislature, executive, and judiciary. And the periphery is made up of the highly differentiated spheres of opinion formation, regular and informal associations, mass media, etc. Here the separation between the two tracks becomes starker. Whereas the strong–weak distinction holds a place for the public sphere within the walls of the state, the center–periphery divide relegates the public sphere to outsider status. The sphere of public discourse, mass media, citizen gatherings, and informal discussions does not only have a different purpose than the center of government administration, its structure is completely different to the point of incompatibility: the center and periphery operate according to incompatible codes. The center operates through the medium of administrative power, not communicative power, making interaction between the two spheres very difficult. Here the domains of the two-track model are completely separate, with only the medium of law to bridge the chasm between them.

In *Between Facts and Norms* Habermas vacillates between these two models of the public sphere: from structurally similar, connected strong and weak publics – both operating according to the logic of communicative power – to structurally different and autonomous center and periphery.[64] And this produces a tension surrounding the question of democratic efficacy: What influence does the participation of the people have on the decision-making structures of government administration? Peters's model encourages a "siege" structure, in which the best the forces of popular sovereignty can do is to lie in wait outside the political system, pound on the door with threats, and hope to influence the happenings within. This is in fact the relational structure Habermas provides in earlier formulations, most notably in "Popular Sovereignty as Procedure" and "Further Reflections on the Public Sphere."[65] "Communicative power," he wrote, "is exercised in the manner of a siege."[66]

However, Habermas has since indicated that the siege metaphor was misleading.[67] And at the end of *Between Facts and Norms* Habermas appears closer to Fraser's significantly more democratic model, which holds on to the possibility of greater interaction between the informal public sphere at large and the formal public sphere of decision-making bodies near the center of state power. In the final chapter of *Between Facts and Norms* Habermas describes the "procedural paradigm of law" as one that supports an active concept of citizenship that builds public legitimation filters into the administrative apparatus. Communicative power is developed not only in the periphery of weak publics but from within the center of strong publics as well. He discusses the prospect of a "'democratization' of the administration" that would facilitate the flow of communicative power within the administrative system through "hearings," "ombudspersons," "quasi-judicial procedures," or other undefined "participatory administrative practices."[68] Thus the strict separation of powers between center and periphery becomes notably softened.

Nevertheless, the distinction does remain, for the political system is both a functionally specified action system limited by other functional systems, operating under its own code distinct from communicative power, *and* a constitutionally regulated action system concerned with general problems of integration, and thus *connected* to the informal public sphere and dependent upon the lifeworld sources of communicative power.[69] There is a division between the two spheres, yet they are closely interrelated; and how the tension between the two is constantly rearticulated defines deliberative politics in complex societies. There is a separation between center and periphery, between strong publics and weak publics – between the two tracks – but only together do they make up a comprehensive model of deliberative popular sovereignty.

Rather than undermining popular sovereignty, the discourse theory of deliberative democracy in this way modernizes it, adapting it to contemporary complex, functionally differentiated societies, drawing upon both participatory republican and institutional liberal understandings of democratic legitimacy. It navigates the historical tension between the republican freedom of collective self-determination and the liberal freedom of limited government, combining the informal domain of free, open-ended discussion where opinions develop and the formal mechanisms of time-constrained decision-making in a single procedural model of collective self-determination and human rights.

As we have seen, for Locke, popular sovereignty represents a principle of right formulated to check the powers of government, while for Rousseau it personifies the direct rule of the people through the generalized will of all. Finally, for Habermas, the concept of popular sovereignty represents the participatory procedures of a multilayered democratic practice *and* the rights that secure its conditions of possibility. We can say that, for Habermas, sovereignty – the structure of final authority – is located in the very legal procedures formulated out of the pragmatic insights of the consensus-oriented discourse principle. Indeed, for Habermas, popular sovereignty is synonymous with the *procedures* of democratic opinion- and will-formation *both* within the decision-making corridors of government *and* in the informal discussions of the public at large.

Thus, to return to Bohman's critique, while public opinion and formal decision-making are operative on two separate tracks, as Bohman charges, it is only in the relation between the two that the full deliberative model of popular sovereignty emerges. Popular sovereignty is not limited by the two-track model but, rather, enabled by it. Habermas's concept of popular sovereignty combines the protective capacity of the liberal model with the collective self-determination of the republican model. It is only through the constitutional combination of "the *guaranteed autonomy of public spheres*" and the "parliamentary principle" – including the presence of competing parties and representative legislatures – that the content of the deliberative model of popular sovereignty is fulfilled.[70]

The co-originality of rights and popular sovereignty

For Habermas, popular sovereignty no longer signifies the body of the people standing in for the deposed monarch, but defines the normative basis and "formal conditions for the legal institutionalization of those discursive processes ... in which the sovereignty of the people assumes a binding character."[71] It identifies the general principles that structure the procedures by which the people can freely formulate opinions and express their will – such as rights to equal participation and due process – and it guides the institutionalization of the conditions in which democratic will-formation is made possible.

For Habermas, rights do not limit the exercise of popular sovereignty but rather provide its condition of possibility. Rights do not restrain the political power of popular sovereignty but rather enable it. Public participation in the collective self-determination of society remains central to democratic legitimation; but effective participation is possible only in the context of a system that secures the basic rights of public and private autonomy necessary for the legitimate regulation of a common social life by means of positive law.[72]

Similarly, rights are not effectively prior to or independent of the exercise of popular sovereignty: In order for rights to gain the specificity necessary for their effective implementation, they must be articulated and justified publicly. Rights and popular sovereignty are not opposed to one another but rather they exist – to use the phrasing of Ingeborg Maus – in a relation of "mutual optimization."[73] Popular sovereignty and human rights mutually presuppose and support one another: private autonomy is necessary for the exercise of public autonomy, and public autonomy is necessary for the protection of private autonomy. In Habermas's often-repeated terms, popular sovereignty and human rights are in effect "co-original."[74]

Situated between republicanism and liberalism, Habermas understands democratic rights not as elements of individual property but rather as products of mutual recognition, legally institutionalized.[75] The democratic principle identifies an ongoing collective process of intersubjective recognition. It describes "the performative meaning of the practice of self-determination on the part of legal consociates who recognize one another as free and equal members of an association they have joined voluntarily."[76] In reconstructing the internal relation between democratic self-determination and the rule of law, Habermas – similar to Locke – evokes a two-stage process at the conceptual origin of civil society and constitutional government.

The mutual accordance of rights between free and equal individuals is conceptually prior to the formal institution of the state. One begins with an informal horizontal relationship among people who decide to regulate their lives by means of positive law. In order to do so they mutually grant each other rights, "recognizing *one another* as equals."[77] Only then does the administrative power of the state come into consideration. As such, Habermas is in keeping with the general principle of popular sovereignty that understands all governmental authority as emanating from the power of the people. That is, rights are not handed down by the state – nor, for that matter, naturally possessed by atomistic men and women – rather, they are reciprocally accorded among free and equal individuals committed to a process of collective self-determination regulated by positive law.

However, this does not mean that Habermas places the *constitutive authority* in "the people" as such. Unlike Locke, Habermas does not place the constitutive authority in the aggregation of separate individuals come together to form civil society in the mutual interest of protecting rights. Nor, like Rousseau, does he place it directly in the hands of a collective participatory people. Rather, as is to be expected, Habermas provides a procedural account of constitutive authority.

The very process of deliberative popular sovereignty articulates a continual open-ended instantiation of the fallible and ever-transforming constitutive authority of the people. The procedural model of constitutive authority is found in the historically developing spiral that begins with the idea of the democratic rule of law and the pragmatic presuppositions of the discourse principle.[78] The recognition of the need to regulate life by democratically legitimate positive law sets in motion a process that over time establishes a "self-correcting learning process" through the open-ended processes of a constitutional politics that is always necessarily open to reform and amendment.[79]

The discourse theoretical principle of popular sovereignty holds that all governmental authority is derived specifically from the communicative power of the people. Based on the procedural model of constitutive authority, popular legitimacy does not refer back to some mythic founding moment, rather it refers to a process that works to enable and maintain the possibility of popular participation in the *collective self-determination* of the political sphere. Habermas argues popular sovereignty need not refer back to a specific collective will or to a concrete sovereign body ruling itself directly. Rather, it may refer to the "general accessibility of a deliberative process whose structure grounds expectation for rationally acceptable results."[80] This does not abandon the participatory, radical impulse of popular sovereignty, but reinterprets it *intersubjectively*. It relocates it to the procedural level of debate and deliberation, of public opinion and public assembly, of informal gathering *and* official parliament.

The deliberative model of popular sovereignty thus defines the procedure by which the communicative power of a loosely related plurality of public spheres, protected by a system of rights, may serve to direct the exercise of administrative power in a constitutionally constituted political system.[81] Now, in so far as this is a theory of popular sovereignty, one may ask: What happens to the concept of the people in this equation? For Habermas, "popular sovereignty no longer concentrates in a collectivity"; it is dispersed along intersubjective networks of communication.[82] But is it indeed possible for the

80 *Globalization and Popular Sovereignty*

concept of popular sovereignty to operate without some sense of the collective people? It is to this question we must now turn.

The deliberative people

As we have seen, any consideration of the concept of popular sovereignty must address the definition of the people. Who are they? And how are they constituted? It has often been noted that the German understanding of the people, or *Volk*, in contrast to the French, is based in the sense of belonging to an ethnic community of descent. Historically, whereas the French developed an "assimilationist" model of nationhood based in the practice of republican citizenship, the Germans developed a "differentialist" understanding of the nation as organically rooted in German culture independent from – and prior to – the politics of the state.[83] Habermas, having grown up in the shadow of Nazi ethnocentrism, may be understood as above all seeking to expel that tradition from the horizon of the modern polity.

In what follows I will first, pp. 81–83, briefly examine the relationship between nation and citizenship and the historical tension between the two. Then, pp. 83–84, I will show how Habermas develops the concept of constitutional patriotism as a response to this tension. Finally, pp. 84–88, I will argue that Habermas's concept of constitutional patriotism does not elide completely the tensions of national culture and democratic citizenship. It remains dependent upon a common liberal democratic horizon of historical interpretation. And this will have consequences for our discussion of Habermas's response to globalization in Chapter 6.

Nation and citizenship

While the original Roman usage of the term *natio*, or nations, referred to geographically integrated "communities of shared decent" it was a concept understood in opposition to the Roman *civitas* – citizenship or the state.[84] The nations were peoples who had yet to be organized into coherent legal-political units: citizenship and national identity were opposite terms. Even in their modern usage the terms are not by necessity related at the conceptual level. The freedom of the republican citizen is internal, relating to the practice of political autonomy in the course of a participatory process of collective self-determination. The freedom of the nation, on the other hand, is external, relating to its sovereign independence from foreign interference.[85]

It was only after the late eighteenth century that citizenship and national identity came together in the figure of nationalism for the functional purpose of providing a principle of integration that could serve to mobilize the transition from royal sovereignty to popular sovereignty. Nationalism provided the solution to the twin problems of secular legitimation and complex integration in the wake of religious schism and republican revolution.[86] As Habermas writes, "only the consciousness of belonging to 'the same' people, makes subjects into citizens of a single political community – into members who can feel responsible *for one another*."[87] Thus, while citizenship describes a purely legal relation within a political community, in modern times the tendency has been to tie it to an identity that points beyond the political sphere. In this way citizenship becomes "double coded," representing both the possession of political rights and the membership in a culturally defined community.[88] And this, Habermas argues, presents a serious danger.

Political membership based upon the principle of a unique national culture presupposes an existential difference between peoples. In the Herderian sense it suggests that each people contains within itself a unique quality which cannot be compared to others. And, according to this logic, in order for the nation to be free it must remain homogeneous and independent from alien influence, necessitating not only separation but also suspicion of others as corrupting forces. According to this logic, diversity becomes a threat. If democratic identity were to require homogeneity, then, as Carl Schmitt was apt to point out, at times it must also require "the elimination or eradication of heterogeneity."[89] It is such logic that lies at the root of some of the most heinous crimes of the twentieth century, including acts of ethnic cleansing and state-sponsored genocide.

Furthermore, the logic of national homogeneity lends itself to the development of authoritarian leadership. If democratic self-determination is defined as the univocal will of a homogeneous people, then it may sever any connection to the principles of individual autonomy, opening the door to the "democratic" justification of repression or popular dictatorship. A political community that understands itself as naturally unified may tend to bypass the role of plural debate in articulating the national will in favor of the immediate expression of a charismatic leader. Indeed, according to Schmitt, as long as the governed identify with the governing, a solitary dictator may serve "democratic" rule just as well as – or better than – a representative assembly.[90]

However, Habermas is quick to illustrate that a commitment to ethnic nationalism is not at all necessary to the organization of modern social integration. In theorizing the transition from royal sovereignty to popular sovereignty Rousseau, for one, focused on the process of collective self-determination as the integrating principle of republican citizenship rather than national identity. We have seen that both Locke and Rousseau articulate a political concept of the people. However, whereas Locke's notion of the people is based in the instrumental relation of individuals seeking to protect private property, Rousseau's is a model for the collective self-determination of society as a whole. Neither one of these contains a necessary connection to a pre-political national ethnic culture.

Again, Habermas retains elements of both traditions. He hangs on to liberal principles of individual rights but articulates a more actively participatory model. He retains the republican tradition of process but eschews the holistic macro-subject model of the univocal general will – and the subsequent tendency toward homogeneity we saw in Chapter 4. According to Habermas, in modern complex societies, claims to cultural homogeneity generally mask the dominance of a majority culture in what is in reality a heterogeneous society.[91] In modern complex societies we must confront what John Rawls called "the fact of pluralism" while at the same time working to ensure social integration.[92] Habermas argues that the fundamental principles of constitutional democracy may form the basis of a liberal political culture that serves this purpose. Specifically, he argues that a form of patriotism may develop whose focus is not an ancient monolithic nation, but an evolving constitutional tradition uniting a diverse society in the common practice of collective self-determination.

Constitutional patriotism and the democratic ethos

As societies become more complex, and life histories more diverse, an unchallenged domain of common values becomes increasingly difficult to maintain, putting pressure on the process of social integration. According to Habermas, increasing complexity causes the *fact* of social norms to separate from their *validity*. In simple societies traditional social norms may generally go unchallenged. However, confronted by diversity in modern societies, traditional norms increasingly come under question: what is basic to one may be foreign to another. A primary function of law in complex societies is to make the practical force of social norms once again concomitant with legitimacy. Law is precisely that which bridges the gap "between facts and norms."[93] And this becomes possible, according to Habermas, only through a legal process that may serve to provide a common space for the production of political solidarity within a diverse society. That is, an open and fair democratic process can itself serve to guarantee the production of social integration independent of ethnic national identity.[94]

In complex societies, Habermas argues, people no longer share substantive ethical views over such basic components of social life as, for example, religion, family structure, educational practice, etc. However, in the context of such value-pluralism, it is possible to arrive at a consensus over a set of general principles that are necessary to establish a process of democratic legislation that claims neutrality with respect to diverse communities and identities. The basic principles of constitutional democracy in turn can form the center of a notion of democratic citizenship that may become the focus of a political culture that serves to integrate a multicultural, value-plural polity.

From the standpoint of discourse theory, the basic principles of constitutional democracy develop out of the intertwining of the discourse principle and the legal form, defining the basic categories of rights necessary to the democratic regulation of society by means of positive law. They include (1) negative *rights of privacy* which protect individual liberty; (2) citizenship rights, or *rights of membership* in a finite voluntary association delimited by law; (3) *rights of due process* and legal protection; and (4) positive *rights to equal participation* in the exercise of political autonomy.[95] While these basic principles can be interpreted in a seemingly endless number of ways, in their abstract form, according to Habermas, they can serve as a "fixed point of reference" around which a "constitutional patriotism" may develop within the horizon of a particular country's history, serving to reproduce solidarity in the face of diversity. That is to say, a form of civic patriotism based in pride for the democratic process and active citizenship over time may come to perform the unifying function previously served by nationalism itself.[96]

Thus the "deliberative people" are defined through the practice of collective self-determination mediated by the institution of positive law. And independent from that practice there is no shared identity – ethnic or otherwise – required. However, constitutional patriotism does name a common commitment to a democratic "way of life" in modern complex societies. And thus we must ask whether the principle of constitutional patriotism itself does not at some level presuppose a form of substantive cultural commitment.

While Habermas is clear about forging the pre-political commitments of ethnic nationalism, does he in fact retain other substantive commitments? For example, Richard Bernstein has argued that at the very least Habermas must presuppose the presence of a political culture that is amenable to democratic practice. In order for constitutional patriotism to take root, a *democratic ethos* – a tendency to be open to the rights and opinions of others, and to respect majority decision-making – must already be present within society. The deliberative model of popular sovereignty depends upon the respect for differences of opinion and the free exchange of ideas. Bernstein writes, "There is no adequate discourse theory of democratic procedure that avoids presupposing a democratic ethos – an ethos that conditions and affects *how* discussion, debate, and argumentation are *practiced*."[97] He thus argues that Habermas's concern for the absence of contentious ethical considerations during a preliminary consensus oriented metadiscourse is inconsequential, because any theory of procedural democracy already presupposes the ethical political culture necessary to make democratic practice possible.

In arguing for the separation of the moral/consensual component of political discourse from the contentious ethical and pragmatic components, Habermas is concerned with the *fairness* of the democratic process. He wishes to assure that decisions about the structure of democratic procedure are made from a generalized impartial perspective from which all affected by the procedure could agree. But, as Bernstein argues, such a consideration presupposes a context where the conditions of open debate and discussion are already a part of the existing political culture.

The people's common horizon of interpretation

Indeed, Habermas fully allows that deliberative politics depend "on a liberal political culture and an enlightened political socialization."[98] The deliberative model of popular sovereignty is a product of a "postconventional *Sittlichkeit*" and would find difficulty in any other social setting (and this, as we will see in the next chapter, raises serious questions concerning the model's application to a potentially global political order). However, Habermas rejects the assertion that as a result deliberative politics is dependent upon the strong republican virtue of individual citizens. Or that constitutional patriotism is thus just another name for a civic nationalism that produces an exclusionary identity based upon a common political history in place of ethnicity. Rather, again, for Habermas the burden lies with the constitution of democratic *procedure*, not with the personal virtue or identity of the people. "[D]iscourse theory," he writes, "employs a structuralist argument that relieves citizens of the Rousseauian expectation of virtue ... insofar as practical reason withdraws from the hearts and heads of collective or individual actors into the procedures and forms of communication of political opinion- and will-formation."[99]

Habermas argues, while an effective constitutional patriotism emerges out of a people's relation to a particular political history they call their own, this does not mean that it requires the cultivation of a sense of a common past narrated in a *national* history made substantial by an exclusionary collective identity. Rather, Habermas is insistent that "what first makes for a 'liberal' political culture, able to create and sustain a shared civic consciousness across all differences of a pluralistic society, is still the common *reference* to universalistic constitutional principles that promise equal rights."[100] Yet this is not an entirely satisfactory answer, for, as Frank Michelman argues, in order to effect consensus, such principles must become so abstract that it is hard to understand them as indeed "fixed" in any way. "It is not clear how we can say that a constitutional norm such as 'equality of concern and respect' remains invariant – remains one and the same norm – under reasonably contesting major interpretations of it[.]"[101] And thus it would appear that more must be at work for the centripetal function of constitutional patriotism to be successful.

For example, according to Michelman, in order for such abstract principles to serve the purpose of social integration they must be understood against the background of a common tradition of interpretation. Disagreements over constitutional law generally do not concern the delineation of essential principles. These are for the most part agreed upon in advance. Rather, such disagreements concern the specifics of their concrete application, and in the process they reflect contemporary deliberation over the meaning of the principles for the body politic. Thus for Michelman constitutional disputes do not reflect divisions over the basic principles of democracy, but rather uncertainty over "who we think we are and aim to be as a politically constituted people."[102] For example, are the American people a people that believe capital punishment is "cruel and unusual"? Are the American people a people that believe the right to privacy includes a woman's "right to choose"? Etc.

In Michelman's sense, constitutional patriotism is defined as the willingness to accept broad disagreement over the *application* of essential constitutional principles, with the understanding that the basic principles themselves are not

The deliberative model of popular sovereignty 85

in dispute. And that when we struggle over their concrete application we are engaged in a debate over where we as a collective body want to go, and thus over who we are as a people. It is a struggle over the evolving character of an enduring collective identity. That is, when we struggle over the meaning of the right to "due process" we are struggling over what it means to be an American. But the fact that we are all Americans is not in question and that must *mean* something.

For Michelman, if constitutional patriotism is thus "the morally necessitated readiness of a country's people to accept disagreement over the *application* of core constitutional principles ... without loss of confidence in the *univocal content* of the principles[,]" it is because there is "a level of confidence that the struggle *over* corporate identity occurs *within* a corporate identity that is already incompletely, but to a sufficient degree, known and fixed."[103] Thus for Michelman it is ultimately the collective identity that is the constant, not the concrete constitutional principles. And therefore, from this view, *pace* Habermas, a functioning constitutional patriotism does indeed depend upon a form of enduring collective identity.

Habermas is predictably critical of Michelman's claim that deliberative democracy thus relies on the "common traditions" of a republican collective identity.[104] Yet it is not clear how far apart they in fact stand. Indeed, they have recognized their debate as a "family quarrel."[105] Habermas allows that in practice, abstract political rights and principles can not become manifest independent from historically available interpretations. Even those basic constitutional rights and principles which, according to Habermas, serve as "the fixed point of reference" for the purposes of political integration must in practice become infused with context-dependent considerations. Political culture, according to Habermas, "is rooted in an interpretation of constitutional principles from the perspective of the nation's historical experience."[106] And in this way Habermas is closer to Michelman than might be immediately apparent.

Thus the following must be considered: Can a political culture that is unavoidably situated in a particular historical perspective remain independent from association with a particular substantive collective identity, as Habermas would have it? Habermas has argued that it is not necessary for a single interpretation of a nation's historical experience to predominate. Rather he suggests it is better to speak in terms of "a common horizon of interpretation within which current issues give rise to public debates about the citizen's political self-understanding."[107] According to Habermas, although articulating a variety of perspectives, the debates maintain cohesion because they always center upon different interpretations of constitutional principles that, in the abstract, citizens agree upon in common. Thus within the common political frame there is room for a multiplicity of collective identities.

Yet to understand such debates as taking place in a political culture that is completely set apart from any partial collective identity in a multicultural society sets aside the possibility that a majority culture may, over time, set the

86 *Globalization and Popular Sovereignty*

parameters of the "common horizon of interpretation." National narratives often minimize the reality of cultural divisions in the course of articulating the history of a unified people. In this way minority cultures may be left at a distinct disadvantage. However, Habermas takes strong exception to this possibility. He argues:

> ... the ethical substance of a constitutional patriotism cannot detract from the legal system's neutrality *vis-à-vis* communities that are ethically integrated at a subpolitical level. Rather, it has to sharpen sensitivity to the diversity and integrity of the different forms of life coexisting within a multicultural society.[108]

Thus constitutional patriotism signifies a first-order principle of political integration within which the coexistence of a variety of "subpolitical" spheres of social integration is possible. This first-order principle of integration is "procedural" to the extent that it concerns a consensus over the procedures of legitimate lawmaking and political authority in a multicultural, complex society. But this does not mean it is completely desubstantialized. While within the "common horizon of interpretation" many diverse communities can exist, that common horizon must define a liberal democratic community:

> Citizens who are politically integrated in this way share the rationally based conviction that unrestrained freedom of communication in the political public sphere, a democratic process for settling conflicts, and the constitutional channeling of political power together provide a basis for checking illegitimate power and ensuring that administrative power is used in the equal interest of all.[109]

The deliberative people are unified in their common relation to the liberal constitutional order, and not as common parts of a social whole predetermined by ethnocultural identity. The deliberative model of popular sovereignty breaks with holistic models of "society" or "the people" as constituting a form of macro-subject consciously steering itself as a single unit.[110] Yet the deliberative people do share a sense of commonality to the extent they are engaged in the practice of self-determination within a liberal democratic polity. The deliberative model is network-based: the people as individuals are in a relation of solidarity to the extent that they are connected by access to common public spheres mediated by the legal order to which they belong as citizens.

The Lockean people, we found, are separate individuals instrumentally come together to protect their rights, and the Rousseauian people are an egalitarian, relatively homogeneous group engaged in a participatory process of collective self-determination. The deliberative model again mediates between the two. It depends upon a fundamental commitment to the protection of individual rights in a plural society. But it also relies upon the political socialization inherent to the discursive relation of public spheres connected to a participatory legal order that must distinguish between members and non-members through the assignation of common citizenship. Therefore the deliberative people, we may say, are first and foremost "a determinate association of citizens" linked by the public spheres of a liberal democratic society.[111]

Challenges of globalization III

Habermas's model of popular sovereignty thus refers to the deliberative procedure by which the communicative power of an association of citizens – loosely connected by the public spheres of a liberal society and protected and enabled by a system of rights – serves to constitute and direct the exercise of administrative power in a constitutionally governed political system of collective self-determination. It clearly represents an advance over the Lockean and Rousseauian models in so far as it is participatory, and thus avoids the antidemocratic limitations of Locke, and in so far as it is decentered and pluralist, and thus avoids the totalizing dangers present in Rousseau. However, it is not clear whether the deliberative model of popular sovereignty proves more capable of responding to the challenges of globalization.

At this stage in the argument the general parameters of the phenomenon of globalization ought to be familiar. And the next chapter, Chapter 6, will analyze in detail Habermas's response to the challenges of globalization. So this section will be comparatively brief. I will focus on three points: First (pp. 88–90), while, in principle, the deliberative model of popular sovereignty, due to its decentered structure, is compatible with a post-nation-state environment, at present its institutional dependence upon the functioning of strong publics poses a problem for its compatibility with the global domain. Second (pp. 90–92), the absence of strong publics in the transnational sphere results in the breakdown of the co-originality of rights and popular sovereignty. And finally (pp. 92–94), the concept of constitutional patriotism and the model's dependence on the cultivation of a common horizon of interpretation conflicts with the reality of a global order defined by multiple histories, extreme asymmetries, and conflicting traditions.

Discourse theory and globalization: what strong publics?

Politics in the context of globalization must confront the proliferation of centers of power and the pluralization of political identities. In principle, the discourse theory of democracy has the flexibility to adapt to this situation. The discourse theory of democracy and the deliberative model of popular sovereignty correspond to the image of society as decentered – meaning it is no longer intelligible as a single unit capable of being steered as a whole from a central set of command institutions.[112] In so far as a "global society" would be far too large, diverse, and functionally differentiated to ever be controlled from a single power center, it would not inherently conflict with the discourse-theoretic image of society.

In this sense, with respect to the challenges of globalization, the deliberative model of popular sovereignty represents an advance from the liberal and republican models. Whereas, from the first step, the Lockean and the Rousseauian models are immediately incompatible with the globalization of politics, in principle the deliberative model is not. Whereas the deliberative model of popular sovereignty refers to a "determinate association of citizens," the scale of the citizen set is not inherently limited to the nation-state form. What is most important is that those affected by political decision-making may be incorporated into the appropriate deliberative processes at whatever level they may occur. If that requires extending the political sphere out beyond previously considered limits, from a purely abstract discourse-theoretic perspective there is no conceptual reason why this should not be possible. Furthermore, while deliberative politics are always situated within a particular political community or set of communities, discourse theory points toward the possibility of a "context-transcending moment" by reference to the endlessly extended community of interlocutors – the "ideally inclusive community" that emerges out of the universalizing orientation of the discourse principle.[113]

That said, the deliberative model of popular sovereignty could not remain at the level of abstract discourse theory. The discourse theory of democracy turns on the idea that all affected by a particular norm or law have the opportunity to register their consent or dissent in meaningful terms with the potential for effecting results. Practically speaking, a globalized political context does present a formidable obstacle to the efficient functioning of politics in this manner. The democratic principle of the deliberative model of popular sovereignty requires legally constituted systems for the effective channeling of communicative power. In spite of those who claim that the transnational sphere can be democratized by a proliferation of discursive networks alone, the deliberative model of popular sovereignty requires that communicative power do more than "influence" the structures of authority, it must have a role in the "exercise" of authority.[114]

The deliberative model of popular sovereignty depends upon the development of strong publics. The problem, as has been indicated, is that decisions taken beyond the nation-state are increasingly having an effect on the domestic sphere, alienating the people from institutions of decision-making. It is the problem of "juridification" and regulation in the transnational sphere in the absence of a unified sovereign or institutional structure open to the input of public opinion.[115] Anne-Marie Slaughter has documented how transgovernmental networks of regulators have established regular informal connections to harmonize national rules with transnational standards, independent of centralized transnational authority.[116]

Such networks make decisions according to standards of "technical expertise" apart from engagement with opposing political views or considerations of public opinion. They are not international proto-democratic-legislative-bodies-in-the-making. Rather they are the functional mechanisms of a new form of global governance established independent from central state authority or traditional treaty-based international law.[117] They do not aspire toward greater formalization or democratic legitimation. As Habermas has noted, despite their influence over the domestic sphere, they are satisfied with remaining "uncoupled from popular sovereignty in the nation-state."[118]

The supranational domain exhibits an absence of strong publics open to the petitions of civil society. In order for the communicative power of the people to affect policy and legislation, constitutional principles must be institutionalized and formal parliamentary bodies must be established. Informal transnational public spheres of social movements, civil society organizations and the like must have formal institutional bodies to serve as the addressees of protest and petition. Extending the deliberative model of popular sovereignty out to the transnational level presents the challenge of constituting transnational strong publics. There is no such institutional framework at the global level, and as we have seen with the defeat of the European constitution in France and the Netherlands and the subsequent defeat of the Lisbon Treaty in Ireland, such frameworks are a difficult thing to achieve even at the regional level.[119]

Rights without popular sovereignty

Nevertheless, in the absence of strong global publics, a significant regime of universal human rights has developed, making respect for human rights one of the fundamental principles of international law. And this has at times come into conflict with the historic bedrock of modern international law – the sovereign equality of states and the principle of non-intervention in national affairs. Some elements of the international human rights regime – for example the Genocide Convention – in fact, have risen to the status of *jus cogens*. They are recognized as "peremptory norm[s] of general international law" which in principle suffice to void contravening interstate treaties or justify intervention to stop an offending domestic state activity.[120] This establishes a level of international law that supersedes the sovereignty of national states.

This is, of course, a matter of some controversy. The idea that international law may supersede the sovereignty of states is greatly resisted in many parts of the world, especially in Asia and parts of Africa. Recent developments on the prevention of genocide and mass atrocities have sought to frame the issue in positive terms as a responsibility of sovereign governments to be supported, rather than in the negative terms of threatened military intervention against outlaw regimes to be opposed. This particular round of the debate has stemmed from the 2005 World Summit Outcome Document adopted by the UN General Assembly, which in part established the principle of the state's "responsibility to protect" its people against genocide, war crimes, ethnic cleansing and crimes against humanity.[121]

From the perspective of the deliberative model as articulated above, the problem is not that such norms transcend the nation-state but that, in the absence of strong publics in the transnational sphere, rights develop without the necessary correlate of popular sovereignty. And as a result two problems arise: First, in the absence of a constitutionally proceduralized popular sovereignty, rights become merely moral or easily coopted rhetorical claims without substance or strong institutional backing. While the European Convention on Human Rights does establish a regional mechanism for the enforcement of human rights, and the International Criminal Court does begin to establish procedures for the punishment of human rights violators, the post-war human rights regime has for the most part developed independent from enforcement mechanisms.[122]

International human rights suggest that every individual has the right to be treated *as if* they were members of an effective sovereign authority, even if reality reflects otherwise. They are, in effect, wishes for a system to come – "placeholder[s]" for a future "democratic autonomy" in the absence of one in the present tense.[123] Without a coherent authoritative structure of supranational institutions that operate according to a regular procedure, Habermas observes, "human rights provide the sole recognized basis of legitimation for the politics of the international community." Yet, while the Universal Declaration of Human Rights has been in principle accepted by most every state in the world, the specific meaning of each right and their general ranking in order of priority is subject to often bitter dispute.[124] According to the co-originality thesis, without a procedure for the democratic articulation of the particular meaning of rights when applied to real world problems, they remain insubstantial, too general to be consistently effective, and of ultimately arbitrary content.

Second, in the absence of legally constituted procedures for the articulation and application of rights, the legitimation gap may tend to be filled on the domestic level by authoritarian populist leaders, and internationally by an imperial power asserting the prerogative to intervene in the name of rights defined to suit its own narrow interests.[125] "Humanitarian intervention" – military intervention in the name of human rights or the alleviation of human suffering – is always an act of power, and yet, despite claims to the contrary, the motivations for such interventions are always mixed.[126] Although they are seldom if ever simply cynical gambits of military adventurism or solely motivated by capitalist interests as critics like Noam Chomsky would have, neither are they ever completely void of self-interest from either a domestic or geopolitical perspective.[127]

While Habermas read the Kosovo intervention in 1999 as anticipating a future cosmopolitan order, the 2003 invasion of Iraq suggests another possible development. In the absence of a strengthened system of international law and the articulation of clear procedures for the enforcement of human rights, the weakening of state sovereignty may lead not to a cosmopolitan legal order but to the rise of imperial domination.[128] From the perspective of the deliberative model of popular sovereignty, the solution must be a greater constitutionalization of the international domain, such that human rights may become situated within a "global democratic legal order" that could limit the abuse of power and allow the addressees of human rights to understand themselves as also their authors.[129]

Thus the challenge of globalization does not lead to the breakdown of the deliberative model but to the question of whether it could be established on a greater scale – the establishment of a postnational, or even global, constitutionalism. This does not necessarily mean a world state; Habermas for one is clear that that is not the type of system he foresees. One can imagine a multilevel system of subnational, national, and supranational political organizations connected by the mutual recognition of a cosmopolitan legal order. The next two chapters will examine two different approaches to this type of arrangement and the problems they encounter. But first, to establish a greater role for supranational institutions within the deliberative model of popular sovereignty means one must interrogate the role of the deliberative people and the concept of constitutional patriotism in the international domain. Is the concept of constitutional patriotism compatible with supranational institutions?

The challenge to constitutional patriotism

The deliberative people, I have argued, refers to a "determinate association of citizens" linked by the public spheres of a liberal democratic society. Can such a definition of the people remain useful beyond the national domain of politics? Unlike the Rousseauian model, the deliberative model of the people is compatible with considerable amounts of cultural diversity within the same political system. Thus the domestic heterogeneity precipitated by globalization is not a direct challenge to the deliberative model; nor should global heterogeneity represent an inherent impediment to the extension of the deliberative model of popular sovereignty beyond the nation-state. As Habermas notes, "… the conflict of cultures takes place today in the framework of a world society … the autarkic isolation against external influences is no longer an option in today's world."[130] However, if the goal were to seek the development of a cosmopolitan legal order that could incorporate the entire globe – that could establish a global association of citizens – one would have to assume the presence of common principles around which the world could find some sense of agreement. This suggests – in the terms of the deliberative model of popular sovereignty – the extension of the principle of constitutional patriotism to the supranational level, or the extension of a first-order principle of political integration based on a broad consensus over constitutional norms.

That is, from the strict Habermasian perspective, one would have to understand some correlate to the function of domestic-based constitutional patriotism in the supranational domain. Yet, as we saw, the principle of constitutional patriotism depends upon the development of a common historical horizon of political interpretation. A sense of constitutional patriotism develops out of the sense of sharing a common political history. In fact, as we will see in the next chapter, this is precisely the perspective Habermas takes in discussing the need for a European constitution. But, clearly, the establishment of such a common horizon for the entire world is not a serious possibility.

While some have criticized globalization as a homogenizing force – especially when taken to be synonymous with "Americanization" – globalization has an equal claim to creating more diversity through processes of cultural "hybridization," and to stimulating reactionary forces of division in response to increased inequality or perceptions of cultural imperialism. To some, the logic of global capitalism goes far towards the creation of a homogeneous consumer culture that tends to paper over regional and national differences for the purpose of creating accessible markets of uniform tastes, precipitating the emergence of a "McWorld," as it was described by Benjamin Barber in the mid-1990s. However, as Barber realized, such processes of homogenization tend to come in dialectical pairs; the counterpart to "McWorld" being "Jihad" – greater nationalism, "tribalism", ethnocentric chauvinism, or religious fundamentalism.[131]

Others have observed that processes of globalization have brought greater cultural complexity.[132] The globalization of the culture industry, whether through movies, fashion, music, fast food, or other consumer products, becomes manifest in different local contexts in different ways. In some places it inspires a reactionary reassertion of local traditions, in others it inspires the appropriation of foreign cultural elements into local arts and practices, thus creating new "hybrid" forms.[133] Roland Robertson has called this intertwining of the global and the local "glocalization."[134]

Furthermore, according to the 1999 and 2000 UN *Human Development Reports*, globalization in the form of market liberalization and free trade increased economic inequality across the globe.[135] And a 2008 report by the International Labour Organization documents a widening of income inequality as economies around the world grew rapidly through 2007 in the "age of financial globalization."[136] Thus while, to some degree, more and more people understand their present situation in relation to the contours of a larger "global society," they are experiencing this relation asymmetrically.[137] For example, while internet access has become increasingly commonplace in North America and Europe, the mere access to a regular source of electricity remains a struggle for many in parts of the southern hemisphere. And while according to the 2004 *A.T. Kearney/Foreign Policy Globalization Index*, six out of the ten "most globally integrated countries" were located in Western Europe, not one of the top twenty was from Africa, East Asia, South Asia, Latin America or the Middle East.[138]

Thus while in some sense globalization creates homogeneity, bringing the world together, in others it creates more divisions, separating the interpretive horizons of the world's peoples. This does in fact present a challenge to attempts to apply the national form of the deliberative model of popular sovereignty directly to the transnational scale. And it begins to reveal what I will argue in the next two chapters constitutes *the problem of cosmopolitan founding* – the inherent tension between the particular contexts of democratic legitimacy and the universalism of a global political order. It is the difficulty posed by the attempt to articulate the proper constitutive authority for transnational democratic governance.

However, first, we must consider whether in reality the shift in scale from national to supranational requires something other than a direct application of the domestic model to a new level. In fact, it is not clear that in applying the deliberative model of popular sovereignty to the transnational or supranational domain the constitution of a single political system integrated within a single common horizon of historical experience is at all necessary. Rather more plausible to imagine would be a supranational order comprising of a variety of mutually compatible systems.

Indeed, Habermas has developed such a response to the challenge of globalization, and we will interrogate it in detail in the next chapter. Saskia Sassen has noted: "With the partial unbundling or at least weakening of the national as a spatial unit due to privatization and deregulation and the associated strengthening of globalization, come conditions for the ascendance of other spatial units or scales."[139] She concentrates on the subnational scale, specifically the role of such "global cities" as New York, London, or Tokyo. Habermas, on the other hand, looks to the supranational scale in the form of the regional polity; and thus to understand how the deliberative model of popular sovereignty may respond to the challenges of globalization we must now turn to his work on democratic regionalism and to what he calls the "postnational constellation."

6 Responses to globalization I
Habermas's postnational constellation

The last three chapters have examined the challenges posed by globalization to the theory and practice of popular sovereignty with respect to the liberal, republican, and deliberative models. We have seen how the concept of popular sovereignty is challenged from both sides. The notion of *the people* as the agent of democracy and the concept of *sovereignty* as the form of final authority are both put into question by the phenomena of globalization. The decentering and proliferation of authority structures challenge the very notion of sovereignty as historically understood, while the accelerated mobility and diversity of citizen bodies and the transnationalization of interest groups have called into question the traditional image of a unified national people. Thus globalization, as we have seen, presents extraordinary challenges for each of the primary dimensions of popular sovereignty discussed: *constitutive authority*, *collective self-determination*, and *protective capacity*. This chapter and the next will examine two possible responses to these challenges: Habermas's "postnational constellation" and David Held's "cosmopolitan democracy."

In recent years, the transformations associated with the processes of globalization have stimulated a reconsideration of traditional political forms. In particular, approaches to the concept of democratic governance beyond the nation-state have gained wide attention. David Held and Daniele Archibugi have systematically advocated for a form of cosmopolitan democracy at the global level.[1] And of course Habermas and even the late John Rawls have presented extended thoughts on the prospects of transnational governance and cosmopolitan law.[2] For some, the proper political response to globalization is the consolidation of democracy at the national level – a strengthening of the nation-state in the face of pressures from abroad.[3] But for many the opposite is needed: while strong democratic procedures at the domestic level remain important, it is argued that, in the current context, democratic government can be maintained only by extending its borders outward, beyond the nation-state. For example, as we will see in Chapter 7, David Held envisions the consolidation of a system of cosmopolitan law that would one day cover the globe, providing the legal structure for a truly transnational democratic politics.[4] Still others see the future of global governance as taking form in a process of decentralization, or "disaggregation." Processes of rulemaking are increasingly dispersed along a multiplicity of networks on a variety of levels of political, economic, and cultural organization; thus, according to this view, political systems must come to transverse the boundaries of the local and the global, the public, and the private.[5]

For Habermas, however, the challenges of globalization call for the *re-aggregation* of political authority at a level that goes beyond the national frame but pulls up short of the global. In "the Postnational Constellation and the Future of Democracy" Habermas argues that a democratic regionalism represented by the continuing project of the European Union could provide the necessary infrastructure for the democratic coordination of processes of globalization in the absence of a global government.[6] This chapter will interrogate both dimensions of Habermas's formulation. What is the status of the "postnational" in Habermas's model for a regional polity? And to what extent can it serve as a general model for the practice of popular sovereignty beyond the nation-state? In the context of globalization can the postnational polity indeed represent "the future of democracy?"

The next section will review the challenges posed by globalization to the modern nation-state, arguing that the challenges are substantial and do in fact merit a reexamination of the institutional form of popular sovereignty. And it will address the project of regionalism as one such political response, indicating the challenges presented by political integration on the regional scale. Clearly, large regional political organizations must transcend ties between central state authority and ethnonational belonging. In this sense they must be "postnational." However, in the following section I will suggest that European democratic integration as described by Habermas maintains elements of an *extended civic nationalism*; political solidarity in the postnational polity is premised upon a territorially based political identity situated in a shared history; and in this sense it does not transcend the national model completely. The last section will explore how this affects the model's claim to represent a general form of democratic practice beyond the nation-state, and it will examine the tensions thus revealed between the particular contexts of popular sovereignty and the broader project of cosmopolitan global governance.

Regionalism and globalization

Capacities of the nation-state

As previously described, David Held and Anthony McGrew have depicted recent debates over globalization as divided among three general positions: the hyperglobalist, the skeptic, and the transformationalist.[7] In the context of this debate Habermas may be understood as a *transformationalist*. Globalization, Habermas asserts, "describe[s] a process, not an end-state."[8] He agrees that something new is certainly happening; and, while such developments are neither inevitable nor necessarily incompatible with democratic practice *per se*, they do, he argues, challenge the nation-state as the primary institutional form of democratic practice.[9]

Habermas defines the modern democratic nation-state by four basic characteristics: First, it is formed by an administrative system constituted by positive law.[10] The origins of the nation-state in Europe lie in the development of systems of administrative power that were well established long before they were brought under democratic control. Second, this administrative system is defined territorially. An effective system of positive law must have a clear object of control; territorial boundaries serve to define the law's "sphere of validity", and identify the population from which the relevant political community will form. Territoriality serves as the focus of the principle of state sovereignty, understood as the state's external autonomy from foreign powers and its internal monopoly on the legitimate use of violence, or the capacity to maintain "law and order."

Third, the development of the administrative state into a modern democratic nation-state depends upon the constitution of national identity. "Only the symbolic construction of 'a people' makes the modern state into a nation-state."[11] National consciousness provides the solidarity that transforms a disparate population into a body of citizens involved in the common practice of democratic self-determination. And fourth, the legitimacy of the modern democratic state is characterized by the progressive development of civil, political, *and* social rights. Basic to effective democratic practice, civil and political rights constitute the spheres of private and public autonomy. And, in the context of social inequality in capitalist society, social rights become necessary to secure the very conditions for the equal exercise of civil and political rights.

As we have seen, globalization challenges the modern democratic nation-state in each of its four basic components: It is challenged (1) in its administrative effectiveness, (2) in its territorial sovereignty, (3) in its collective identity, and (4) in its democratic legitimacy. As a result, Habermas argues, democratic politics must seek ways to respond. It is not possible to turn back the clock and reassert the autonomy of the nation-state. But a total transcendence of the nation-state is also unlikely. In fact, the influence of emerging powers such as China and India demonstrates the enduring significance of the nation-state in international affairs. Yet political, economic, cultural, technological and military forces are establishing connections across national and regional borders with increasing facility. As a result, if the practice of popular sovereignty is to remain viable it must not limit itself to the frame of the nation-state. The container has been breached, and democratic practice must seek new forms or risk being overcome.

The history of modernization reflects the extension of new networks of functional integration challenging the coordination capacities of societies, confronting them with new horizons, and precipitating social and political crises. Historically, such crises are generally followed by a renewed closure characterized by new modes of social integration. Thus, Habermas argues, the project at hand becomes the constitution of a new political-institutional enclosure by which the democratic capacity for making collectively binding decisions could be extended to the transnational sphere. Habermas offers a theory of a democratized European Union as a model for such a new political framework. He argues that, as a *postnational* polity, the EU would transcend the national frame in the interest of regaining the regulatory and steering capacities currently being lost by the nation-state. And he offers the postnational model as a starting point for a new democratic international order.

The regional polity

If under conditions of globalization the state has begun to lose its capacity to protect its people from the exigencies of the world economy, and if processes of globalization have left influential forces beyond the steering capacities of the democratic nation-state, then political change is clearly on the agenda. The integration of separate nation-states into new political and economic units is seen as one way to respond to this new conjuncture. Habermas's version of the postnational constellation presents a form of *regionalism* as an attempt to demonstrate how democratic politics might be reconfigured to regain some of its regulatory and steering capacity *vis-à-vis* transnational economic and political actors. *Regionalism* is thus understood as a political project that goes beyond the evolutionary integration of a geographical unit. It is a response to a political and economic context that can be generalized to represent a normative project for the articulation of a new global order.

For the discussion that follows it will be helpful to make some distinctions regarding the concept of regionalism and the regional polity. First of all, in speaking about a region in the context of globalization I will primarily be concerned with "macroregions," regions that today comprise more than one nation-state, as opposed to micro- or sub-state regions – e.g., South East Asia as opposed to the American southwest, the Andes rather than Catalonia. Second, it is important to distinguish between Cold War strategic regionalism constructed by exogenous hegemonic powers – such as the case of the South East Asia Treaty Organization (SEATO) – and what Björn Hettne calls the "new regionalism," endogenous projects of regional political and economic integration – most notably the recent stages in the consolidation of the EU.[12] Clearly the Habermasian project falls under the latter, "new regionalism."

The idea of a functioning democratic polity uniting all of Europe is indeed daunting. However, understood in the model of deliberative democracy, Habermas argues, there is no reason that the constitution of democratic legitimacy beyond the plane of the nation-state should be inconceivable. As we saw in Chapter 5, according to Habermas's discourse model of democracy, democratic will-formation is understood not primarily in the exercise of political freedom through direct participation but, more important, in the use of *public reason*. Most important is not the expressed will of the people *per se*, but the extent, quality, and accessibility of networks of communication where political opinions are debated and political wills are formed.[13] Given modern communication technology and mass media, Habermas argues there are no insurmountable structural barriers to conceiving the functioning of such networks in an expanded territory such as the European Union.

Applying the Habermasian standard of the deliberative model of popular sovereignty to the regional polity presents extraordinary institutional and social challenges. First, it clearly necessitates the constitution of transnational political institutions that could be responsive to the communicative power of an extremely diverse European civil society.[14] And, second, in its focus on the intersubjectivity of popular sovereignty and the role of the public sphere, it further reveals the structural dependence of democratic practice upon forms of social solidarity. The pursuit of common citizenship and the cultivation of a sense of collectivity thus remain vital to the success of the democratic polity even at the regional or transnational level.

In order for this to develop fully, the treaty basis of the Union would have to be rearticulated into a type of constitution that would establish the foundations of democratic citizenship and representation, cultivating a more democratic transnational decision-making procedure, complete with direct elections of representatives to the European Parliament, as indeed was recommended by the European Convention in June of 2003 in the notoriously defeated *Draft Treaty establishing a Constitution for Europe*.[15] In addition, according to Habermas, regional democratization will require the development of transnational political parties, along with increased avenues for the proliferation of informal political debate on a transnational scale. While political debates will continue to be largely located within national publics, the development of a continental public sphere would be essential to the development of democratic practice at the supranational level.[16]

To be successful in the long run, Europeans will have to understand themselves as participants in a collective project that transcends national borders; former competitors will need to become fellow citizens. As the Preamble to the Draft Constitution states, Europeans must be "determined to transcend their ancient divisions and, united ever more closely, to forge a common destiny …"[17] Yet this assumes the presence of a common source of integration uniting an extremely diverse population. According to the discourse theory of democracy, this should not necessarily present a problem, for solidarity may develop in the course of "a practice of self-legislation that includes all citizens equally."[18]

To the extent that people from a variety of backgrounds may understand themselves to be both the authors and the subjects of the law within the same polity, a common ethnocultural identity is unnecessary for democratic practice. A homogeneous collective identity becomes unnecessary "to the extent that public, discursively structured processes of opinion- and will-formation make a reasonable political understanding possible, even among strangers."[19] And thus, Habermas argues, with political reform, solidarity on the regional level of Europe is certainly within the realm of possibility, if however difficult, as attested by the defeat of the EU constitution in France and the Netherlands and, subsequently, the failure of the Lisbon Treaty to be ratified in Ireland.

The postnational people

Habermas seeks to retrieve the collective capacity to make legitimately binding decisions to steer the course of society. Doing so on the regional level presupposes social integration beyond the nation-state. Habermas invites us to understand this form of regional solidarity as *post*national; it clearly seeks to transcend the long-standing ethnic or linguistic divisions of Europe: the French and Germans, the Spanish and British, the Czechs and the Poles all to share a common citizenship. However, it must be asked whether democratic institutional reform is the only prerequisite for cultivating a postnational or transnational common citizenship? As Habermas has noted, the relationship between nationalism and modern democratic practice has long been intertwined. Thus history would suggest it could not be as simple as substituting democratic identity for national identity.

In what follows I will argue that while Habermas does provide a model for a post-ethno-national polity, he remains tied to a civic-national frame on the regional level, or rather he provides us with a model of an "extended nationalism."[20] Understanding the model in this way has consequences for its applicability beyond the European case, and helps to illuminate some of the substantial obstacles to the founding of a cosmopolitan democratic world order in the context of globalization.

Cosmopolitan republicanism versus ethnocentric nationalism

As a member of the first generation of post-war German intellectuals seeking to overcome the catastrophe of Nazism, Habermas is keenly suspicious of any links between ethnicity and citizenship.[21] However, he recognizes the historic function this link has played in providing the requisite principle of integration necessary to the rise of popular sovereignty. The history of the liberal democratic nation-state is characterized by a tension between civic-republicanism and nationalism, and, according to Habermas, the fate of democracy depends upon which tendency predominates.[22]

Civic-republicanism demarcates political membership according to a legal definition of citizenship that emphasizes universal legal equality. On the other hand, nationalism understands the political community to be constituted by a particular cultural identity that is prepolitical or given "independent of and prior to the political opinion or the will-formation of the citizens themselves."[23] At the close of the eighteenth century, republicanism allied with nationalism in order to advance democratic citizenship as the integrating principle of the state. However, democratization becomes threatened whenever ethnic nationalism encroaches upon the political sphere claiming to be the primary integrative force independent of republican political practice.[24] According to Habermas, this tension can be resolved only "as long as a cosmopolitan understanding of the nation of citizens is accorded priority over an ethnocentric interpretation of the nation."[25]

Thus, as we saw in Chapter 5, democratic citizenship articulates more than a legal status for Habermas; it provides the foundation of a shared political culture that can serve the purpose of integration often provided for by ethnocentric nationalism. In order for the democratic integration of a regional polity to be successful it must be able to cultivate a common political culture among an extremely diverse array of peoples. Habermas argues that in a liberal democratic nation-state political culture may arise from a rational consensus over the general principles of legitimate democratic practice. Basic constitutional rights and principles can serve as a "fixed point of reference" around which a "'constitutional patriotism' may develop, politically integrating people from a variety of world-views."[26] These basic rights and principles stand apart from the *level of subcultures and prepolitical identities* to the extent that the legal definition of citizenship is based upon the notion of universal equality before the law. There is no conceptual reason why this could not ultimately take place on a continental level.

However, while the principles of *universal* legal equality may transcend national divisions in a regional polity, to become operational they must be situated within a *particular* historical context. According to Habermas, in a complex multicultural, value-plural world, basic political rights and principles pertain to those that "… citizens must confer on one another if they want to legitimately regulate their interactions and life contexts by means of positive law."[27] However, as we saw in our analysis of the deliberative model of popular sovereignty, the basic categories of positive and negative rights (free speech, assembly, etc.) are in Habermas's terms, "unsaturated;" they are not infused with the concerns of particular historical, political or social contexts. And, as a result, they cannot become the "driving force" behind the project of democratic political integration "until they are situated in the historical context of the history of a nation of citizens …"[28] This applies equally to the project of regional popular sovereignty.

Postnationalism or extended nationalism?

Writing on the need for a European constitution, Habermas argues what is needed is not simply abstract allegiance to broad principles but "interest in and affective attachment to a particular ethos: in other words, the attraction of a specific way of life."[29] Regional political integration thus depends not only on a shared commitment to the values of liberal democratic practice but on a shared historical experience which may provide a common backdrop for the interpretation of basic constitutional principles and to a specific shared way of life. Sharing the values of liberal democratic practice is not the same as sharing a "specific way of life." American society is clearly committed to liberal democracy, but there are sharp distinctions between the broadly speaking American and the broadly speaking European ethos. And I would argue such distinctions, not least the European concern for social rights, are foremost in many Europeans' minds, including that of Habermas. A central concern for Habermas is to reframe social policy in the wake of neoliberalism's attack on the European welfare state, the goal being to articulate a viable alternative to the now greatly discredited "Washington Consensus."[30]

Habermas argues that the nations of Europe already share a certain historical horizon based in the shared experiences of modernization and violent upheaval. After centuries of conflict – between religions and between nations – culminating in two disastrous international wars in "the age of extremes,"[31] Europe has come to share a common tendency toward toleration, "the overcoming of particularisms ... and the institutionalization of disputes."[32] It is not only that the European nations share a geographic and thus historical contiguity, but that, according to Habermas, they have lived a shared history that particularly prepares them for regional political integration.[33] While Habermas is thus optimistic about the solidarity-producing effects of a common European history, there are many reasons to be less sanguine. For many, it is precisely the variety of the European experience that calls into question the viability of political integration on the regional scale. This has become all the more apparent with the the expansion of the European Union to include former Communist bloc countries. How will the different state traditions and historical experiences of the north and the south, or the east and west, affect the cultivation of a common regional political culture in Europe? And ultimately where does the European border lie? Why is Turkey potentially in, while Russia is out? As the debates surrounding "the Draft Treaty establishing a Constitution for Europe" and its defeat in France and the Netherlands would suggest, such questions are very difficult to answer.

Nevertheless, Habermas argues, the course of European history reflects a general process of modernization that forms a common value horizon, providing the shared context for the interpretation and application of basic constitutional rights and principles, making possible the development of a common political culture across the diverse peoples of Europe. According to Habermas, in spite of the variety of political traditions found on the continent, the experiences of European history "have shaped the normative self-understanding of European modernity into an egalitarian universalism that can ease the transition to postnational democracy's demanding contexts of mutual recognition ..."[34]

Regional political integration requires an expansion of civil solidarity beyond the nation-state; and the basis of this solidarity is a shared political culture that can succeed only within the common horizon of a shared course of history and a sense of common fate. While regional political integration does not require homogenization – Europe will never be a "melting pot" – it does require the cultivation of a regional political identity that "goes beyond mere legal classification."[35] According to Habermas's own terms, European political integration depends upon a territorially based political identity situated in a shared history. In the sense that the shared history occurs on the regional level, and entails solidarity among a variety of ethnic groups, it is understood as *post*national. Yet one could equally discuss this in terms of an "extended nationalism," or a regional civic-nationalism.[36]

Habermas tends to equate nationalism with ethnonationalism.[37] Yet "constitutional patriotism" in another manner of speaking is the civic-nationalism inspired by the principles of liberal democracy at work in a multicultural polity. While ethnonationalism places the basis for political membership in a collective identity existentially prior to state institutions, civic-nationalism understands the origins of political membership intertwined with political institutions. In the midst of the French Revolution, Sieyès defined the nation as a "body of associates living under *common* laws and *represented* by the same legislative assembly."[38] The nation is composed of citizens, equal before the law without reference to prepolitical ethnic identity.

This portrait of the nation is quite compatible with the political culture of Habermas's regional polity.[39] A democratized European Union would be animated by a spirit of "extended nationalism" in that its integration would depend upon a territorially based political identity, situated in a shared history, and cultivated by the constitution of a political process that enabled a continental collective capacity to make legitimately binding decisions.

Understanding democratic regionalism as a form of *extended nationalism*, however, has implications for its potential to embody "the future of democracy" as promised. It raises questions concerning both the potential applications of the model beyond Europe and its compatibility with the project of constituting a broader democratic world order, as well as the more general project of responding to the challenges of globalization by expanding the deliberative model of popular sovereignty beyond the nation-state form. The specific characteristics of any particular democratic regional integration must arise from the particular constellation of historical processes experienced in any given region. While the basic principles of liberal democratic governance may be the same across regions, their interpretation and institutional application remain situated in the particular historical horizons of a specific context. Thus one may expect the form of prospective regional polities to differ across regions. In what follows I will argue that, while Habermas makes a strong case for the possibility of a post-nation-state European democracy, the model's generality as the "initial form" of a democratic response to globalization is ultimately less convincing.

Regionalism as democratic world order: the future of democracy?

The European Union remains easily the most developed form of regional integration in the world, and it will continue to be so far into the foreseeable future. Thus it is logical that scholars turn to it to analyze regionalism's general feasibility as a form of economic and political organization. Habermas presents his model of the postnational polity, not simply as an argument for the democratization of the European Union, but as an attempt to understand how the practice of popular sovereignty might in general remain effective beyond the frame of the nation-state in the context of globalization.[40]

This approach leads to the following questions. First, is regionalism as a political project an adequate response to the challenges presented by globalization? More specifically, could a democratized EU indeed compensate for the lost competence and protective capacity of the nation-state? Second, does Habermas provide a general model as suggested – "the initial form" of the "future of democracy" – or is the form of his regional polity specific to Europe and not generally applicable to other regions in the world? And third, what is the relation between Habermas's regional model and the larger project of advancing a more democratic world order in the context of globalization? How does understanding the regional polity as an "extended nation" complicate the relation between the particular contexts of popular sovereignty and the universalism of a cosmopolitan world order?

The capacity of a regional polity

In economic terms, a successfully integrated European Union would certainly be strong enough to insulate itself from the risks of capital flight and fluctuations in the global market, so devastating to smaller nation-state economies. For example, Habermas argues that vibrant intraregional trade and direct investment in Europe would make the pursuit of strong social policies by the EU possible if the political will indeed existed. But if the potential effectiveness of a regional polity is greatly to be measured by the strength of its balance sheet, could such a model serve to redress the general inequities of the neoliberal global economy? Or would it simply be yet another tool – cost-prohibitive to most – to improve a developed region's competitive position in the transnational order, leaving the general architecture of the global political economy untouched? A world order dominated by self-sufficient regional blocs would risk devolving into a "neo-mercantilism"[41] in which protectionist rich region-states compete over access to the cheap materials and labor of the developing world.

However, Habermas recognizes that "the creation of larger political unities in itself changes nothing about the mode of locational competition as such..."[42] A regionalism of self-sufficient inward-looking "extended nationalisms" could easily slip into a system of defensive alliances, dividing the world into competitive blocs. But such a scenario would not take into account the important ways in which economic regionalization serves not simply as a bulwark *against* globalization but as a mediating, *complementary* process.[43] The speed, complexity, and flexibility of economic activity in the context of globalization means that simply expanding the territorial unit from nation-state to region-state is not sufficient to encompass the economic and political phenomena of the twenty-first century. As Manuel Castells has observed, many of the most significant social and economic practices of our time take place via networks that transcend the necessity of territorial contiguity. Multinational corporations spread their production processes across the globe, and brokers in New York trade in London and Tokyo.[44]

The idea of a democratic regionalism is not to establish a viable "fortress" closed off from the rest of the world, but rather to constitute a democratically governed polity with the capacity to act effectively in the transnational sphere. The constitution of such regional polities could represent a necessary step in reinvigorating the political capacity to regulate markets, and to protect labor from the exigencies of the global economy. And at the very least an economically vigorous, politically coherent and democratic European Union could serve as a check on American hegemony. But, in order to be effective, regional polities must be theorized in relation to a broader transnational order.

The constitution of the regional polity seeks to regain democratic regulatory and steering capacities at the transnational level. Regional polities, according to Habermas, could effectively take part in an "international negotiations system" which would seek to politically influence the global economic order. In cooperation with international organizations and global civil society actors, cosmopolitan regional polities could represent "at least a prospect for a world domestic policy without a world government."[45] That is to say, supranational regimes could with time become vital contributors to a transnational commitment to social justice within a decentralized cosmopolitan order. However, to be effective, the system would have to be characterized by a network of likeminded regional polities animated by a cosmopolitan commitment to transnational law – needless to say, not an easy achievement. Thus, at the very least, it remains important to consider whether Habermas's model of the post-nation-state democracy is applicable beyond the European case and into the cosmopolitan sphere.

Alternative paths to regionalism

Habermas's model of the regional polity clearly aspires to relevance beyond the European context, but he justifies it in particularly European terms. European history has developed along a path that particularly prepares Europe for the postnational moment: "The learning process that can lead toward European civil solidarity encompasses a series of *specifically* European experiences."[46] If, according to Habermas, the postnational polity develops out of a specific European experience, how are we to understand the project of democratic regionalism in other parts of the world? Have the histories of other parts of the world, such as Asia, Africa, or Latin America, developed along broadly similar lines? Clearly Europe is the furthest along on the path to regional integration, but are other regions simply at earlier stages or are they on different paths altogether? While Habermas's normative discourse theory of democracy has applications beyond the European sphere, clearly there are substantial differences among the regions of the world that would seem to prevent any simple correspondence between the European experience and other regional projects.

If, for Habermas, the signature event of European regional popular sovereignty has been the gradual "overcoming of particularisms" – or the triumph over religious and ethnonational chauvinism – faced with obstacles of a different sort, what form might regionalism take elsewhere? How might different political constellations effect the development of alternative forms of democratic regionalism? For example, the South American nation-states of the Andean Community have always shared a common religion, and they have never defined nationality by ethnicity, yet the exclusion and exploitation of indigenous populations has been an integral part of the region's complex history. Recognizing and redressing the special tragic history of indigenous groups in the region could result in the establishment of a regime of group rights in any future Andean democratic regionalism.

For example, Colombia incorporated special representation rights for indigenous groups into its new constitution of 1991; and throughout the 1990s indigenous movements in Ecuador and Bolivia made special claims on the state regarding agrarian reform and local autonomy.[47] In fact the transition from dictatorship to democracy in Latin America has brought with it a concomitant rise in ethnic-based movements in all of the countries in the region with large indigenous populations, with the exception of Peru.[48] Thus, *pace* Habermas, in some regions achieving the postnational polity may require accepting that, at times, democratic progress means the recognition of ethnic specificity, not necessarily its transcendence.

Farther afield, many have noted the differences between the process of regionalism in Asia and that in Europe.[49] Whereas European regionalism is based on a Weberian framework of "legal state integration," regionalization in the Asian Pacific is principally organized around rhetorical "community building" and informal "ethnic market capitalism."[50] While analysts observe the rise of "Asia's new regionalism" and ASEAN continues to develop regional ties,[51] economic regionalization in Asia depends less on interstate agreements and more on business networks that seek out comparative advantage and the benefits of informal ethnic solidarity. Japanese companies export production processes throughout the region. And the large body of "Overseas Chinese" living throughout South East Asia and Indonesia maintain a vast web of economic relations based on kinship and ethnicity, establishing finance, trade, and production networks that transcend state borders.[52]

Whereas the creation of a single integrated market and polity is the long-term goal of the European Union, "Asian governments see the complete elimination of economic barriers as more of a threat than an opportunity."[53] Asian governments see regionalization as a way to strengthen national sovereignty in the face of globalization. The end goal is not regional political union but, rather, heightened global competitiveness. Thus in comparison to

Europe, Asian nations are not simply at an earlier stage on the path to an EU style of regional integration; rather, they are on a different path altogether.

This can also be said about other processes of regionalization around the world. For one, it is important to note that different state traditions would tend to produce different forms of regional integration. The framework of an interstate treaty-based process of legal-state integration in Europe arises out of a strong Weberian state tradition. Weber famously defined the state as a political order whose "administrative staff successfully upholds a claim to the *monopoly* of the *legitimate* use of physical force in enforcement of its order."[54] And further: a modern state "possesses an administrative and legal order subject to change by legislation... [which] claims binding authority... over all action taking place in the area of its jurisdiction. It is thus a compulsory association with a territorial basis."[55] Habermas's definition of the state lies securely in this tradition, and it is particularly this vision of the state that is most challenged by processes of globalization.

However, the image of the state as a unified administrative order successfully integrating a particular territory under a single system of authority finds scant relation to reality in many parts of the world. Often national territory is only partially controlled by central government, as for example in the case of the long-standing autonomy of tribal groups on the Pakistani border with Afghanistan, or throughout the conflict plagued regions of Africa, for example in the Democratic Republic of Congo or Sudan. In fact, a primary concern of the African Union is the development of mechanisms to respond to civil conflicts within divided states on the continent, a concern far from the central preoccupation of the EU – a union of solidly consolidated nation-states.

Furthermore, the state often has to compete with other systems of authority in society, such as religious institutions, tribal councils, kinship structures, etc. Thus many states' traditions do not even approximate the Weberian ideal and are better understood under a different model.[56] For example, Joel Migdal's "state in society" approach understands the state as a *field* of multi-dimensional contestation that contends with multiple spheres of rule-governed behavior. In society the state is necessarily one actor among many. Furthermore, while the state may project an *image* of unity and control, its component parts tend to compete, engaging in *practices* that divide and undermine administrative coherence.[57]

Migdal is insistent that such contradictory states be understood not as failed Weberian states but as embodiments of a different *idea* of the state altogether. The "state in society" approach identifies a distinct tradition of state development often found in the developing world. Consequently, this would have to be taken into account when theorizing projects of democratic regionalism in many regions of the world. At the very least, it suggests a very different starting point from which to negotiate the transition to regional integration. And as a result, one might expect resulting forms of democratic regionalism to take alternative forms to the one theorized by Habermas.

Regionalism and cosmopolitan democracy

Understood here, regionalism is concerned with reinvigorating the democratic capacity to govern in the context of globalization. Integral to the project of democratic regionalism is the potential for transnational coordination between regional polities, civil society actors, and international organizations. The consolidation of regional polities, for Habermas, represents the possibility of providing an effective, democratically legitimate infrastructure to the international system for the first time. Like many before him, Habermas is skeptical about the normative justifiability and practical feasibility of a comprehensive World State.[58] He argues that an international system composed of regional polities, global civil society actors, and international organizations such as the UN would be preferable and more likely to succeed than a more comprehensive and integrated cosmopolitan democracy like the one proposed by David Held.[59] Habermas proposes a system of cosmopolitan *harmonization* rather than administrative institutional *consolidation*.[60]

According to Habermas, unlike the nation-state or the regional polity, a global political structure could not provide a strong enough basis in civic solidarity necessary to support the legitimacy conditions of an adequate social policy. In order to inspire the sense of collective identity necessary for the constitution of solidarity and the practice of popular sovereignty, a political community needs to distinguish between members and non-members, defining the group, and identifying the relevant shared history. A cosmopolitan community of world citizens, by definition, has no outside; all people are members. It cannot inspire the "ethical-political self-understanding of citizens" necessary for the cultivation of civic solidarity.[61] It cannot constitute the ethos of a shared way of life. Thus, Habermas argues, if there were to be an extension of policies of redistribution beyond the nation-state, it would have to occur at the level of regional polities like the European Union in conjunction with civil society actors and international institutions, rather than in a comprehensive World State.

Yet Habermas clearly seeks an international system regulated by more than the inconsistencies of transnational power politics and generalized commitments to human rights. In reflecting on Kant's *Perpetual Peace* with "the benefit of two hundred years' hindsight," Habermas argues that to be effective cosmopolitan law must have *force*:

> Cosmopolitan law must be institutionalized in such a way that it is binding on the individual governments. The community of peoples must be able to ensure that its members act at least in conformity with the law through the threat of sanctions... [62] The point of cosmopolitan law is... that it bypasses the collective subjects of international law and directly establishes the legal status of the individual subjects by granting them unmediated membership in the association of free and equal world citizens.[63]

At its best, for Habermas, the present is a transition between the Westphalian system of nation-states and a future decentered cosmopolitan legal order characterized by the broad acceptance of human rights and a transnational commitment to social justice.[64] Democratic regional polities offer the best practical stepping-stones to this cosmopolitan future. Yet Habermas's model presents a certain difficulty: achieving cosmopolitan legal harmony necessitates convergence upon a political identity he suggests lacks the ethical-political foundations necessary to produce democratic legitimacy. For "[e]ven a world-wide consensus on human rights could not serve as the basis for a strong equivalent to the *civic* solidarity that emerged in the framework of the nation-state."[65]

Habermas envisions a system where processes of democratic political identity formation remain tied to national and regional historical experience. Yet it is unclear, in Habermas's own terms, how cosmopolitan law would be able to gain democratic legitimacy, given that world citizenship cannot constitute the requisite sense of civic solidarity, something he recognizes is necessary even in the discourse model of the regional polity. For Habermas, "constitutional patriotism" may serve to reconcile the universality of cosmopolitan right and the particularity of democratic legitimacy. Yet "constitutional patriotism" proves to be either too strong or too weak to succeed at the global level. Either it strongly binds a political community together around vigorous particular interpretations of abstract constitutional rights at the cost of cosmopolitan identification, or its content remains at such a level of generality that it allows for cosmopolitan identification but fails to produce the "ethic of solidarity" on the domestic level necessary for the production of democratic legitimacy.[66]

Thus the transition from an emerging "international negotiation system" (where regional polities may serve to provide an effective infrastructure for a decentered global governance) to a future cosmopolitan legal order (where a universal law holds individuals and institutions accountable for the protection of human rights) entails a more radical leap than Habermas is willing to concede. While Habermas claims to oppose a world state, the force-backed binding nature of cosmopolitan law he seeks does suggest a greater level of institutional consolidation than he lets on. William Scheuerman has argued that, in order for Habermas's system of "multilayered governance" to work, entities such as the European Union or the United Nations would indeed have to take on more state-like properties than Habermas cares to admit. For one, if peace and human rights law are going to be consistently and non-politically enforced, some form of transnational independent military capacity would seem necessary.[67]

Habermas offers a form of democratic regional politics as the best practical stepping-stone between national present and cosmopolitan future. Yet the stone path falls one step short: the ethical foundations of democratic legitimacy remain unable to extend the final distance to a globalized system of law. The project is subject to a serious conceptual problem. Popular sovereignty and democratic legitimacy depend upon the cultivation of a common political culture and the solidarity that arises from it. Yet the conditions for the constitution of such a culture are incompatible with the global domain of cosmopolitan governance.

Recent economic, political, technological and cultural developments have put pressure on the traditional institutions of modern representative democracy. Referred to collectively as "globalization," these processes are said to give impetus to the restructuring of modern democratic practice. Habermas presents a democratized European Union as a model for the reinstitutionalization of democracy beyond the nation-state form. I have argued that, while Habermas makes a good case for the potential democratization of the Union, the application of the model beyond the European case requires substantial additional theorization.

Regional democratic political integration depends upon the development of a common political culture that can transcend ethnonational solidarity; in this sense it must be "postnational." However, as Habermas argues, in order to be successful, regional civil solidarity must remain situated in a shared history, and it must be animated by an "affective attachment to a particular ethos... a specific way of life."[68] Regional political solidarity thus remains dependent upon a territorially based political identity situated in a common historical horizon. It must constitute what is in effect an "extended nation," and as a result the specific form of democratic regional integration must arise out of the particular historical processes experienced in any given region. It would follow that if a process of democratic regionalization were to take hold beyond the European continent it would have to develop in relation to the specific political, economic and social traditions of the region. While different regional democratic projects may maintain common liberal democratic principles at their core, their manifestation within alternative state and economic traditions would necessitate alternative political structures.

Regionalism is a political project that seeks to regain the capacity for the effective practice of popular sovereignty in the face of global processes that transcend the borders of current democratic institutions. In order to be effective, regional polities must be understood in relation to a broader global order of multiple regions, civil society actors and international institutions. Thus it is important to understand how a variety of transnational and regional political structures might develop, and how such structures may remain compatible with the project of advancing a more broadly democratic world order in the context of globalization. Habermas's "postnational constellation" provides an important step in understanding the potential for regional democratization in Europe, but "the future of democracy" beyond the European continent, by Habermas's own reasoning, must entail a further diversification of forms.

Given a fortuitous history and a determined political will there is no definitive reason why a transnational deliberative process of self-legislation could not function to reproduce the political solidarity necessary for the constitution of democratic legitimacy on the macro-regional scale. However, the historic tension between the ideal of universal democratic citizenship and the necessarily particular contexts in which it becomes situated is surely exacerbated when extended to the global domain. Thus either the normative legitimacy of a coercive cosmopolitan legal order may not be understood in the terms of popular sovereignty, as Habermas intends it, or its legitimacy must remain rooted in the local, national, and regional practice of popular sovereignty and democratic legitimation. In this case, understanding how a variety of political arrangements and processes of legitimation may maintain their social and historical particularity while remaining compatible with a broader system of transnational law must become an integral component of cosmopolitan theorizing.

Realizing the potential for a democratic coordination of globalization in the absence of world government requires theorizing further the interrelation between such diverse political forms; and it requires investigating how each particular context of democratic legitimation may be brought to bear on the coordination of global governance. This of course presents an extraordinary challenge for theory and practice at all levels: local, national, regional and transnational.

Perhaps no theorist has taken up the project of rethinking democracy in the context of globalization more so than David Held. In a series of articles and book-length studies since the mid-1990s he has delineated the institutional and normative bases for a decentralized but integrated political and legal system that could one day cover the globe. According to Held the constitution of such a global order would be multilayered and heterogeneous, and it would thus remain sensitive to the particularities of local political traditions. In fact, he argues, the establishment of a cosmopolitan level of democratic practice would reinvigorate participatory politics on the local and national levels. It is thus to his theory of cosmopolitan democracy that we must now turn.

7 Responses to globalization II
David Held's cosmopolitan democracy and global civil society

No political theorist has engaged in a more sustained and thorough consideration of the consequences of globalization than David Held. In addition to contributions in democratic theory he has also contributed to some of the most comprehensive empirical studies of globalization as a historical, political, economic and cultural phenomenon.[1] In his theory of cosmopolitan democracy Held articulates a comprehensive global system of governance. He lays out the institutional and normative basis for a common structure of action that would in theory cover the entire globe in a decentralized but integrated political and legal system. Such a structure of cosmopolitan sovereignty, he argues, could serve as the final authority at the global level while at the same time reinvigorating popular sovereignty at the local and national levels.

Held's concerns regarding globalization and the nation-state fall into three general categories familiar to our discussion thus far. First, Held argues that the regulatory and protective capacity of the state is being transformed – and in many cases reduced – by expanding political, economic, military, and cultural connections across borders. Second, he argues, such connections create chain reactions in political and economic institutions that transcend national borders. Decisions made at a distance have a profound effect on the political and economic development of nation-states, and as a result domestic constituencies experience a narrowing of the passage through which they may steer the course of government, thus limiting their capacity for collective self-determination. And, third, processes of globalization transform political identities in myriad ways, causing regional, subregional or local groups to reevaluate the representative capacity of their central governments, stimulating the constitutive authority of the people to seek change.[2] For Held, the solution lies in the gradual institution of a form of cosmopolitan sovereignty that would one day cover the globe.

In what follows I will argue that while the transformation and weakening of the state's protective capacity may indeed lead to the need for a form of cosmopolitan sovereignty, Held's model raises two important questions for the concept of popular sovereignty as discussed here. First, to what extent would local and national collective self-determination be limited under a global structure of cosmopolitan law? And, second, how are we to identify and mobilize the proper constitutive authority necessary for the legitimate constitution of such a system of global governance?

The next section will discuss the system of cosmopolitan sovereignty as described by Held. The following one will articulate what I call *the problem of cosmopolitan founding*, the difficulty of articulating the proper constitutive authority for the constitution of cosmopolitan global governance. And, finally, the closing section will interrogate the concept of global civil society as a proposed form of democratic politics that could serve to bring legitimacy to the constitution of cosmopolitan global governance.

Cosmopolitan sovereignty

A global democracy

As we saw in Chapters 3–5, globalization poses many challenges to the model of the independent democratic nation-state. While the vision of the sovereign Westphalian state – defined as completely free from the confines of external authority – was from the beginning an exaggeration, or in Stephen Krasner's terms a form of "organized hypocrisy," today the international domain is faced with a proliferation of centers of authority that clearly undermine the relative autonomy of the nation-state in unprecedented ways.[3]

According to Held the development of a system of cosmopolitan sovereignty is both required to adapt democratic practice to a changing world and remarkably consistent with the trajectory of international law established after World War II. In contrast to a model of sovereignty based on the presence of a single consolidated final authority, or manifest "effective control" over a given state or delimited territory, the post-war order has increasingly focused on the principle of "legitimate authority," defined by a reinvigorated commitment to human rights and democratic governance.[4] In contrast to the classic Realist position that the international sphere is defined by anarchy, Held argues, states have increasingly initiated and promoted the establishment of supranational levels of regulations, rights, and duties that, in effect, extend the liberal concern with limiting sovereign government to the international domain.[5] Whereas previously international law took the independent self-interest and autonomy of states as its starting point, much international law beginning in the second half of the twentieth century and continuing into the twenty-first – for example, commitments to human rights and environmentalism – proceeds from the principle of universal humanity and a shared duty to care for the globe and its inhabitants.[6]

Most dramatically, the UN General Assembly expressly approved "the responsibility to protect" in the World Summit Outcome Document of 2005. There it declared that while "[e]ach individual State has the responsibility to protect its populations from genocide, war crimes, ethnic cleansing and crimes against humanity," if states fail to do so, "[t]he international community, through the United Nations, also has the responsibility" and must be prepared "to take collective action, in a timely and decisive manner." Such action includes supporting state efforts through peaceful, diplomatic, and humanitarian means, but clearly may in the last resort also include force. This principle was later reaffirmed by the UN Security Council in 2006. While it remains by no means settled or uncontroversial, the responsibility to protect articulates the idea that state sovereignty entails positive duties that, if not met, may be borne by the international community as a whole, superseding the government of an individual nation-state.[7]

No matter how contingent or precarious such developments may be, Held argues, it is but a short if mighty jump to the establishment of a cosmopolitan order which he defines as "nothing more or less than the entrenchment and enforcement of democratic public law across all peoples[.]"[8] The particulars of this political order conceived by Held are complex and burdensome. Yet this should not discourage, for its seeds, Held argues, have been planted in the post-war regime of international institutions and the Universal Declaration of Human Rights. The task is thus to develop them further, to follow them through to their logical fulfillment. And he argues this is in fact necessary if we wish to maintain the practice of democratic governance in the context of globalization.[9] A system of "cosmopolitan democratic law" would provide a "common structure of action" to protect people's rights and secure the conditions for the possibility of democratic participation at the local, national, regional, and even international levels.[10]

Starting with an ambitious, some might say utopian, reform of the UN system, Held envisions the establishment of a Global Parliament and a globally interconnected legal system. A "Boundary Court" would have to be established when disputes of jurisdiction (local, national, regional, cosmopolitan) needed resolution; and an effective international military force would have to be organized, diminishing reliance on a national hegemonic military power like the United States.[11] While the nation-state in some form would remain, according to Held, in such a cosmopolitan order the *sovereign* nation-state "would, in due course, 'wither away'."[12]

Most recently he has described this project as the pursuit of a "global social democracy."[13] For Held, the pursuit of economic justice is an integral part of the democratization of global governance. Liberal internationalism is primarily concerned with limiting the abuses of *political* power. A cosmopolitan social democracy would be equally concerned with the abuses of *economic* power; and, as such, it would further expand the current liberal human rights regime to include the entrenchment of social rights. For Held, the principles of social justice must be incorporated into the structure of global governance in order for the project of economic globalization to continue without resulting in catastrophic divisions that would inevitably undermine the entire project. In this way he holds on to the Rousseauian concern for the dangers of inequality that was discussed in Chapter 4. Held thus calls for a new "global covenant" that would "reduce the economic vulnerability of the poorest countries by transforming market access, eliminating unsustainable debt, reversing the outflow of net capital assets from the South to the North, and creating new finance facilities for development purposes."[14]

Assuming such a comprehensive and progressive order could be realized, and would not collapse under its own weight, it could represent a serious response to the economic, political, and environmental challenges of globalization. For now one can only speculate. However, serious questions arise when considering the conceptual ramifications of Held's project, independent of concerns about the questionable practicality of its institutional architecture or the doubtful geopolitical possibility of its being realized. For example, how could such a comprehensive polity incorporate the many levels of solidarity and identity that necessarily remain within the cosmopolitan system? How does Held make room for a variety of processes of collective self-determination? The institution of *cosmopolitan* sovereignty leads to the question of *popular* sovereignty and *collective self-determination* on the local and national levels. After all, his project is not simply to reinvigorate the capacity of government, but to understand how processes of democratic legitimation may be extended beyond the nation-state. If, as Held says, "the idea of democracy derives its power and significance... from the idea of self-determination..."[15] how are we to understand the maintenance of this idea in the context of globalization?

Collectivity, self-determination, democratic autonomy

At their core, democracy and popular sovereignty entail a commitment to the notion of self-determination. They imply the idea that people ought to have the freedom to choose the type of society in which they live; and they ought to be free to contribute to the steering of the political structures that govern their lives and work. In the context of globalization, such governing structures are increasingly disconnected from – or beyond the reach of – the established mechanisms of democratic input and accountability. Thus cosmopolitan democracy seeks to consolidate a new level of public law and communication beyond the nation-state level. But the project of constituting a single legal and political structure to encompass the globe in turn raises a variety of questions concerning the freedom of local or national self-determination. From a broadly communitarian or multiculturalist perspective, cosmopolitan democracy appears to lack the capacity to incorporate diverse political practices and traditions. It is charged with misunderstanding the importance of identity to the foundations of political obligation and solidarity; or with being too abstract or disconnected from the social structures of local contexts.[16] Yet clearly cosmopolitan democracy could not require absolute homogeneity on a global scale; this would represent an obvious impossibility.

Held's response lies in the principle of democratic autonomy, its recognition of community, and its implicit commitment to cosmopolitan law. In the liberal tradition, a commitment to self-determination presupposes the normativity of

David Held's cosmopolitan democracy 115

individual autonomy. Simply put, it states that individuals "should be free and equal in the determination of the conditions of their own lives."[17] However, given that individuals always live in groups or among other individuals, the principle needs to be qualified: People ought to be free in so far as they don't violate the rights of others – liberty is not license. Thus for Held the principle of "democratic autonomy" is not the right of atomistic individuals to greedily pursue self-interest without constraint; rather, it is a "structural principle of self-determination where 'the self' is part of the collectivity or 'the majority'..." It is "autonomy within the constraints of community."[18]

For Held, the primary unit of moral concern remains the individual; but individuals are always found within particular communities that frame and enable – or at times inhibit – self-determination. Thus, Held argues, while we may depend upon and encourage a "persistence of a plurality of frames of political meaning" there are justifiable limits to the moral acceptability of relations established between individuals and their communities.[19] Individual self-determination does not require independence from tradition, but it does signify the capacity and freedom to choose alternative life paths whether through reinterpretation, critique, or exit.

Yet there is nothing inherent to a community-based interpretation of political authority that is necessarily antithetical to the recognition of the normative and practical benefits of extending the rule of law to the transnational domain. Possessing a primary political attachment to one's own community does not signify an *ipso facto* rejection of general normative commitments to human rights and representative democracy. Rather it signifies that such commitments must be understood as rooted and substantiated in specific social contexts that inform and motivate people's various levels of commitment to the pursuit of transnational democratic politics. In fact, a consideration of globalization stemming from this insight could encourage the project of cosmopolitanism, as more and more communities come into regular contact, intertwine, and learn from one another, expanding the awareness of diverse ways of life. Held is aware that there is no emerging "common global pool of memories" to constitute a single global political community. In fact he argues that cosmopolitan democracy, remaining consistent with the principle of democratic autonomy, creates greater possibilities for a diverse and reinvigorated participatory politics in the local sphere.[20]

Held envisions cosmopolitan democracy to be a system of overlapping authorities and divided loyalties.[21] In a cosmopolitan democracy individuals would remain connected to their local communities, but political participation also would be structured along national, regional, and even global lines. Admittedly, this would likely result in boundary conflicts regarding what issue is to be settled where. At the very least, it would demand a rigorous system for determining the jurisdiction of particular issues. For example, distinguishing a national issue from a regional one would be an important and often difficult task.[22] According to Held, the key to keeping this system from descending into a chaotic medieval order of multiple overlapping authorities without a clear final arbiter would be the general commitment to the "cosmopolitan model of democratic autonomy."²³ In order to avoid the predominance of centrifugal forces, each level of the system would have to remain compatible with the overall cosmopolitan model.

Held argues that cosmopolitan law would represent "... a binding framework for the political business of states, societies and regions not a detailed regulative framework for the direction of all their affairs."²⁴ With regard to general normative commitments and basic institutional structures, governance at all levels would have to conform to the principles of cosmopolitan democratic law; but, consistent with such principles, there would be an undetermined plurality of approaches and policies possible: self-determination remains manifest in the details.

In fact, Held argues, in relation to the current context, cosmopolitan law would liberate self-determination. Held claims that a commitment to democratic autonomy embedded in a cosmopolitan legal structure is a *necessary* condition of collective self-determination in the context of globalization. The claim being if we choose democracy in the context of globalization we must choose some form of "cosmopolitan democracy," given the shortcomings of the nation-state to regulate transnational affairs and protect the people from the exigencies of a globalizing economy.

Nevertheless, the requirement of cosmopolitan compatibility does suggest a remainder of uncertainty in Held's model: How much latitude could each particular collectivity maintain for distinguishing itself from the general political structure of the cosmopolitan whole? If we could assume that a form of liberal or social democracy indeed would be the world's choice, I would be inclined to gladly accept a version of Held's model. However, unfortunately, this is not a reasonable assumption; there is too much evidence to the contrary. And this presents a political and conceptual problem that Held does not sufficiently address.

While Held clearly recognizes the persistence of pluralism, his model requires convergence upon a global overlapping consensus: the development of a common cosmopolitan political culture. Held's cosmopolitan democracy is designed to maximize self-determination; but in the absence of a preexisting consensus the institutional reform necessary to constitute such a system would require coercive means. And a top-down systemic reform executed on an unwilling base would have volatile consequences. Assuming the normativity of Held's model of cosmopolitan democracy, a fundamental question still remains concerning the bridge between globalizing present and cosmopolitan future: What is the mechanism or agent of crossing? Held does not theorize what it would mean to legitimately constitute cosmopolitan democracy, given the fact many would not freely choose it. James Mittelman poses this question in terms of agency: Who are the agents of cosmopolitan democracy? What are the social forces that could begin to bring this development about, not in some distant possible future, but now within the context of contemporary processes of globalization?²⁵ In the language of popular sovereignty, Held does not define a legitimate *constitutive authority* for such an order, giving rise to what I call *the problem of cosmopolitan founding*.

The problem of cosmopolitan founding

Obstacles to transnational democratization

The normative core of a cosmopolitan democratic order is firmly rooted in the liberal tradition. Those who find this tradition distasteful will tend to oppose Held's cosmopolitan democracy. Those who resist the language of autonomy and self-determination may resist the cosmopolitan democratic project altogether. This is true not simply for some non-Western traditions, but for tendencies within the West as well. Indeed, Held suggests that at their core the Rousseauian and Marxist traditions – not to mention conservative Judeo-Christian traditions – do not entail a commitment to the principle of individual autonomy.[26]

To what extent does Held presuppose convergence into a global political society? He makes clear that he does not see globalization inevitably leading toward a "world society," a single integrated global community.[27] However, he remains dependent on a thinner notion of political society. Cosmopolitan governance depends upon a fundamental agreement over the need to regulate association by democratically legitimate law on a global scale, and for Held this must include an international commitment to social justice as the organizing principle of the global economy.[28] Currently, none of the principal actors in the international arena – not states, peoples, or capital – would participate in such an agreement. None has an immediate interest in the transnational democratization of power.[29]

For example, a new level of regulation and oversight is antithetical to the libertarian instincts of capital, the driving force behind neoliberal ideology. While capital benefits from international legal agreements guaranteeing property relations and processes of exchange, it opposes regulatory procedures that might restrict labor or trade policies in the name of social interests. States, as the major actors in the international arena, have a strong interest in maintaining their *de jure* sovereignty; sovereign status remains the foundation of state identity and agency in the international arena. This is never to be given up lightly. And, perhaps most troublesome for the cosmopolitan vision, while individuals are set to benefit the most from cosmopolitan democratic law, *peoples* are often the most reactionary forces regarding notions of world community and transnational solidarity. Popular opinion is often more nationalistic and parochial than that of political, social, and economic elites – witness, again, the rejection of the European constitution by the people of France and the Netherlands.

In the terminology of international regime theory, Held's model is "knowledge-based."[30] It arises from a deep appreciation of the history of political theory, and a strong normative commitment to the potential of international institutions. However, more "interest-based" or "power-based" theories emphasize the difficulty in consolidating international institutions, especially those that would establish levels of authority superior to the nation-state. They draw attention to the historically self-interested nature of states and capital, categorically impeding the development of cosmopolitan sovereignty.[31] Held would argue that such models, especially the power-based Realist school, employ a too narrow, rational-choice method when analyzing the international system. And as such they are limited in their understanding of how change might be brought about based upon the normative commitments of national leaders and policymakers.

According to Held, if the trajectory of the twentieth century continues from a power-based state system to a regime of liberal international law, the development of cosmopolitan sovereignty ought to follow. Yet the effectiveness with which the United States subverted the mechanisms of international law in the pursuit of the War on Terror, and the general resistance of the Bush administration to the constraints of international law, suggest the trajectory of the twenty-first century may be tragically other. In developing a model for the democratic constitution of cosmopolitan sovereignty, geopolitics and state power relations – and, in general, forces antagonistic to the development of rigorous regimes of international law – must be taken further into account. If international law is to move beyond its traditional foundation in state sovereignty, the path to a cosmopolitan order is anything but predetermined; in fact, at the height of the Bush Doctrine's defiance it appeared the end result of the fall of the Westphalian system could just as easily be the growth of a global empire.[32]

To be fair, Held's later work does attempt to address the hegemonic status of the Washington-based security and economic agendas. He argues that a coalition of European social democrats, liberal Americans, and developing countries seeking fair trade and debt relief, allied with powerful NGOs, could provide the impulse to push the international agenda toward a "global social democracy." In this spirit he has striven to provide detailed policy recommendations for the project of reforming global governance in the direction of a more social democratic future. Doing so in accessible terms, he has provided an invaluable service for the practitioners of global policy. Nevertheless, while the formation of such a powerful coalition for cosmopolitan social democracy is certainly within the realm of possibility, after even the most cursory survey of the contemporary scene one would be hard pressed to call it likely. And the rise of authoritarian China as a global player and consistent critic of the Western human rights regime only complicates matters further. Held is admittedly an optimist.[33]

The conditions for the establishment of a common political culture on a global scale do not exist. While this must not spell doom for the project of cosmopolitan democracy as a normative ideal, it does raise tough questions concerning the constitution of the global political culture necessary to legitimately institute a system of cosmopolitan democratic law. How does the system incorporate groups that reject its normative appeal? This is more than a practical or institutional question. The acceleration of globalization and the spread of cosmopolitan ideals have witnessed a concomitant rise in reactionary and extremist activism. To institute cosmopolitan law without a broad-based supportive politics is to invite violent, energetic counteraction. Held is at his best when he theorizes either the global reality of contemporary affairs or the ideal of a cosmopolitan future. But it is the road between that is the most challenging and vital. For Held, the short-term project is to reform the international system according to its inherent principles, which, he argues, logically lead toward cosmopolitan social democracy. However, he does not provide a sufficient conceptualization of the political process that could achieve this end in the context of vigorous dissent and extreme asymmetries of power.

Disaggregated citizenship

Held seeks to understand the constitution of cosmopolitan law with the same conceptual apparatus as the democratic nation-state. Yet in such terms democratic legitimacy remains dependent upon the cultivation of a common political culture that is incompatible with the global domain. In such case, either the normative legitimacy of cosmopolitan governance cannot be understood with the same conceptual apparatus as the democratic polity; or we must understand cosmopolitan democracy as a regulative ideal, eternally suspended into the future, never realized, but capable of guiding present practice. In the case of the first, a critical democratic theory must articulate how the normative elements of each level of politics are distinguished and how they are interrelated. In the second case, a critical democratic theory must turn to the conceptualization of political practice in the moment between globalizing present and cosmopolitan future. Jean Cohen takes a version of the first route. In the last section and the concluding Chapter 8 I take a version of the second.

Faced with globalization's challenges to democratic governance, Jean Cohen advocates a disaggregated model of citizenship. We may transcend the perceived tensions between cosmopolitanism and democracy, she argues, by separating the component parts of the traditional model of citizenship: (1) the *democratic* element related to political participation, (2) the *juridical* element of legal personhood, and (3) the *identity* component of political membership. Whereas the juridical component of citizenship, conferring legal status on individuals as equal before the law, is compatible with universal inclusion, the *democratic* and *identity* components always entail some form of exclusion. The members of a polity with rights to participation will always be less then those possessing general legal rights, and recognition of the status of political *members* presupposes the existence of non-members.[34]

For Habermas and Held these component parts remain normatively intertwined. But Cohen argues that it is only in separating the democratic, juridical, and identity components that cosmopolitan citizenship becomes feasible. We could imagine a cosmopolitan system of juridical citizenship securing the status of all individuals as legal persons protected by cosmopolitan law and universal human rights on a global scale, supported by a variety of democratic political practices on the local, national, and perhaps even regional levels.

This approach points toward a potentially rich and dynamic model of citizenship. However, questions remain concerning the problem of cosmopolitan founding. The notion of "legal person" refers to individuals in relation to a system of coercive rules and authoritative protections as opposed to the abstract normativity of universal human rights, referring to humanity as such.[35] However, given the potential for legal systems to be abused or appropriated by self-interested actors, the legitimacy question must be raised once the institution of a *coercive* system of cosmopolitan law is introduced. If necessarily disconnected from democratic procedures, how are we to understand the origins of cosmopolitan legal authority? Cohen suggests the justification of a global human rights regime "lies in the end in our willingness to publicly acknowledge global interdependency and to shape our worldwide interrelations *justly.*"[36]

Thus a juridical notion of cosmopolitan citizenship separated from the democratic and identity components would still depend upon a global consensus on the need to regulate our interactions by means of a cosmopolitan system of law. It would still depend upon the negotiation of treaties, charters, protocols, and the like to provide the necessary sense of legitimacy. Thus it does not overcome the difficulties encountered in Held's cosmopolitan democracy; the problem of securing a requisite consensus among a vast, diverse and recalcitrant global society continues. Separating the juridical component of cosmopolitan citizenship from the democratic and identity components does not bypass the necessity of constituting a sense of global commonality that could somehow animate the development of a transnational civil society. Hence the problem of legitimate cosmopolitan founding remains.

Held diagnoses the threat to traditional forms of democratic politics posed by processes of globalization, and he articulates a normative and institutional vision of cosmopolitan democracy as a response to that threat. However, I have argued that he does not sufficiently theorize the democratic constitution of such a system. One is left with the impression that cosmopolitan democracy is an elite project constituted from the top down.[37] Habermas, as we saw, offers a form of democratic regional politics as the best bridge to the constitution of cosmopolitan democratic law. But the bridge falls short of the far side: the ethical foundations of popular sovereignty and democratic legitimacy remain unable to expand to the global domain. We are left to inquire, How might a form of popular sovereignty be incorporated into the formation of cosmopolitan democracy? How are we to identify the proper constitutive authority necessary for the legitimate institution of such an order?

Global civil society

Both Habermas and Held encounter a tension between the particular contexts of democratic legitimacy and the universalism demanded of a global political culture. In part this is the result of conceiving cosmopolitan democracy in the vein of a unified system with clearly defined levels of jurisdiction, vertically integrated by a general commitment to cosmopolitan law. In order to think of democratic processes as either prior to or independent of such vertical integration, one must conceptualize a horizontal non-hierarchical form of political organization. One potentially fruitful way of doing so is through the form of the network.

Network governance

Cosmopolitan democracy and democratic regionalism are strategies to regain lost capacities for collective self-government by establishing new levels of political integration, either on the regional or global scale. Theories of global *network governance* on the other hand attempt to elude the tensions inherent to projects of integration by operating under the assumption that social and political institutions must adapt to an environment of increasingly decentered authority.[38] Theorists of global governance reject the traditional state-centered view of international relations and global politics. They argue that in the last quarter of the twentieth century the world witnessed a proliferation of centers of authority whose sources are neither the individual nation-state nor the state-based treaties of international law. Instead they develop out of interest-based functional networks that either bypass or establish equal partnerships with government in the international sphere. For example, the International Accounting Standards Committee has set international accountancy standards independently of state regulation since 1973. And since 1998 the committee's authority has been officially recognized by the G-7.[39]

In contrast to the hierarchical model of state authority, the model of global governance is based on the horizontal form of the "network." While, as we have seen, the contributing factors to the decline of state capacities are many, James Rosenau has argued, "one of the most important of these has been the shifting balance between hierarchical and network forms of organization."[40] Manual Castells's pioneering work in this field is instructive: simply put, "a network is a set of interconnected nodes."[41] The character of the individual node depends upon the specific network: a currency trader's office in London is a node in the global financial market; a local gathering of International ANSWER, a node in the anti-war movement; an Al-Qaeda cell in Pakistan, a node in the global terrorism network.

This manner of decentering transnational practice away from the nation-state has clearly been amplified and accelerated by the revolution in information and communication technology. Most important, the development of the world wide web has vastly improved the capacity of networks to coordinate action, disseminate information, and recruit new members. In the information age of the internet and satellite communications, networks have the capacity to all but transcend distance completely. For the academic organizing a conference or editing a book, a colleague overseas who checks his e-mail regularly is ironically "closer" than the emeritus professor down the hall who still refuses to "get connected." Distance in the information age, Castells argues, ranges from zero, between any two nodes on the same network, to the infinite distance to a point outside of a given network. In this way political action and authority based in the network form are *deterritorialized*. Distance or proximity becomes detached from territorial space, thus undermining the paradigm of the state, categorically organized around the geographic limits of "national territory."

The network form clearly raises the ability of non-state actors to accumulate political power. But does this signify a redistribution of power to the historically powerless? Is it a form of transnational democratization? Could it represent the form of a transnational constitutive authority in the process of founding a cosmopolitan democracy? Can we speak of it as a form of transnational popular sovereignty in the same way we have discussed cosmopolitan politics or democratic regionalism? The movement against the war in Iraq indeed established "chains of equivalence" across a broad swath of humanity, creating a potent political solidarity where there was none previously.[42] And yet, while network-based governance does perhaps carry such a potential for inclusion, it doesn't necessarily do so. For example, one can observe an emerging pattern in which the governance of technical issues is given over to networks of experts. Ngaire Woods argues that an emerging form of "technocratic network governance" devolves regulatory procedures away from traditionally representative institutions and processes of transparency into the inaccessible, jargon-filled board rooms of technical elite rule. In such cases, legitimacy becomes detached from democratic procedure. The technical quality of results comes to matter more than the status of "democratic inputs."[43] Thus network forms, while non-hierarchical, are not necessarily inclusive; they are in effect normatively ambivalent. They may serve as tools of exclusion as easily as they can provide avenues for the proliferation of political participation.

As we have seen, recent years have witnessed the accelerated evolution of a complex system of decentered transnational regulation and rulemaking on a near global scale. This system includes states, international organizations, treaty regimes, security relationships, transnational networks, private agencies, public–private partnerships, financial institutions and more. Serving an important function in an increasingly interconnected world, this complex of mechanisms and organizations, however, lacks a coherent structure for the consideration of democratic will-formation. That is to say, global governance suffers from a clear democratic deficit. As Held has argued, "global governance is said to be distorted in so far as it promotes the interests of the most powerful states and global social forces, and restricts the realization of greater global social justice and human security."[44]

If network governance is only potentially a democratic form of transnational politics, how do we distinguish its democratic form from its exclusionary cousin? May we specify "global civil society" as the democratic form of network based global governance? While the meaning of the term "civil society" has shifted over time, in the post-Cold War world it has come largely to signify the sphere of "social interaction," independent from the state and the market, encompassing formal and informal associations, non-governmental organizations (NGOs), social movements, and other processes of public communication.[45]

Concomitant with processes of globalization and the spread of information technology, civil society in this sense has transcended national and regional borders. The 1990s witnessed the vast growth in the number of transnational social movements, NGOs, and international citizen networks, for the first time contributing to the sense that a truly global civil society was in the making. Such movements and organizations contributed to the growing emphasis on human rights and social justice in the international agenda in the late 1990s. At times they have proven to be genuinely effective in changing international policy, for example, in the case of the campaign against land mines.[46] The strong presence of civil society organizations at the large global forums of the 1990s such as the Rio Earth Summit or the Beijing conference on Women and Development, and the subsequent advent of the annual World Social Forum have also elevated the presence and influence of such actors on the global stage.

However, does this then mean that the continued spread of civil society organizations represents the democratization of global governance? Does global civil society represent the constitutive authority of cosmopolitan democracy? Some have argued that the central role played by civil society organizations in the Ottawa Convention Banning Landmines served for the first time to democratize the process of international legislation.[47] Could perhaps a vibrant global civil society provide the necessary democratic legitimacy to a decentered form of global governance? Could it extend the conditions for the constitution of democratic governance all the way out to the global domain, thus overcoming the tensions encountered by Habermas and Held?

Global civil society as agent of democratization

A strong version of the civil society argument would suggest that a vibrant, diverse global civil society could democratize global governance, independent of reform at the level of states or international law. James Rosenau has argued that the more global civil society becomes populated with a variety of social movements, NGOs, and international institutions the more global governance will in fact exhibit "democratic tendencies." Empowered by the information and communication revolution, such grassroots networks and social movements can provide a counterbalance to transnational "technical networks" that support or reproduce the agenda of entrenched interests. As global civil society becomes more populated with a diversity of movements and organizations making specific demands on specific institutions and articulating previously excluded political perspectives the more receptive to popular concerns and the more transparent the mechanisms of global governance will become.[48]

Similarly, John Dryzek argues that, in the absence of global government, transnational democratization is achievable at the discursive level through the capacity of global civil society to control the terms of debate. He argues that the "network form can play a key part in establishing deliberative democratic control over the terms of political discourse and so the operation of governance in the international system."[49] This represents the claim that a version of the deliberative model of popular sovereignty could still function without the existence of strong publics. But this reduces popular sovereignty to the status of mere force of influence, rather than essential constitutive authority or primary mechanism of collective self-determination. It relegates popular sovereignty to the weak public sphere, disconnected from the mechanisms of rulemaking and governance.

Dryzek's view, in fact, represents a very ideal vision of the position and potential of global civil society. In many respects, global civil society is extremely limited and often does not live up to its normative expectations. Global civil society organizations are often Eurocentric, frequently coopted by powerful interests, and of questionable representative status, their policies often developed behind closed doors, far from public debate. The claim that in international affairs the mere presence of global civil society organizations represents a democratization of the international domain must be treated with extreme caution.

For one, global civil society institutions arise out of the same political economy as other international institutions. Thus you find the same inequalities reproduced in civil society institutions as elsewhere.[50] For example, civil society resources are much higher in the countries of the Organization of Economic Cooperation and Development (OECD), thus tipping the scale of influence heavily in their favor. In fact, predictably, the only city outside of Europe or America in the top ten centers for international NGOs is Tokyo.[51] Furthermore, clearly not every civil society organization directly or indirectly promotes values consistent with liberal or social democracy. What about associations promoting extreme sectarian or fundamentalist causes? Consideration certainly must be given to what Simone Chambers and Jeff Kopstein have called "bad civil society."[52]

A more moderate form of the global civil society argument understands its role within the context of domestic reform and international agreement. It argues that civil society has an important role in bringing issues of global concern to the top of the international agenda. For example, civil society played a vital role in the international anti-apartheid movement, and in providing the momentum for the creation of the International Criminal Court,[53] and as mentioned it was also instrumental in the signing of the Ottawa Convention Banning Landmines. Furthermore, international civil society organizations have proven successful in reforming national institutions by establishing solidarity networks with domestic movements. In such cases civil society stimulates what Keck and Sikkink call "transnational advocacy networks" which petition third-party states and intergovernmental organizations to pressure violating governments to change.[54] In this sense, the participation of civil society organizations in the process of international legislation is understood as a major factor in democratizing the constitution of global governance.

Yet, again, this position entails considerable idealization, eliding the normative ambivalence of the network form. For one, as indicated, civil society institutions can be gradually coopted by powerful interests. The international environmental movement is a case in point. After the Rio Earth Summit in 1992 the environmental movement gained tremendous influence. Green parties joined coalition governments in Europe and corporations hired environmental advisors. Yet in July of 2001 when the parties to the UN Framework Convention on Climate Change met in Bonn they systematically rolled back the commitments made in Rio in 1992. And global civil society organizations such as Greenpeace and Friends of the Earth International were left to applaud as historic an agreement they would have found completely unacceptable only ten years earlier.[55]

There are also questions concerning the representative status of civil society institutions. Who do they in fact speak for? And how do they set their agendas? NGOs at the global level can be very large, complex organizations highly removed from any basic social or political community. Their only true constituency, so to speak, is their member base, people who send in a check from time to time – a financial contribution being the only form of participation expected from the general public – their policies often the product of specialist professionals and not public deliberation. Furthermore, often those people most in need of articulating their needs outside of state institutions live in hostile political environments that restrict peaceful protest and free association, making the functioning of civil society associations all but impossible.

Thus in order for the sum effect of global civil society to be the democratization of global governance, it must exist within a framework of normative rules and egalitarian institutions that ensures equal access to all and compensates for broad differentials of power. Organizations and movements from around the world must have the capacity and freedom to articulate their diverse interests as they simultaneously cultivate the sense of global interdependence necessary to address issues of common concern for the entire planet. However, then we must ask, How would this framework be constituted? And then have we thus come full circle, back to the problem of cosmopolitan founding? In the interest of democratic legitimacy, the constitution of global governance must incorporate the input of civil society. And yet civil society, in order to live up to its normative expectations, requires an already existing framework of governance to provide the relatively level and inclusive playing field necessary to establish its conditions of possibility.

Democratic legitimacy remains tied to particular contexts of interest and historical perspective. Transnational democratic legitimacy even for a decentered global civil society depends upon the cultivation of a minimal common frame of action, necessary to avoid the perception that transnational politics benefit only powerful states at the expense of the weak – or the developed states of the global North against the developing states of the global South – a charge at times leveled against environmental or human rights accords. Global civil society is caught in an infinite regress: it must play a constitutive role in cultivating the recognition of a common planetary project for the democratization of global governance; but this awareness must already be present in order to produce the "democratic tendencies" necessary for it to gain legitimacy. Global civil society must construct its own conditions of possibility. It is a ship at sea, still under construction.

New forms of global governance and transnational legal structures are now emerging in a decentered "evolutionary process." The question for popular sovereignty is how to instill this process with democratic legitimacy. Is it possible for a form of democratic practice to take part in the constitution of the emerging forms of global governance? Can the collective capacity to steer the social, political and economic institutions that affect our lives be reinvigorated on a transnational scale? Democratic regionalism, cosmopolitan democracy, and democratic network governance represent three forms of politics that attempt just that.

In the context of globalization no form of politics may be thought of in isolation: Regionalism must be thought of in the context of the broader world order; cosmopolitanism implies transformations at the local, national, and regional levels. And global networks are enabled or hindered depending upon the character of national and international politics as they traverse national and regional boundaries. I have argued that each model of transnational politics encounters a tension between the particular contexts of democratic legitimacy and the universalism demanded of a political culture that can address the myriad issues in need of transnational governance revealed by our increasingly global interdependence. I call this *the problem of cosmopolitan founding*.

The world is now indeed a community of shared risks – environmental disaster, international terror and crime, nuclear proliferation, the interrelation of financial markets, all have transnational effects. A transnational politics must indeed build bridges across borders to address these problems. Such a politics must achieve real results for a wide breadth of humanity; a globalization of heightened inequality is doomed to disaster. Raising awareness to that effect is perhaps the most important role for global civil society today. Only such a politics could establish the conditions for the democratic constitution of global governance.

For global governance to remain consistent with the principle of popular sovereignty, however, it must entail a commitment to the process of self-determination at a variety of levels, reflecting the divisions and asymmetries characterizing twenty-first-century globalization. Chapter 8 will conclude by addressing how the problem of cosmopolitan founding may be overcome in part through a decentered, multilayered and process-oriented model of popular sovereignty as a particularly efficient and progressive way of conceptualizing the bridge between globalizing present and cosmopolitan future.

8 Conclusion
Toward a transnational politics of popular sovereignty

On February 15, 2003, across North America, Europe, the Middle East, Asia, and Australia as many as 30 million people took to city streets to express opposition to the planned invasion of Iraq.[1] It seemed an extraordinary moment for global civil society, perhaps for the first time living up to its name. The anti-war movement appeared to accomplish in a day what four years of transnational activism against neoliberal globalization could not. It brought together constituencies from East and West, North and South into a broad-based movement with a common clear objective: Stop the US-led drive for war. The next weeks saw what was, in effect, a pyrrhic victory for global civil society. The protests no doubt contributed to the Bush administration's defeat in the UN Security Council. But, in the end, they also contributed to the heightened sense that the United Nations and global civil society were impotent next to the hegemonic power of the United States. President Bush made clear the US would follow its own course regardless of global public opinion.

My concern here is not with the intricacies of such high-stakes diplomacy, nor with the hard realities of the long conflict in Iraq, but rather with what these events reveal about the state of politics in the international sphere. Global public opinion, as best it could be determined, was overwhelmingly opposed to the war, and yet by most accounts war seemed nearly inevitable from the very start. For all the advances in international communications and the spread of international law in the twentieth century, there remains no institutional mechanism to effectively channel the transnational communicative power of an emerging global civil society. Popular sovereignty, it would seem, carries no purchase in the transnational domain.

What is more, these events reveal the extent to which the historic trend toward a greater consolidation – even "constitutionalization" – of international law is increasingly at risk. From the establishment of the League of Nations, through the founding of the United Nations and the signing of the Universal Declaration of Human Rights, to the establishment of the International Criminal Court, the twentieth century developed along a path pointed toward a future cosmopolitan juridification of international affairs. The early twenty-first century, however, has already established troublesome counter-trends.

The project of international law is now challenged by more than its traditional skeptics – those national isolationists or doctrinaire realists who have long claimed that effective law is possible only within the confines of states armed with the power of sanction, and not within the international domain itself. Regrettably, challenges have also come recently from a once proud sponsor of international law: the United States. The US under George W. Bush challenged the cause of international law, however, without denying the need or possibility of a rule-governed international order. The vision of the Bush Doctrine was by no means isolationist; it was equally global in scope, and it recognized the need for the establishment of international security. Yet it represented a counter-vision of world order and global governance, premised not upon legal procedures, but upon the supposedly "benevolent" might of a global superpower.[2] According to this view, the rule to govern the world is not that of international law but that of liberal imperialism. And as the doors closed on the Bush administration, the extended disaster in Iraq, the moral stain of Abu-Ghraib, and the legal black hole of Guantánamo Bay all provided strong indications to where such unilateral extra-legal "benevolence" must lead. Meanwhile, the emerging – or reemerging – powers of Russia and China promise to alter the calculus further. As we move beyond a brief unipolar moment in international affairs, dominated by a declining liberal democratic power, to a multipolar moment characterized by economic uncertainty and the emergence of the authoritarian giant China and the newly assertive Russia, the cause of democratically legitimate global governance will be challenged further.

Such developments, I argue, continue to make clear the stakes of globalization's challenge to popular sovereignty. Recall that, for Rousseau, the prevention of tyranny was an important function of popular sovereignty. In that spirit, I argue that the normative claims and practices of popular sovereignty represent vital mechanisms to counter the threats of transnational militarism, ascendant authoritarianism, and liberal imperialism. Thus it is all the more imperative to ask: In an increasingly globalized world, where political, military, social, financial, and environmental policies have transnational effects, how do we address the need for an invigorated transnational capacity for democratically legitimate collective action?

We are living at a time of transformation in which new political arrangements are being formed and old political arrangements appear insufficient. In this context one can perceive alternative forms of authority gaining strength, putting pressure on the normative currency of democratic politics. The authoritative weights of security, functionalism, and religion are all advancing, representing potentially profound antidemocratic tendencies. Fears of vulnerability and calls for tighter security can trump critical opposition and overwhelm public debate. Technical elite rule by bureaucracy, technocrats, and a stubborn faith in the long-term efficiency of the market –

notwithstanding global financial crises – poise to take over steering functions once reserved for processes of democratic representation. And appeals to the "higher" authority of religion threaten to legitimate exclusionary practices.

At the start of the twenty-first century we can see that the end of the Cold War did not bring about an "end of history" with the triumph of liberal democratic regimes the world over, as Francis Fukuyama once predicted.[3] Rather, we see the proliferation of "hybrid" regimes: China and Russia have opened to capitalism, but continue to develop their own distinct forms of authoritarianism; Europe balances between social democracy and neoliberalism, as the well known democratic deficit becomes increasingly entrenched after the defeat of the EU constitution; politics rooted in religious-based authority is becoming only stronger throughout the Middle East; populism is on the rise in Latin America; and in the United States, even after the historic election of Barack Obama, the legacy of eight years of assertive militarism after a bitterly disputed election reveals the potentially precarious status of democratic legitimacy even in the world's oldest republic.[4]

In such a context, the central categories of democratic theory need to be reexamined or they risk becoming coopted and diminished. We must rethink the concept of popular sovereignty in this reconfigured political context. In spite of all its contradictions and historical ambiguities, I have argued that popular sovereignty remains a necessary principle of modern democratic political thought and practice. Again, it signifies the general principle that "the people," broadly defined, play a central role in the constitution, steering, and occasional disruption or transformation of the laws and institutions that govern their lives; and that the controlling reason for the foundation of law and government is the protection of individuals and groups from the abuses of power common to conditions of lawlessness.

Popular sovereignty signifies that the people remain, in the words of Etienne Balibar, "the last instance of legitimacy and political decision making."[5] And in fact it proves very difficult to think about democracy without some reference to this horizon of popular legitimacy. Even when denied, the principle of popular sovereignty remains implicit in democratic theory. To discount it completely is to undermine the commitment to the future of democratic government. Thus any reconsideration of the basic categories of democratic theory and the fate of democratic forms of authority in the context of globalization must address the concept of popular sovereignty.

In conclusion, I will briefly review the challenges posed by globalization (pp. 132–34), revisit the possible solutions and the problem of cosmopolitan founding described in the last two chapters (pp. 134–36), and then I will defend the concept of popular sovereignty as a normative principle that may illuminate the way to help navigate, critique and theorize the tensions and dilemmas inherent to the democratic constitution of global governance (pp. 136–42).

Challenging popular sovereignty

As we have seen, the current historical context presents extraordinary challenges to the concept of popular sovereignty. I have examined these challenges by breaking down the term into its component parts, examining both the concept of sovereignty as the structure of final authority and the notion of the people as a unified democratic subject. The notion of the people and the concept of sovereignty are both undergoing radical transformations in the context of an incomplete process of globalization. To analyze the various dimensions of these transformations I have addressed three models of popular sovereignty: the Lockean, the Rousseauian, and the Habermasian.

If you recall, sovereignty for Locke refers to the authority to institute government for the protection of natural right and the authority to dissolve or alter government when its original ends are betrayed, or to reconstitute government after it falls. The people for Locke are a political community formed for the instrumental purpose of protecting private property, including the rights to life and liberty. And they are sovereign in that they are the constitutive authority behind all civil society. As a result, government is instituted to protect their interests, such that political legitimacy must be based upon their consent.

Globalization, we found, clearly presents a challenge to each of the fundamental dimensions of the Lockean model of popular sovereignty. It bypasses the popular constitutive authority by constituting mechanisms of governance far beyond the domain of the people, for example, through the formation of global systems of private law such as the newly expanding *lex mercatoria* or the nascent *lex digitalis mundialis*. Similarly, it undermines the consensual foundation of authority by obfuscating the centers of power. As economic production and control become increasingly transnational it becomes more and more difficult to know who or what is behind the forces that determine our life chances, or influence our opportunities to choose a better life. Under such conditions, the national procedures for registering consent or dissent are increasingly limited.

Furthermore, in the event that the people do mobilize sufficient dissent to overthrow a corrupt, incompetent, or tyrannical government the forces of globalization limit the people's ability to radically reconstitute government independent from geopolitical concerns or restrictions imposed by international capital. In sum, from the perspective of the Lockean model of popular sovereignty, globalization restricts the people's authority to constitute government as it expands the domain of law and governance beyond established mechanisms of consent or dissent. It challenges the capacity of the state to protect the rights and interests of the people, shifting the seats of power out of the people's view, while at the same time diminishing the people's capacity to respond by effecting radical change.

Similarly, we found, globalization presents extraordinary challenges to the Rousseauian model of popular sovereignty. Rousseau's model of popular sovereignty is collective and participatory, and it depends upon the constitution of a small, unified, homogeneous society. Globalization challenges each of the central elements of the Rousseauian model: the principles of collective self-determination, social homogeneity, and political participation.

Rousseau's model of collective self-determination was premised upon society's autarkic relation to others. Yet globalization, I argued, is marked by increasing levels of interdependence, calling into question any model of collective self-determination that requires isolationism. Similarly, globalization calls into question any model of popular sovereignty that is premised upon social homogeneity. Globalization disrupts social homogeneity in two ways of specific concern to Rousseau: it stimulates economic inequality, and it gives rise to increased cultural diversity in the domestic sphere. Finally, the model of direct participation is clearly incompatible with a political domain that spans the globe. The transnational scale is too large and too irregular to accommodate a republican model of citizenship and political participation.

Yet this is not to argue that globalization signals the demise of the participatory public. Taken literally, both the Lockean and the Rousseauian models were already under considerable stress long before an accelerating globalization became a concern. Rousseau and Locke both provide fundamental ideas and normative inspiration to the concept of modern democracy, not ready-made blueprints. Thus, I turned to an examination of the deliberative model of popular sovereignty to explore the ways in which a combination of liberal and republican norms may be operationalized in a discourse model of popular sovereignty compatible with modern, complex societies. I argued that Habermas's deliberative model of popular sovereignty represents an advance over the Lockean and Rousseauian models in that it is participatory – and so avoids the undemocratic limitations of Lockean liberalism – and in so far as it is pluralist – and so it avoids the stifling homogeneity of Rousseauian republicanism. However, globalization presents challenges for the Habermasian deliberative model as well.

I argued, while in principle the decentered structure of the deliberative model makes it more compatible with transnational politics, its structural dependence upon the constitution of strong public spheres capable of making legally binding decisions presents an obstacle for its immediate application to a global domain void of such structures. Second, I argued that, in the absence of strong publics, the development of an international human rights regime occasions a problematic breakdown of the co-originality of popular sovereignty and rights, integral to the deliberative synthesis of liberal and republican norms. Finally, I argued that extending the Habermasian deliberative model to the transnational sphere requires a rearticulation of the key concept of constitutional patriotism; and this proves incompatible with a transnational domain characterized by multiple histories, conflicting traditions, and extreme socioeconomic and technological asymmetry.

In many respects, globalization's challenge to all three models of popular sovereignty relates to the expansion of politics beyond the domain of the nation-state. However, again, to be clear, this is not an argument about the demise of the nation-state: states still matter profoundly. Domestically, they continue to wield powerful mechanisms for the distribution of power and resources; and internationally, notwithstanding the post-Cold War expansion of NATO's mission, states are the only entities capable of projecting large-scale military force, and a select few states still control the principal levers of global governance (e.g., the UN Security Council, the World Bank, the IMF, etc.)

However, the very real social, political and economic developments currently discussed under the heading of globalization signify an altered context in which the state exercises its power. For example, sovereign wealth funds represent the new financial power of a few individual states at the expense of global institutions like the IMF;[6] yet they also draw attention to the interdependence of even the most powerful nation-states – like the United States, which relies on such funds in addition to foreign central banks to finance its ballooning external debt, and more so than ever after the financial meltdown of September 2008.[7] While states remain powerful actors capable of shaping the social, economic, and security contexts within their borders, the model of the sovereign state independent from external influence is under increasing pressure. And the consistent capacity to draw clear distinctions between the domestic and the foreign has become increasingly difficult to maintain.

In such case, the concept of popular sovereignty must be rethought beyond the scope of the nation-state if it is to retain any coherence as a category of democratic theory. As the domain of governance transcends the reach of national institutions the space for effective popular political input narrows; thus, I have argued, in order for processes of globalization to continue without resulting in a corresponding loss of the capacity for collective self-determination, new mechanisms of democratic politics need to be developed.

Popular sovereignty and the problem of cosmopolitan founding

New forms of global governance and transnational legal structures are now taking form beyond the reach of national democratic procedures or processes of public oversight. The question *vis-à-vis* popular sovereignty is how to incorporate the constitutive authority of the people into the formation of global governance and international legislation. Is it possible for a form of democratic practice to take part in the constitution of emerging forms of global governance? Can the collective capacity to constitute, guide, and transform the social, political and economic institutions that affect our lives be made effective at the transnational level? I presented cosmopolitan democracy, democratic regionalism, and democratic network governance as three forms of politics that work exactly toward that end.

For some, the challenge of globalization requires reinforcing the capacities of the nation-state to provide for its more effective intervention in the fast developing international domain. Others, as we saw, call for the abandonment of the independent nation-state in favor of a globalized system of rule. Habermas seeks to respond to the challenges of globalization by reconstituting political space beyond the nation-state, but not in the form of a global polity. Rather, he argues that the absence of strong publics at the transnational level could be remedied by the constitution of strong regional polities with a reformed European Union as a model.

For Habermas, the postnational constellation would be composed of democratic regional polities interacting with international institutions and global civil society to effect a decentered system of cosmopolitan law that could respond to public demands via deliberative processes based at the local, national, and regional levels. However, I argued, tensions arise for Habermas when attempting to reconcile the necessarily "local" foundations of democratic legitimacy with an obviously broader, universal system of cosmopolitan law. For Habermas, popular sovereignty and democratic legitimacy remain rooted in the cultivation of a common political culture, yet the conditions for such shared politics are currently incompatible with the global domain.

This presents a serious problem for David Held as well, for he envisions an even more consolidated and entrenched system of cosmopolitan democratic law. Held's cosmopolitan democracy would cover the globe in a single legal structure for political action, leading to the eventual end of the sovereign nation-state as we know it. Held envisions the constitution of a global parliament, a global judicial system to adjudicate issues of cosmopolitan jurisdiction, a vast social justice program for the redistribution of wealth and opportunity, and the realization of an effective standing international military force. While Held's model of cosmopolitan democracy presents an attractive vision of global social justice, I argued, he lacks even a minimally sufficient conceptualization of the political process that could accomplish the constitution of a global system of social democracy, especially in the context of extreme asymmetries of wealth and power. In the language of popular sovereignty, Held does not theorize the constitutive authority of cosmopolitan democracy.

I then examined the concept of democratic network governance and the rise of global civil society as a potential vehicle for the transnational constitutive authority of cosmopolitan democracy. However, I argued that in order for global civil society to result in a democratization of global affairs it would have to be itself situated in a framework of normative rules and egalitarian institutions that would ensure equal access to all. Thus I argued that each model of transnational politics encounters a tension between the particular contexts of democratic legitimacy and the universalism demanded of a political culture that could address the myriad issues in need of transnational governance revealed by our increasingly global interdependence. I call this tension *the problem of cosmopolitan founding*. The idea of a democratic global governance would appear to entail a contradiction: it can not be constituted democratically.

I began this project by arguing for the need to reevaluate the concept of popular sovereignty. However, while a consideration of the concept of popular sovereignty may assist us in illuminating the problem of cosmopolitan founding, it is not clear how it may assist in its resolution. The problem of cosmopolitan founding results in part from the sense that the development of a common global human community is required for the extension of democratic authority into the supranational domain. Stated again in the language of popular sovereignty, the intractable problem is the seeming impossibility of the constitution of a global people. This is a particularly unavoidable problem when working with a simplified model of popular sovereignty structured around the image of a centralized macro-subject engaged in self-government. But, as we saw, even a decentered deliberative notion of the people, if it remains tied to a concept of constitutional patriotism, fails to overcome this difficulty.

Nevertheless, independent from the dimension of collective self-government in a future cosmopolitan system, the problem of cosmopolitan founding refers to the process of constituting such a system. It points toward the need to examine constitutive processes. The problem of cosmopolitan founding, I argue, does not indicate the impossibility of cosmopolitan democracy, but asks whether it can be legitimately constituted. Models of transnational democracy have not sufficiently theorized a constitutive authority capable of driving the formation of a system of democratic global governance. They have not properly theorized the middle stage between globalizing present and cosmopolitan future, instead focusing on either analyses of contemporary politics or the articulation of a future ideal. In conclusion, I will put forward the principle of transnational popular sovereignty as an important normative conceptual resource for theorizing and critiquing the politics of this middle stage: the constitutive politics between globalizing present and cosmopolitan future.

Toward a transnational politics of popular sovereignty

The tensions identified by the problem of cosmopolitan founding suggest that comprehensive democratic global governance will not be a reality any time soon. Nation-state-based government will remain vitally important for the foreseeable future, and any commitment to the improvement of the mechanisms of popular sovereignty must engage with domestic reform. Nevertheless, the increasing awareness that crises quickly cross borders makes imperative the search for improved global governance and multilateral cooperation. This was made patently clear as ripple effects from the US financial crisis shook markets around the globe in the fall of 2008 and world leaders gathering for the sixty-third UN General Assembly chastised the US for the global consequences of the debacle. As C. Fred Bergsten of the Peterson Institute of International Economics said, with fears of global recession rising, "The globalization of the crisis means we need a globalization of responses."[8] Yet this presents a dilemma: at a time when the constitution of global governance is most in demand, we must admit, there is no way to constitute it democratically; at a time when democratic authority is most needed to provide for a legitimate response to global crises, it seems most out of reach. There seems an unbridgeable gap between global governance and democratic governance. Could the concept of transnational popular sovereignty help to fill that gap?

In contrast to the traditional model of a centralized, macro-subject engaged in self-government through the expression of will, a transnational form of popular sovereignty is decentered and multilayered. Global governance is an inherently complex affair. Modern complex societies, let alone the entire world, cannot be deliberately steered as a whole from a single command center. The traditional metaphor of popular sovereignty is that of the individual body. It is to consider the will of the people in the singular. It incorporates the ideal of the unified *demos* with a center of power capable of speaking in a single voice.[9] The decentered model as we have seen recognizes the simplification this entails and incorporates a consideration of the multiple sources of power – in the state, in civil society, and in the economic sphere. And, in the contemporary context, it recognizes the degree to which states and citizenship are becoming increasingly disaggregated.[10]

Thus a transnational popular sovereignty must be able to incorporate new modes of political agency. That is, it must be possible to understand popular sovereignty as operative on multiple, at times overlapping, but not always congruent, layers. Popular sovereignty in the context of globalization "means multiplying sites of citizenship at the sub-national, national, and transnational levels."[11] National state structures of citizenship and representation remain important: a secure state characterized by a separation of powers and the rule of law remains the best guarantee for the protection of basic human rights; but key to understanding popular sovereignty in the context of globalization is considering political agency at the subnational as well as the national and transnational levels, and how they are interrelated.

Understanding how these multiple layers of political agency are constituted becomes central to the transnational theory of popular sovereignty. It concerns the processes by which jurisdictions are formed and interested parties are identified. In the context of globalization, for every process of economic redistribution, legal recognition, or political representation the question of *who* is to be considered and at *what* level of authority defines a significant dimension of the politics involved. Under such conditions, struggles over the "frame" of particular issues – whether they are local, national, regional, global, etc. – become of increasingly central importance. And understood within the context of a transnational popular sovereignty, "the people" become precisely those that are affected by any given policy or practice under consideration irrespective of national citizenship.[12]

In such case, the interaction among layers becomes essential; how would local demands be heard at the regional level and how would transnational authority be legitimated at the national level? There is a temptation here to

Conclusion 137

speculate about what such an institutional architecture would look like. Yet such an impulse is misplaced if it results in a general schema. There is no one size fits all. The organ-a-gram of transnational democracy cannot be devised through a top-down academic exercise. It must come out of a multilateral process of a historically diverse set of political approaches. How regional and national processes, for example, in West Africa, northern Europe, Central America, and South East Asia respond to the demands of globalization, and the necessity of devising multilateral responses to the challenges of our age, will vary considerably over time and geography. Each region and political tradition has its own history that provides the background and storied waters that must be navigated in ways that generate internal legitimacy in order to find success.

How a post-Soviet state or a postcolonial state responds to the burgeoning norms of international law is likely to differ from the responses of a historically independent state or a former imperial power. Similarly, the political tools and vocabularies at the disposal of a centralized state versus a federal state, or a contentious multinational state, vary. For example, regional differences related to past experiences are emerging in responses to the principle of the "responsibility to protect" (i.e., the idea that states have a duty to protect their people from atrocities and the international community must support them or respond if they fail). Western European states, having already softened the barriers of state sovereignty through the European Union, are generally supportive; Asian countries wary of past Western interference in the region are suspicious; Africa and Latin America are more ambivalent, skeptical of outside influence, but Africa's recent history of genocide and conflict, and Latin America's history of overcoming dictatorship and grave human rights abuses, make them both sensitive to the issue.[13]

Of course, such a decentered and multilayered perspective does not so conveniently overcome the problems of cosmopolitan founding. As we have seen, the multilayered models of cosmopolitan democracy and democratic regionalism, and the decentered model of global civil society, in the long run still remain dependent upon the constitution of a universalist common frame of action that comes into tension with the particular contexts of democratic legitimacy. However, the conceptual focus on the principle of popular sovereignty rather than on a specific institutional model of transnational politics or mechanism of democratic legitimacy shifts the analysis in important ways. Most important, it shifts away from the articulation of a distant ideal or utopian institutional framework and toward a concentration on the political processes of constituting democratic global governance in the present tense.

As I have discussed it, popular sovereignty is well suited for this purpose, particularly in the following three respects. Popular sovereignty is a (1) constitutive, (2) emancipatory, and (3) process-focused category:

1. Popular sovereignty is a *constitutive category* especially suited to the consideration of moments of transformation such as the current one. While the concept of democratic legitimacy, for example, assumes an existing object

to be legitimated, the concept of popular sovereignty encompasses the act of creation or extraordinary change. It is a productive concept. Popular sovereignty articulates the form of authority involved in the constitution of democratic institutions. As we saw in Chapter 2, the concept of popular sovereignty moves away from the original command model of sovereignty stemming from the Roman notion of *imperium*, toward a concept of the constituent power, most famously articulated by Emmanuel Sieyés. And, as we saw, the principle of constitutive authority was central to both the Lockean and the Rousseaian models of popular sovereignty.[14]

2. Popular sovereignty is an emancipatory category, especially suited to moments of exclusion and abuse. It entails an equation of "asymmetry" between the people as political sovereign and the institutionalized governing powers.[15] Recall the important distinction in Rousseau between the popular sovereign and the administrative government, or the Lockean place of the people independent of the state, ready to revolt if their most fundamental trust is betrayed. The principle of popular sovereignty protects against abusive power: if government turns against the popular interest, the people as sovereign authority have the right to oppose government – or, as the case may be, call for outside intervention – for the purpose of emancipation.

Furthermore, popular sovereignty entails a dual structure comprising a present-focused politics and a normative future-orientation pointed toward the goal of inclusion. James Fishkin, for example, chronicles how the evocation of popular sovereignty at the start of the American Revolution initiated a process in which over time larger and larger proportions of the population were included in "We the People," beyond its original narrow interpretation.[16] Once the people as a whole are declared sovereign, leverage is created for the excluded to claim political rights, setting in motion the logic of inclusion. The speed and comprehensiveness of such a process is contingent upon many factors, and it is not immune to setbacks or antidemocratic populist detours; but evidence of its operation is apparent in the United States, for example, from Jacksonian democracy to the women's suffrage movement, and on through the civil rights era.[17]

3. Finally, the concept of popular sovereignty is process-focused in two ways. First, it is procedural in the Habermasian sense: it refers to the "general accessibility" of a discursive process of debate and deliberation in the public sphere, including both informal gatherings and official parliaments. And it defines the formal conditions for the juridification of those processes, making possible the legal "rule" of the people.[18] And thus it entails the articulation of normative principles that can help distinguish between expressions of popular will and the conclusions of technocratic elites or the manipulations of populist demagogues. Second, it is focused on present-tense political processes for the positive influence over the constitution and functioning of mechanisms of redistribution, recognition, and representation. It identifies not just the structure of deliberation but the total effect of individual assertions of right and local struggles over the distribution of resources. That is, it does not

presuppose an existing common frame, but is concerned with the bottom-up politics that result in the indirect constitution of the frame itself over time.

Thus the concept of *transnational* popular sovereignty advances the idea that local struggles over rights and needs are also a part of the larger transnational process of constituting a "new world order," a transformed global governance. For example, Sidney Tarrow has analyzed the phenomenon of transnational activism within the "contentious politics" model he articulated with Charles Tilly and Doug McAdam.[19] Tarrow identifies three sets of processes by which domestic activism can connect the global and the local: these include "global framing," where domestic actors mobilize international symbols to frame domestic issues; "scale shifts," where a locally or nationally based movement, such as ATTAC, becomes reborn at the transnational level; and "transnational coalition formation," where distinct national or local groups form transnational networks of cooperation with the purpose of effecting the character of global governance.[20]

Of course a norm of transnational popular sovereignty does not solve once and for all the problems associated with constituting democratic transnational governance. But it can help us to evaluate the process as it unfolds, to articulate the political tasks ahead, measure accomplishments, and critique shortcomings. Most important, it realigns the focus of research and analysis away from speculations about the ideal structure of a future cosmopolitan order, and toward an examination of the political processes by which global governance structures are being constituted today. It sharpens the analytic lens on the political processes involved in the struggle over transnational governance in a manner consistent with the democratic ideals of popular constitutive authority and collective self-determination. And it helps to push beyond the stalemate by which cosmopolitan democrats critique our contemporary distance from the Kantian ideal, and Realists in turn charge them with naive utopianism, incapable of grasping the power structures that make the democratization of global governance impossible.

Looking at the constitution of global governance from the perspective of traditional models of sovereignty suggests that popular participation has no role to play beyond the domestic frontier. The people have no choice but to sit on the sidelines while the global political elite negotiate the new structures of governance; any movement that seeks to reorient the process toward popular concerns immediately becomes understood as anachronistic or nostalgic. Rather, understood within a normative concept of transnational popular sovereignty, for example, protesters outside the WTO no longer appear simply as visionless protectionists or lawless Luddites, but as activists with the potential to articulate a progressive future alternative to the status quo. Or the rejection of the EU constitution in France and the Netherlands may be revealed to be as much about a critique of the exclusionary process of the constitutional convention as about the defects of the constitution itself.

Historically, the concept of popular sovereignty has been considered a category that encompassed exclusively domestic concerns, whereas the principle of state sovereignty encompassed the international domain. The principle of state sovereignty makes no assumptions about the form of domestic governance, beyond its capacity to establish law and order within a bounded territory. The concept of popular sovereignty, on the other hand, entails a normative claim to the right of self-determination. Considering popular sovereignty as a principle operative in the realm of international and transnational governance entails the recognition that international actors do have an effect on domestic governance and that this results in normative pressure on transnational governance to include avenues for popular participation or public input.

For example, the development of additional avenues for the communication of wider constituent concerns within the existing structures of global governance would improve their real and perceived legitimacy, adding to their potential for success and continued relevance in a changing world. To put it in the Habermasian terms discussed in Chapter 5, the decision-making bodies of global governance – including the United Nations and global economic institutions – need additional public legitimation filters to facilitate the flow of communicative power between the center and the periphery, between the North and the South, or between the local, national, regional, and transnational levels.

Less than the immediate overhaul of international institutions – after all, even a minimal UN Security Council reform has proven to be little more than wishful thinking in the short term – this requires the strengthening of popular sovereignty at the local and national levels in communication with regional institutions and the networks of a growing transnational civil society. Over time, real-world responses to real problems shift transnational norms affecting elite opinion in key capital cities, making the practical transformation of international institutions more likely.

Transnational challenges require transnational solutions. The challenges of climate change, financial crisis, nuclear proliferation, pandemic disease, and extreme poverty, among others, cannot be addressed by a go-it-alone politics. The problem of cosmopolitan founding should not force a choice between democratic governance and global governance, but rather encourage the search for innovative, legitimate solutions to the practical problems that are common to all. Structures of global governance and cosmopolitan international law are already in the process of being formed.[21] Thus the task before democratic theory is not the wholesale design of new institutional architectures. Rather, the task of democratic theory is to articulate the principles by which an evolving decentered system of global governance may be subject to democratic authority as it is being constituted by actors responding to the demands of our time. And this is not simply an abstract normative project. There are very real consequences at stake. The challenges of globalization demand better global governance and enhanced multilateral cooperation. And a sense of legitimacy will be integral to their success – integral to getting everyone "on board."

Habermas has suggested the unity between the particular context-embedded democratic will and the abstract, universal rule of law "can only develop in the dimension of time."²² If we can understand the constitution of transnational democracy as an ongoing, tradition-building process based in local, national, and regional democratic projects, over time the tension between the particularity of popular sovereignty and the universality of cosmopolitanism may be reconciled. Yet again, this depends upon a growing awareness of global interdependence, the cultivation of the perception that we are in effect all "on board" *and* "in the same boat."²³

In the meantime, while we increasingly inhabit a global community of shared risks, the universal recognition of a planetary common good remains an elusive goal, to say the very least. More than expressing the unity of humanity, the rise of global civil society highlights the complexity and asymmetry of the world. Global civil society does not constitute a single world community; it is complex, stratified, and endlessly diverse. Yet this need not present an impassable obstacle to the democratic constitution of global governance. For, *pace* Rousseau, popular sovereignty has seldom if ever concerned the governance of unified societies, but rather struggles for power in divided societies.²⁴ The key is not simply a chicken–egg question of which comes first, cosmopolitan governance or transnational solidarity. Rather, it is the challenge of a concomitant innovative democratization of institutions *and* the cultivation of democratic norms, or the formation of democratic political culture – how they can begin to happen simultaneously, not in some distant future but now, in the middle stage between globalizing present and cosmopolitan future. Threading this needle, of course, presents an extraordinary challenge for politics at all levels: local, national, regional, and transnational. How this challenge is met will determine the shape of the world in the years to come.

Notes

1 Introduction

1 Andrew Arato, "Sistani v. Bush: Constitutional Politics in Iraq," *Constellations* 11:2 (June 2004).
2 "Democracy in Latin America: Towards a Citizens' Democracy" (UNDP 2004).
3 John Glenn, "Global Governance and the Democratic Deficit: Stifling the Voice of the South," *Third World Quarterly* 29:2 (2008). Thomas W. Pogge, "Creating Supranational Institutions Democratically: Reflections on the European Union's 'Democratic Deficit'," *Journal of Political Philosophy* 5:2 (June 1997). Richard Bellamy and Dario Castiglione, "The Uses of Democracy: Reflections on the European Democratic Deficit," in E.O. Eriksen and J.E. Fossum Tarrow, eds., *Democracy in the European Union: Integration through Deliberation?* (London: Routledge, 2000). Frank Decker, "Governance beyond the Nation-State: Reflections on the Democratic Deficit of the European Union," *Journal of European Public Policy* 9:2 (April 2002). Jan Aart Scholte, "The WTO and Civil Society," *Journal of World Trade* 33:1 (February 1999).
4 David Held and Anthony McGrew, "The Great Globalization Debate: an Introduction," in *The Global Transformations Reader*, second edition (Cambridge: Polity Press, 2003), 14.
5 Ian Bremmer, "The Return of State Capitalism," *Survival* 50:3 (June–July 2008).
6 David Held, Anthony McGrew, David Goldblatt, and Jonathan Perraton, *Global Transformations: Politics, Economics and Culture* (Stanford, CA: Stanford University Press, 1999).
7 Immanuel Wallerstein, "States? Sovereignty?" in D.A. Smith, D.J. Solinger, and S.C. Topik, eds., *States and Sovereignty in the Global Economy* (New York: Routledge, 1999), 22–23.
8 Stephen Krasner, "Globalization and Sovereignty," in Smith et al., *States and Sovereignty*. Stephen Krasner, *Sovereignty: Organized Hypocrisy* (Princeton, NJ: Princeton University Press, 1999).
9 David Held, *Democracy and the Global Order* (Stanford, CA: Stanford University Press, 1995), Chapters 5–6. On challenge to the nation-state see Kenichi Ohmae, *The End of the Nation-State: The Rise of Regional Economies* (New York: Free Press, 1995), Saskia Sassen, *Losing Control? Sovereignty in an Age of Globalization* (New York: Columbia University Press, 1996), Jan Aart Scholte, "Global Capitalism and the State," *International Affairs* 73:3 (July 1997), and Susan Strange, *The Retreat of the State* (Cambridge: Cambridge University Press, 1996).
10 It should be noted that according to some figures openness to global markets provides greater economic growth which in the long term may enhance state

capacities, and others point to a lack of clear evidence of the preclusion of welfare state policies. Held and McGrew, "The Great Globalization Debate," 23.
11 See, for example, Joseph E. Stiglitz, *Globalization and its Discontents* (New York: Norton, 2003), ix.
12 Held et al., *Global Transformations*.
13 Kanishka Jayasuriya, "Globalization, Sovereignty, and the Rule of Law: From Political to Economic Constitutionalism?" *Constellations* 8:4 (December 2001), 447.
14 Anne-Marie Slaughter, "The Real New World Order," *Foreign Affairs* 76:5 (September–October 1997). See also James Rosenau, *Along the Domestic–Foreign Frontier* (Cambridge: Cambridge University Press, 1997).
15 Anthony Giddens, *The Consequences of Modernity* (Cambridge: Polity Press, 1990).
16 Held et al., *Global Transformations*.
17 See, for example, Alain Touraine, "Meaningless Politics," *Constellations* 10:3 (September 2003).
18 Held and McGrew, "The Great Globalization Debate," 1, 4.
19 See, for example, Chalmers Johnson, *The Sorrows of Empire: Militarism, Secrecy and the End of the Republic* (New York: Holt, 2004), David Harvey, *The New Imperialism* (Oxford: Oxford University Press, 2003), and James Tully, "On Law, Democracy and Imperialism," twenty-first annual public lecture, Centre for Law and Society, University of Edinburgh, March 10–11, 2005.
20 Held et al., *Global Transformations*, 2–10. David Held and Anthony McGrew, *Globalization/Anti-globalization* (Oxford: Polity Press, 2002).
21 Gareth Evans, *The Responsibility to Protect* (Washington, DC: Brookings Institution, 2008).
22 This movement from the liberal to the republican to the deliberative mirrors Habermas, in Jürgen Habermas, "Three Normative Models of Democracy," in *The Inclusion of the Other* (Cambridge, MA: MIT Press, 1998).
23 Although the topic of popular sovereignty and globalization may appear to warrant special attention for John Rawls's *The Law of Peoples*, I have chosen not to consider it in a chapter of its own – the most important reason being that Rawls remains focused on a nation-state framework, while my interest is to consider thinking beyond it. See John Rawls, *The Law of Peoples* (Cambridge, MA: Harvard University Press, 1999).

2 Trajectories of popular sovereignty

1 F.H. Hinsley, *Sovereignty*, second edition (Cambridge: Cambridge University Press, 1986), 17.
2 For example, Norberto Bobbio, *The Future of Democracy* (Minneapolis: University of Minnesota Press, 1987), 28.
3 Stephen Krasner breaks the concept down further, adding a notion of "interdependence sovereignty" and "Westphalian sovereignty" to the more general domestic–international divide. Stephen D. Krasner, *Sovereignty: Organized Hypocrisy* (Princeton, NJ: Princeton University Press, 1999), 9–25.
4 Hannah Arendt, *On Violence* (New York: Harcourt Brace, 1969), 44.
5 Hannah Arendt, *On Revolution* (New York: Penguin, 1963), 175.
6 Arendt, *On Revolution*, 182.
7 Aristotle, *The Politics of Aristotle*, ed. and trans. Ernest Barker (London: Oxford University Press, 1958), Book III, Chapter 7.
8 Charles Merriam, Jr., *History of the Theory of Sovereignty since Rousseau* (New York: Garland Publishing, 1972 [1900]). Quentin Skinner, *The Foundations of Modern Political Thought* (Cambridge: Cambridge University Press, 1978).

144 *Globalization and Popular Sovereignty*

9 Merriam, *History of the Theory of Sovereignty*, 11–12. Hinsley, *Sovereignty*, 36–41.
10 Hinsley, *Sovereignty*, 126.
11 Hinsley, *Sovereignty*, 71. Skinner, *Foundations*, 291.
12 These are two different formulations from two different versions of the text. The first comes from the now standard French edition of 1583, and the second from Bodin's own Latin translation of 1586. See Jean Bodin, *On Sovereignty: Four Chapters from the Six Books of the Commonwealth*, ed. and trans. Julian H. Franklin (Cambridge: Cambridge University Press, 1992), 1.
13 The extent to which the sovereign could actually be bound by customary law, according to Bodin, is quite narrow and specific. Namely, custom forbids a change in the rule of succession, and forbids the abdication of the royal domain to a foreign power. Both of these restrictions are intended to secure the integrity of the state and not to strictly limit sovereign power. Bodin, *On Sovereignty*, xxv.
14 The parties to the compact for Bodin were the Ruler and the Ruled. In effect, individuals agreed to be subject to sovereign power with the expectation of receiving stability and security in return. As opposed to tyrannical absolutism, good government for Bodin entailed two limitations on sovereignty: (1) those dictated by divine or natural law, including the sanctity of private property, and (2) those established by ancient political tradition, or custom. The extent to which Bodin saw natural law actually restricting sovereign power, however, is ambiguous. At times the limitations contradict the concept of absolute sovereignty, at others they define sovereignty's very condition of possibility. Natural law, according to Bodin, signifies a "merely" moral limitation on the sovereign; it is indicative of good government but not legally enforceable and certainly not to be taken as grounds for legitimate resistance. If a sovereign legitimately ascends the throne, according to Bodin, his subjects have no right to rise up against him, no matter how tyrannical his rule. They have no recourse to challenge his sovereign authority. Hinsley, *Sovereignty*, 122–23. Bodin, *On Sovereignty*, 120. Bodin does, however, argue that it is the duty of all subjects and magistrates to disobey the sovereign if he rules in violation of natural law, for no one must knowingly disobey the will of God. Nevertheless, those who disobey the sovereign do so under risk of severe punishment. See Bodin, *On Sovereignty*, Book III, Chapter 3, and Skinner, *Foundations*, 295.
15 Thomas Hobbes, *Leviathan*, ed. Richard Tuck (Cambridge University Press: Cambridge, 1996), 88.
16 Hobbes, *Leviathan*, 120.
17 Hobbes, *Leviathan*, 150.
18 Hobbes, *Leviathan*, 121.
19 Hobbes, *Leviathan*, 94.
20 Hobbes *Leviathan*, 123–24, 148.
21 Hobbes was not in fact the first to make the shift from ruler contract to social contract. That distinction belongs to Johannes Althusius, a German Calvinist, who did so some forty years prior to the publication of the *Leviathan*. However, whereas for Hobbes the social contract resulted in the constitution of a people in the person of the sovereign, for Althusius the social contract constituted the people itself, independent of the ruling authority. In essence he provided an early articulation of the inalienability of the sovereignty of the people. However, while Althusius made a coherent argument for the location of sovereignty he did not clearly advance the definition of the concept. Furthermore it was a concept adapted for the less centralized polities of the Netherlands and Germany than France and England, where he was thus ignored for centuries.
22 Hobbes, *Leviathan*, 120.
23 John Locke, *Two Treatises of Government*, ed. Peter Laslett (Cambridge: Cambridge University Press, 1988), Chapter XIX, 406–28.

24 A.V. Dicey, *Introduction to the Study of the Law of the Constitution* (New York: St. Martin's Press, 1961 [1885]), 72–73.
25 J.-J. Rousseau, *The Social Contract and other later Political Writings*, ed. Victor Gourevitch (Cambridge: Cambridge University Press, 1997), 57.
26 Rousseau, *Social Contract*, 61.
27 Rousseau, *Social Contract*, 53.
28 Locke, *Two Treatises*, Chapter XIX, 328.
29 William H. Sewell, Jr., *A Rhetoric of Bourgeois Revolution: The Abbé Sieyés and What is the Third Estate?* (Durham, NC: Duke University Press, 1994), 68. See also Keith Michael Baker, *Inventing the French Revolution* (Cambridge: Cambridge University Press, 1990), 298.
30 Emmanuel Joseph Sieyés, *What is the Third Estate?* trans. M. Blondel, ed. S.E. Finer (New York: Praeger, 1964), 121. For Sieyés the concept of the nation was inseparable from citizenship in a commonwealth. A nation could be defined as "a body of associates living under *common* laws and represented by the same *legislative assembly*, etc." (58). It is this character of commonality irrespective of ethnicity that is the deciding factor in the definition of the nation, for Sieyés. It is the nation's "singleness of will" and the desire to live under a common body of laws that enables it to succeed as the constituent power (58, 121). As a result, Sieyés argued, French aristocrats were in fact not true members of the nation. By reserving for themselves a privileged relation to the law they set themselves apart from the common interest, and thus became enemies of the nation (58, 62–63, 146–47, 164). Sewell, *A Rhetoric of Bourgeois Revolution*, 5. Social privilege for Sieyés was like "a horrible disease eating the living flesh." Sieyés, *What is the Third Estate?* 164. Anything that went against the common interest of the nation in effect divided itself from the community, and thus abdicated all its political rights. In this sense, Sieyés, like Rousseau, understood social unity to be a vital principle of popular sovereignty. Rousseau famously declared, "[e]verything which destroys social unity is worthless." Rousseau, *Social Contract*, 147.
31 Sieyés, *What is the Third Estate?* 119, 127–28.
32 Sieyés, *What is the Third Estate?* 126.
33 Sieyés, *What is the Third Estate?* 128.
34 Sieyés, *What is the Third Estate?* 130.
35 As quoted from the *Archives parlementaires* in Baker, *Inventing the French Revolution*, 300.
36 Sieyés, *What is the Third Estate?* 131.
37 Carl Schmitt, *Die Diktatur* (Leipzig: Duncker & Humblot, 1922). See also Andrew Arato, "Goodbye to Dictatorships?" *Social Research* 67:4 (winter 2000).
38 Sewell, *A Rhetoric of Bourgeois Revolution*, 68.
39 Baker, *Inventing the French Revolution*, 303.
40 Baker, *Inventing the French Revolution*, 303–05.
41 Arato, "Goodbye to Dictatorships?" 930.
42 Baker, *Inventing the French Revolution*, 301.
43 Baker, *Inventing the French Revolution*, 303.
44 Baker, *Inventing the French Revolution*, 304.
45 See Arendt, *On Revolution*, 162–65.
46 Sieyés, *What is the Third Estate?* 123–24.
47 Sewell, *A Rhetoric of Bourgeois Revolution*, 19.
48 Hinsley, *Sovereignty*, 156.
49 Immanuel Kant, *The Metaphysics of Morals*, ed. Mary Gregor (Cambridge: Cambridge University Press, 1996 [1797]), 91.
50 Like other social contract theorists, Kant provided an image of the state as a necessary condition posited by human beings in order to secure their freedom to pursue individual ends. For Kant "Public right is therefore a system of laws for a

146 *Globalization and Popular Sovereignty*

people, that is, a multitude of human beings, or for a multitude of peoples which, because they affect one another, need a rightful condition under a will uniting them, a *constitution* (*constitutio*), so that they may enjoy what is laid down as right." Kant, *Metaphysics*, 89.
51 James Madison, *Federalist* No. 40, in *The Federalist Papers*, ed. Clinton Rossiter (New York: Penguin, 1961), 253.
52 Bruce Ackerman, *We, the People: Foundations* (Cambridge, MA: Harvard University Press, 1991). Gordon Wood, *The Creation of the American Republic, 1776–1787* (New York: Norton, 1998).
53 Arendt, *On Revolution*, 166.
54 Arendt, *On Revolution*, 157. While this may appear to entail a certain amount of circularity, because the constitution in turn rests on a claim to being of the will of the people, the key point is that the people are the origin of the constitution only on the basis of prior agreement. There can be no single instantiation of the popular will. The will of the people is behind the constitution only through the mediation of institutions and legal procedures. Arendt, *On Revolution*, 165–66.
55 Jürgen Habermas, *Between Facts and Norms*, trans. William Rehg (Cambridge, MA: MIT Press, 1996), 104.
56 Carl Schmitt, *Teoría de la constitución*, trans. Francisco Ayala (Madrid: Alianza, 1982), 97–100.
57 Jorge Eliécer Gaitán (1902–48), a populist candidate for President in Colombia, who was assassinated in 1948, provoking the years of civil unrest known as *la Violencia*.
58 With respect to the theory of sovereignty and the law H. L. A. Hart makes this point convincingly. Hart, *The Concept of Law*, second edition (Oxford: Clarendon Press, 1994).
59 Habermas, *Between Facts and Norms*, 463–90.

3 The liberal model of popular sovereignty

1 Richard S. Dunn, *The Age of Religious Wars, 1559–1715*, second edition (New York: Norton, 1979), 1–3.
2 John Locke, *Two Treatises*, ed. Peter Laslett (Cambridge: Cambridge University Press, 1988), 218–19. See also James Tully, *An Approach to Political Philosophy: Locke in Contexts* (Cambridge: Cambridge University Press, 1993), 11–12.
3 See "Measuring Globalization: Economic Reversals, Forward Momentum," *Foreign Policy*, March–April 2004. While the index does reflect a decline in foreign direct investment and portfolio capital flows, it shows that the growth of other indicators of globalization, particularly communications and information technology, more than compensated for the losses.
4 Connie Koch, *2/15: The Day the World said No to War* (Oakland, CA: AK Press, 2003).
5 Moisés Naím, " Think Again: Globalization," *Foreign Policy* Magazine, March–April 2009, 28.
6 David Held, *Models of Democracy*, second edition (Stanford, CA: Stanford University Press, 1996), 81. On Locke's influence on the American Revolution see Paul Rahe, *Republics Ancient and Modern* (Chapel Hill: University of North Carolina Press, 1992), 397, 450–72. And John Gray, *Liberalism* (Minneapolis: University of Minnesota Press, 1986), 11–14.
7 However, that is not to say that Locke's model of popular sovereignty is democratic. In addition to Locke, the conceptual formulation of liberal democracy would need to incorporate at the very least a consideration of Montesquieu, Madison, and Mill. Held, *Models of Democracy*, 82–120.

8 This threefold notion of sovereignty has parallels to Carl Schmitt's theory of the people before, within, and alongside a democratic constitution. See Carl Schmitt, *Teoría de la constitución*, Chapter 18. And Andreas Kalyvas, "Carl Schmitt and the Three Moments of Democracy," *Cardozo Law Review* 21 (2000). However, Locke is clearly not discussing a democratic state and so the role for the people is distinct.
9 Laslett briefly discusses this point. Locke, *Two Treatises*, 100.
10 Ian Shapiro, *The Moral Foundation of Politics* (New Haven, CT: Yale University Press, 2003), 111–13.
11 Locke, *Two Treatises*, 271.
12 Locke, *Two Treatises*, Chapters VII–VIII, 318–50.
13 On the "workmanship" theory of obligation see Shapiro, *Moral Foundations* (New Haven, CT: Yale University Press, 2003), 15. On the centrality of Locke's theological commitments to his political philosophy see John Dunn, *The Political Thought of John Locke* (Cambridge: Cambridge University Press, 1969).
14 Held, *Models of Democracy*, 80.
15 John Dunn, "Consent in the Political Theory of John Locke," in *Political Obligation in its Historical Context* (Cambridge: Cambridge University Press, 2002), 33.
16 Dunn, "Consent in the Political Theory of John Locke," 30.
17 Locke, *Two Treatises*, 330.
18 Locke, *Two Treatises*, 331–33, 354.
19 Locke, *Two Treatises*, 348.
20 Locke, *Two Treatises*, 349.
21 Locke, *Two Treatises*, 363.
22 Dicey, 26–27.
23 Locke, *Two Treatises*, 367.
24 This aspect was specifically taken up by the American Founders. See National Constitution Center definition of popular sovereignty at www.constitutioncenter.org.
25 Tully, *Approach*, 37.
26 See Chapter 2 above, 15. And Hobbes, *Leviathan*, 88.
27 Tully, *Approach*, 29–30.
28 Locke, *Two Treatises*, 326.
29 Locke, *Two Treatises*, 412–13.
30 Locke, *Two Treatises*, 412.
31 Locke, *Two Treatises*, 427. Tully, *Approach*, 319.
32 Carl Schmitt, *Political Theology: Four Chapters on the Concept of Sovereignty*, trans. George Schwab (Cambridge, MA: MIT Press, 1985 [German revised edition, 1934]), Chapter 1.
33 However, again, it is important to note that, in contrast to Schmitt or Sieyés, the moment of exception for Locke is never completely without ground, due to his theological commitment to natural law. The people's authority to institute government is thus limited by the principles of natural law; there are rational limits to the type of government they may install. For example, absolutism is unacceptable because it places the people in a state-of-nature relationship with the ruling parties and thus runs contrary to the rationale of natural law.
34 Tully, *Approach*, 46.
35 Tully, *Approach*, 319.
36 John Austin, *The Province of Jurisprudence Determined, etc.* (London: Weidenfeld & Nicolson, 1954 [1832]). Franklin makes a similar point with respect to George Lawson. Julian Franklin, *John Locke and the Theory of Sovereignty* (Cambridge: Cambridge University Press, 1978), 73.

37 On this question see Etienne Balibar and Immanuel Wallerstein, *Race, Nation, Class* (London: Verso, 1991), and Will Kymlicka, *Multicultural Citizenship* (Oxford: Oxford University Press, 1995).
38 Bernard Yack, "Popular Sovereignty and Nationalism," *Political Theory* 29:4 (August 2001).
39 Locke, *Two Treatises*, 268.
40 Locke, *Two Treatises*, 351.
41 Tully, *Approach*, 315.
42 Tully, *Approach*, 17–19.
43 Locke, *Two Treatises*, 324.
44 Locke, *Two Treatises*, 349.
45 John Gray, *Two Faces of Liberalism* (New York: New Press, 2000).
46 Locke, *A Letter Concerning Toleration* (New York: Prometheus Books, 1990 [1689]), 21.
47 Tully, *Approach*, 57.
48 See, for example, John Rawls, *Political Liberalism* (New York: Columbia University Press, 1993). It is, however, important to note that Locke's famous advocacy for the toleration of religious pluralism did not extend to atheists, because a fear of God was believed to be necessary to motivate people to abide by their contracts and keep their promises. Without this theological underpinning, social order would be in jeopardy, calling into question the very purpose of civil society. Locke, *A Letter Concerning Toleration*. See also Tully, *Approach*, 57.
49 Locke, *Two Treatises*, 404–05.
50 Tully, *Approach*, 46.
51 Franklin, *Locke and the Theory of Sovereignty*, 1. Charles E. Merriam, *History of the Theory of Sovereignty*, 17–21. Althusius.
52 Franklin, *Locke and the Theory of Sovereignty*, 70–75. See also Conal Condren, *George Lawson's Politica and the English Revolution* (Cambridge: Cambridge University Press, 1989).
53 Lawson, Tully *Approach*, 19. Locke, *Two Treatises*, 406 note by Laslett.
54 Tully, *Approach*, 19.
55 Tully, *Approach*, 42.
56 Shapiro, *Moral Foundations to Politics*, 114.
57 Tully, *Approach*, 45.
58 James Rosenau and Ernst-Otto Czempiel, *Governance without Government: Order and Change in World Politics* (Cambridge: Cambridge University Press, 1992). James Rosenau, "Governance in the Twenty-first Century," *Global Governance* 1 (1995). Martin Hewson and Timothy J. Sinclair, eds., *Approaches to Global Governance Theory* (Albany, NY: SUNY Press, 1999). David Held and Anthony McGrew, eds., *Governing Globalization: Power, Authority and Global Governance* (Cambridge: Polity Press, 2002). Paul Kennedy, Dirk Messner and Frank Nuscheler, eds., *Global Trends and Global Governance* (London: Pluto Press, 2002).
59 Anthony Giddens, *Runaway World: How Globalization is Reshaping our Lives* (New York: Routledge, 2003).
60 Robert Gilpin, "A Realist Perspective on International Governance," in Held and McGrew, *Governing Globalization*, 240. See also Wolfgang H. Reinicke, *Global Public Policy: Governing without Government?* (Washington, DC: Brookings Institution, 1989).
61 Susan Strange, *The Retreat of the State* (Cambridge: Cambridge University Press, 1996), Chapter 6.
62 On the "evolutionary process" of constitution-making at the national level see Andrew Arato, *Civil Society, Constitution, and Legitimacy* (New York: Rowman & Littlefield, 2000), Chapter 7.

63 A. Claire Cutler, "Globalization, the Rule of Law, and the Modern Law Merchant: Medieval or Late Capitalist Associations?" *Constellations* 8:4 (December 2001). See also A. Claire Cutler, Virginia Haufler, and Tony Porter, eds., *Private Authority and International Affairs* (New York: SUNY Press, 1999). Gunther Teubner, ed., *Global Law without a State* (Aldershot: Dartmouth, 1997).
64 Vaios Karavas and Gunther Teubner, "http://www.CompanyNameSucks.com: The Horizontal Effect of Fundamental Rights on 'Private Parties' within Autonomous Internet Law," *German Law Journal* 4:12 (2003): 1355.
65 Karavas and Teubner, "http://www.CompanyNameSucks.com," 1355. See also Gilpin, "A Realist Perspective on International Governance," 240.
66 Ngaire Woods, "Global Governance and the Role of Institutions," in Held and McGrew, *Governing Globalization*, 31.
67 Woods, "Global Governance and the Role of Institutions," 31–32.
68 Karavas and Teubner, "http://www.CompanyNameSucks.com," 1356.
69 On intergovernmental networks see Anne-Marie Slaughter, "The Real New World Order," *Foreign Affairs* 76:5 (September–October 1997).
70 David Held and Anthony McGrew, "Introduction," *Governing Globalization*, 13.
71 A. Claire Cutler, "Globalization, the Rule of Law, and the Modern Law Merchant," *Constellations* 8:4 (December 2001): 488.
72 Robert Cox, "Democracy in Hard Times: Economic Globalization and the Limits to Liberal Democracy," in Anthony McGrew, ed., *The Transformation of Democracy?* (Cambridge: Polity Press, 1997), 61.
73 *Global Governance Initiative: Executive Summary 2004* (Washington, DC: Communications Development, 2004), 6.
74 Strange, *Retreat*, 95. David Held, Anthony McGrew, David Goldblatt, and Jonathan Perraton, *Global Transformations: Politics, Economics, and Culture* (Stanford, CA: Stanford University Press, 1999), 85.
75 David Held and Anthony McGrew, "The Great Globalization Debate," in *The Global Transformations Reader*, second edition (Cambridge: Polity Press, 2003), 39.
76 Paul Kennedy, Dirk Messner and Frank Nuscheler, eds., *Global Trends and Global Governance* (London: Pluto Press, 2002), 189.
77 Noberto Bobbio, *The Future of Democracy: A Defense of the Rules of the Game* (Minneapolis: University of Minnesota Press, 1987), 18.
78 Kanishka Jayasuriya, "Globalization, Sovereignty, and the Rule of Law: From Political to Economic Constitutionalism?" *Constellations* 8:4 (December 2001): 453–54.
79 Mathias Koenig-Archibugi, "Mapping Global Governance," in David Held and Anthony McGrew, eds., *Governing Globalization: Power Authority and Global Governance* (Cambridge: Polity Press, 2002), 56.
80 Cutler, "Globalization," 484.
81 On the other hand, globalization does present the potential to increase the capacity for rights protection through the institution of a cosmopolitan human rights regime – and I will have much more to say about that in Chapters 6 and 7 – however, at present it is uneven and its effectiveness is based more on political influence than on the equal application of universal principles. See Chris Brown, *Sovereignty, Rights and Justice* (Cambridge: Polity Press, 2002), Chapter 7.
82 According to a 1999 UNDP report, OECD countries account for 71 percent of all global trade in goods and services while making up only 19 percent of the world's population. And as of 1999 South Asia represented 23 percent of the world's population but was home to only 1 percent of the globe's internet users. See "Patterns of Global Inequality," UNDP Report 1999, in Held and McGrew, *The Global Transformations Reader*, 425, 428.
83 Hewson and Sinclair, *Approaches to Global Governance Theory*, 7.

150 *Globalization and Popular Sovereignty*

84 Ulrich Beck, *What is Globalization?* trans. Patrick Camiller (Cambridge: Polity Press, 2000), 10.
85 Held et al., *Global Transformations*, 228–30.
86 See Seth Mydans, "A Burst of Raw Democracy: Anything Wrong with That?" *New York Times*, Wednesday, January 7, 2004.
87 Koenig-Archibugi, "Mapping Global Governance,", 63.
88 John A. Guidry, Michael D. Kennedy, and Mayer N. Zald, eds., *Globalizations and Social Movements* (Ann Arbor: University of Michigan Press, 2000), 1.
89 Margaret E. Keck and Kathryn Sikkink, *Activists beyond Borders* (Ithaca, NY: Cornell University Press, 1998), 12–28.
90 James N. Rosenau, "Governance and Democracy in a Globalizing World," in Daniele Archibugi, David Held, and Martin Köhler, eds., *Reimagining Political Community* (Stanford, CA: Stanford University Press, 1998), and James N. Rosenau, *Distant Proximities* (Princeton, NJ: Princeton University Press, 2003).
91 Beck, *What is Globalization?* 8.

4 The republican model of popular sovereignty

1 Jean Jacques Rousseau, "Discourse on the Origin and the Foundations of Inequality among Men," *The Discourses and other early Political Writings*, ed. Victor Gourevitch (Cambridge: Cambridge University Press, 1997), 187. [Hereafter, "Second Discourse."] See also Jean Starobinski, *Jean-Jacques Rousseau: Transparency and Obstruction*, trans. Arthur Goldhammer (Chicago: Unversity of Chicago Press, 1988), 4–5.
2 Jean Jacques Rousseau, "The State of War," *The Social Contract and other later Political Writings*, ed. Victor Gourevitch (Cambridge: Cambridge University Press, 1997), 166.
3 "Lettre á Malesherbes," 1249, January 12, 1762, *Correspondance Générale de J.-J. Rousseau*, ed. Dufour and Plan (Paris, 1924–34, 20 vols.), Vol. VII, 5051. Translation quoted in Fred Weinstein and Gerald M. Platt, "Rousseau: the Ambivalent Democrat," in *The Wish to be Free* (Los Angeles: University of California Press, 1969), 85.
4 Rousseau, "Second Discourse," 187.
5 This autonomous solitude was key to natural freedom for Rousseau, and it is his commitment to a fundamentally antisocial nature in man that distinguishes Rousseau from many of the thinkers that he influenced. As Sankar Muthu has explained, while Diderot, Kant, and Herder all appropriated elements of Rousseau's social criticism and philosophy of freedom, they rejected his account of natural solitude in favor of a view of man as a social agent from the start. Sankar Muthu, *Enlightenment against Empire* (Princeton, NJ: Princeton University Press, 2003), 8.
6 Judith Shklar, *Men and Citizens: A Study of Rousseau's Social Theory* (Cambridge: Cambridge University Press, 1969), 76. This transformation from good natural man to wicked man-in-society is represented by the triumph of *amour propre* over *amour soi-même*. *Amour soi-même* is the natural instinct for self-preservation experienced by all animals, moderated in humankind by a natural dispensation to compassion or pity before the suffering of others. *Amour propre* is born of society and is purely relational in so far as its standard is set by comparison to others. It is the sense of pride that leads one to "set greater store by himself than by anyone else, [and] inspires men with the evils they do one another…" See Rousseau, "Second Discourse," 218. However, it is important to note that while some critics such as Judith Shklar see *amour propre* as always a negation of humankind's natural inclinations, its character is in fact more ambivalent. According to Rousseau *amour propre* may be cultivated into a source of

patriotism that would promote social unity, and in a homogeneous society this does not necessarily negate the natural inclinations of *amour soi-même* and compassion. Rather for Rousseau the key is to imagine the society in which man's natural inclinations would develop into social integration as opposed to dislocation. For the practical cultivation of *amour propre* into patriotism see, for example, Jean-Jacques Rousseau, "Considerations on the Government of Poland," *The Social Contract and other later Political Writings*. And for the cultivation of natural inclinations into social virtue see Jean-Jacques Rousseau, *Emile, or, On Education*, trans. Alan Bloom (New York: Basic Books, 1979). And John W. Chapman, *Rousseau: Totalitarian or Liberal?* (New York: Columbia University Press, 1956).
7 Jean-Jacques Rousseau, "Preface to Narcissus," *The Social Contract and other later Political Writings*, 101.
8 Starobinski, *Transparency and Obstruction*, 21, 30. Shklar, *Men and Citizens*, 17.
9 Jean-Jacques Rousseau, "Observations," *The Discourses and other Early Political Writings*, 50–51.
10 William F. Fisher and Thomas Ponniah, eds., *Another World is Possible: Popular Alternatives to Globalization at the World Social Forum* (New York: Zed Books, 2003), 351. On the right to self-determination see also Daniele Archibugi, "A Critical Analysis of the Self-determination of Peoples: A Cosmopolitan Perspective," *Constellations* 10:4 (2003).
11 Álvaro Vargas Llosa, "The Return of Latin America's Left," Op-Ed, *New York Times*, March 22, 2005, A23. Jorge G. Castañeda, "Latin America's Left Turn," *Foreign Affairs* 85:3 (May–June 2006).
12 Rousseau, "Social Contract," 68.
13 Rousseau, "Social Contract," 66–67, 80.
14 Rousseau, "Discourse on Political Economy," *The Social Contract and other later Political Writings*. 6. Rousseau, "Social Contract," 57, 82–83.
15 Rousseau, "Social Contract," 112.
16 In this respect, Rousseau's use of the term "government" differs from much historical as well as contemporary usage. Generally government is understood to include the domain of lawmaking. This is not the case for Rousseau. For a recent discussion of this distinction see John T. Scott, "Rousseau's Anti-agenda-setting Agenda and Contemporary Democratic Theory," *American Political Science Review* 99:1 (February 2005): 138.
17 Rousseau, "Social Contract," 106, 110, 111–12.
18 Chapman, *Rousseau: Totalitarian or Liberal?*
19 Jean-Jacques Rousseau, "On the Social Contract," *The Social Contract and other later Political Writings*, 58.
20 Shklar, *Men and Citizens*, 191.
21 Rousseau, "Social Contract," 62.
22 Patrick Riley, *Will and Political Legitimacy* (Cambridge, MA: Harvard University Press, 1982), 112.
23 Shklar, *Men and Citizens*, 13–16. While Rousseau was a classicist in his admiration for Sparta and republican Rome, Stephen Ellenburg aptly notes that it is important to recall that Rousseau rejected the Ancient Greek notion that man was by nature a political being. As has been said, for Rousseau, man in the state of nature was happily solitary. Stephen Ellenburg, *Rousseau's Political Philosophy: An Interpretation from Within* (Ithaca, NY: Cornell University Press, 1976), 25.
24 Riley, *Will and Political Legitimacy*, 114.
25 Rousseau, "Social Contract," 44.
26 Rousseau, "Social Contract," 60. Charges that Rousseau seeks to suppress individual will are mistaken in this regard. See, for example, John Charvet, *The Social*

Problem in the Philosophy of Rousseau (Cambridge: Cambridge University Press, 1974). Furthermore, while Rousseau preferred consensus as a sign of the presence of the general will, he argued, "For a will to be general it is not always necessary that it be unanimous, but it is necessary that all votes be counted; any formal exclusion destroys generality." Rousseau, "Social Contract," 58 f.

27 Chapman, *Rousseau: Totalitarian or Liberal?* 83.
28 Gourevitch, "Introduction," *The Social Contract*, xiii. Shklar, *Men and Citizens*, 169. Denis Diderot, *"Droit naturel,"* Article de L'Encyclopédie, Paris, 1755. See Denis Diderot, *Political Writings*, John Hope Mason and Robert Wokler, eds. (Cambridge: Cambridge University Press, 1992).
29 Rousseau, "Political Economy," 7.
30 Riley, *Will and Political Legitimacy*, 113.
31 "[T]he most general will is also the most just..." Rousseau, "Political Economy," 8.
32 Rousseau, "Social Contract," 61.
33 Rousseau, "Social Contract," 59–60.
34 Rousseau's term *Législateur* is often transliterated as "the Legislator." However, I prefer Gourevitch's translation of the term as "Lawgiver." It makes clear the distinction between the founding act of constitution-making and later acts of legislation by the people assembled. That said, it is also clear that Rousseau did believe that there was space for statesmen to play the role of lawgiver after the original act of founding in processes of constitutional transformation. See Rousseau, "Considerations on the Government of Poland."
35 Rousseau, "Social Contract," 59. On this problem see also John Charvet, "Rousseau, the Problem of Sovereignty and the Limits of Political Obligation," in Robert Wokler, ed., *Rousseau and Liberty* (New York: St. Martin's Press, 1995).
36 Gourevitch, "Introduction," *The Social Contract*, xxi.
37 Charvet, *The Social Problem in Rousseau*.
38 Rousseau, "Political Economy," 8.
39 Rousseau, "Social Contract," 147.
40 Rousseau, "Social Contract," 49.
41 Nadia Urbinati, "Continuity and Rupture: The Power of Judgment in Democratic Representation," *Constellations* 12:2 (June 2005): 199.
42 Lord Acton, "Nationality" [1862], in *Mapping the Nation*, ed. Gopal Balakrishnan (London: Verso, 1996), 22.
43 See especially Rousseau, "Social Contract," 72–78.
44 Lord Acton, "Nationality," 29.
45 Rousseau, "Social Contract," 50.
46 Rousseau, "Social Contract," 78.
47 See Philip Pettit, *Republicanism: A Theory of Freedom and Government* (Oxford: Oxford University Press, 2000). And Ian Shapiro, *Democratic Justice* (New Haven, CT: Yale University Press, 1999).
48 This is true generally for the size of the republic as well as the diversity of "morals," according to Rousseau. "Now, the smaller the ratio of individual wills to the general will, that is to say, of morals to laws, the more does the repressive force have to increase." Rousseau, "Social Contract," 84.
49 Charvet, *The Social Problem in Rousseau*, 145–46.
50 Rousseau, "Social Contract," 71.
51 Rousseau, "Social Contract," 69.
52 Allan Bloom, "Introduction to *Emile*," in Rousseau (New York: Basic Books, 1979), 5.
53 Rousseau, "Social Contract," 77.
54 Rousseau, "Second Discourse," 165.
55 Rousseau, "Second Discourse," 127.
56 Chapman, *Rousseau: Totalitarian or Liberal?* 59.

Notes 153

57 Shklar, *Men and Citizens*, 161. Shklar makes a similar point to distinguish Rousseau from nineteenth-century nationalists that saw the national identity as grounded in nature.
58 Johann Gottfried von Herder, "Reflections on the Philosophy of the History of Mankind," [1791], in Omar Dahbour and Micheline R. Ishey, eds., *The Nationalism Reader* (New York: Humanities Press, 1995), 54. Important to note that Sankar Muthu has taken issue with the now stereotypical portrayal of Herder as the model counter-Enlightenment Romantic nationalist. Muthu astutely demonstrates the manner in which Herder in fact attempted to balance a universal humanitarian philosophy with a particularstic appreciation for human diversity and national self-determination. See Muthu, *Enlightenment against Empire*, 210–58.
59 Rousseau, "Social Contract," 68.
60 Rousseau, "The Geneva Manuscript," *The Social Contract and other later Political Writings*, 158.
61 The figure of the true lawgiver was indeed rare for Rousseau. Among the modern nations he saw not a single one, and among the ancients only three principal lawgivers: Moses, Lycurgus, and Numa. And, interestingly enough, each one of these is the subject of considerable myth-making. Rousseau, "Considerations on the Government of Poland," 180. To a degree the lawgiver provides a revered symbol of national unity who is often attributed deeds and virtues after the fact that are undeserved. Numa was regularly credited with the establishment of the whole system of Roman religious institutions that were more likely the product of centuries of development. And to the extent that the American "Founding Fathers" may be treated as a collective lawgiver, they are often revered as if they spoke with the authority of a single wise voice, when any cursory examination of the record documents grave disagreements, political maneuvering, and pragmatic compromise among them. Of course, in the American case, the metaphor is not entirely apt in that the "founders" were not lawgivers per se in that they were not outsiders, nor did they exit the political scene but dominated it for years after the constitution was ratified.
62 Rousseau, "Social Contract," 68–72.
63 Rousseau, "The Geneva Manuscript," 156.
64 Rousseau, "Political Economy," 13. Also Rousseau writes, "It is national institutions which form the genius, the character, the tastes, and the morals of a people, which make it be itself and not another...", "Considerations on the Government of Poland," 183
65 Rousseau, "Political Economy," 13.
66 Chapman, *Rousseau: Totalitarian or Liberal?* 59.
67 Rousseau, "Social Contract," 150.
68 Rousseau, "Considerations on the Government of Poland," 189.
69 Rousseau, "Considerations on the Government of Poland," 183–85.
70 Chapman, *Rousseau: Totalitarian or Liberal?* 58. Gourevitch, "Introduction" to *The Social Contract and other later Political Writings*, xxviii–xxix. Rousseau, "Political Economy," 15.
71 Rousseau, "The Social Contract," 146.
72 Rousseau, "Political Economy," 16.
73 Shklar, *Men and Citizens*, 206.
74 Shklar, *Men and Citizens*, 206–07.
75 Jean-Jacques Rousseau, "Essay on the Origin of Languages," *The Discourses and other early Political Writings*, 269.
76 Jean-Jacques Rousseau, "Extrait du projet de paix perpétuelle de Monsieur l'abbé de Saint-Pierre," *Oeuvres Complètes* (Paris: Gallimard, 1964), 563.

154 *Globalization and Popular Sovereignty*

77 Howard Williams, "Rousseau: the Impossibility of International Harmony," in *International Relations in Political Theory* (Philadelphia: Open University Press, 1992).
78 Held et al., *Global Transformations*, 321–26, 370. Thomas Friedman, *The Lexus and the Olive Tree: Understanding Globalization* (New York: Anchor Books, 2000), 67–68. As the Google–China case exemplifies, rigorous forms of electronic censorship do, however, remain possible, and may increase in the future, especially in countries where the government has monopoly control over all Internet Service Providers. The systematic censorship of the internet in China is the product of an official program, the "Golden Shield Project," or the Great Firewall of China. The extent to which American high-tech firms are complicit in such censorship was lambasted by Xeni Jardin in "Exporting Censorship," Op-Ed, *The New York Times*, March 9, 2006, A23.
79 This is what has often been termed "Westphalian sovereignty," see Stephen Krasner, *Sovereignty: Organized Hypocrisy* (Princeton, NJ: Princeton University Press, 1999), 20–25.
80 Antonio Cassese, *International Law*, second edition (Oxford: Oxford University Press, 2005), 28.
81 Charles R. Beitz, *Political Theory and International Relations* (Princeton, NJ: Princeton University Press, 1979), 92.
82 Robert O. Keohane and Joseph S. Nye, eds., *Power and Interdependence: World Politics in Transition*, revised edition (New York: Addison-Wesley, 2001). Robert O. Keohane, "Sovereignty in International Society," in Held and McGrew, *The Global Transformations Reader*, 154.
83 Keohane, "Sovereignty in International Society," 155. See also Habermas, "A Political Constitution for the Pluralist World Society?" He writes: "And what is termed 'external sovereignty' is more the ability to cooperate with partners than the ability to defend oneself against enemies," 10
84 See also Hauke Brunkhorst, *Solidarity: From Civic Friendship to a Global Legal Community*, trans. Jeff Flynn (Cambridge, MA: MIT Press, 2005), 104–05.
85 Seyla Benhabib makes a similar observation about the self-determination of minority groups within multicultural and transnational societies, especially as it relates to gender equality. See Seyla Benhabib, *The Claims of Culture: Equality and Diversity in the Global Era* (Princeton, NJ: Princeton University Press, 2002), 185.
86 Rousseau, *The Social Contract*, 60, 84.
87 United Nations Development Programme (UNDP), *Human Development Report* (New York: Oxford University Press, 1999).
88 David Held, *Global Covenant: The Social Democratic Alternative to the Washington Consensus* (Cambridge: Polity Press, 2004), 34. On the institutional response to the state of inequality in the global economy see also Ngaire Woods, "Global Economic Governance: Strengthening Multilateral Institutions" (New York, International Peace Institute, July 2008).
89 Branko Milanovic, "Global Income Inequality: What it is and Why it Matters," DESA Working Paper No. 26, August 2006, UN Doc. ST/ESA/2006/DWP/26.
90 Jeff Faux, *The Global Class War* (New York: Wiley, 2006).
91 Held, *Global Covenant*, 37. Faux, *The Global Class War*. Inequality in the global North is especially pronounced in the United States. See APSA Task Force on Inequality and American Democracy, "American Democracy in an Age of Rising Inequality" (Washington, DC: American Political Science Association, 2004). Available at www.apsanet.org/imgtest/taskforcereport.pdf. Andrea Brandolini and Timothy M. Smeeding, "Patterns of Economic Inequality in Western Democracies: Some Facts on Levels and Trends," *Political Science and Politics* 39:1 (January 2006).
92 Held, *Global Covenant*, 46.

93 See discussion of Garrett in Held, *Global Covenant*, 47–49, and Geoffrey Garrett, "Globalization's Missing Middle," *Foreign Affairs*, November–December 2004.
94 Sen argues for an understanding of the global economy that appreciates the intimate connection between economic development and substantive freedoms. Thus he argues that poverty must not be understood simply in terms of low income, rather more comprehensively as "capability" deprivation, such as the capacity for individuals to act as self-responsible "agents" able to effect change. Amartya Sen, *Development as Freedom* (New York: Anchor Books, 1999). On poverty see especially Chapter 4.
95 See, for example, "The Bamako Appeal" (Bamako, Mali, January 18, 2006).
96 Held et al., *Global Transformations*, 315.
97 Rainer Muenz, "Europe: Population and Migration in 2005" (Washington, DC: Migration Policy Institute, June 2006).
98 Robert Bernstein, "Coming to America: A Profile of the Nation's Foreign Born (2000 Update)," *Census Brief: Current Population Survey* CENBR/01-1 (Washington, DC: US Census Bureau, 2002). Luke J. Larsen, "The Foreign-born Population in the United States, 2003," *Current Population Reports*, P20-551 (Washington, DC: US Census Bureau, 2004).
99 In fact only 13.7 percent of the foreign-born population in 2003 was from Europe, while 53.3 percent was from Latin America, 25 percent from Asia, and 8 percent from "other regions," including Africa, Canada, the Middle East, and Oceania. Larsen, "The Foreign-born Population in the United States, 2003," 10.
100 Sam Roberts, "Whites to be Minority in New York Area Soon, Data Show," *New York Times*, March 7, 2006, B1. In the study cited here the New York metropolitan area includes New York City, Long Island, northern New Jersey, and northeastern Pennsylvania, but not Connecticut.
101 Rousseau, *The Social Contract*, 147.
102 By hyphenated identities I mean, for example, Mexican-American or Turkish-German, etc.
103 William I. Robinson, *Transnational Conflicts* (London: Verso, 2003), 270–72.
104 Held et al., *Global Transformations*, 283. The traditional description of population movements in terms of center and periphery raises a number of issues in the context of complex processes of globalization. For one, as Arjun Appadurai has argued, it suggests a definite shape – a clear inside and outside – and a certain stability, neither of which characterizes the contemporary condition. Alternatively, Appadurai prefers to speak in terms of "scapes" and "flows" to evoke the irregularity of global processes. See Arjun Appadurai, *Modernity at Large: Cultural Dimensions of Globalization* (Minneapolis: University of Minnesota Press, 1996), 32–34, 44–48.
105 It is important to note that such conflicts are not simply limited to relations between immigrants from the developing world living in Europe or North America. In the context of globalization, such conflicts represent a dynamic familiar to regional economic powers as well. For example, the armed conflict in Côte d'Ivoire between rebel-held north and government controlled south may be understood as an issue of immigration and assimilation. As the historically wealthiest country in West Africa, Côte d'Ivoire has attracted millions of largely Muslim immigrants from poorer neighboring countries such as Burkino Faso and Mali, especially as laborers in the cocoa fields. By the 1990s the foreign population had grown to nearly one-third of the country, and in response, rather than seeking to include the new population as full citizens, the government began instituting restrictive citizenship laws based on the nativist concept of *ivoirité*, precipitating the organization of violent resistance. "Q&A: Ivory Coast's Crisis," BBC News, at http://news.bbc.co.uk/1/hi/world/africa/3567349.stm.

106 Seyla Benhabib, *The Claims of Culture* (Princeton, NJ: Princeton University Press, 2002), 178–86.
107 Benhabib divides the components of citizenship among three elements: "collective identity, political membership, and the right to social entitlements," what I summarize as the identity, political, and social elements. Jean Cohen, who also articulates the notion of disaggregated citizenship, divides it up slightly differently among the juridical, political, and identity components. The juridical component of citizenship is the universal right to be treated as a person under the law. She does not as directly address the issue of social entitlements as does Benhabib. I discuss Cohen's model of disaggregated citizenship in detail in Chapter 7, p. 120–121. Jean Cohen, "Changing Paradigms of Citizenship and the Exclusiveness of the Demos," *International Sociology* 14:3 (September 1999).
108 Benhabib, *The Claims of Culture*, 182.
109 On the importance of "the frame" for questions of global justice see Nancy Fraser, *Reframing Justice* (Amsterdam: Van Gorcum, 2005), or Nancy Fraser, "Reframing Justice in a Globalizing World," *New Left Review* 36 (November–December 2005).
110 As Nadia Urbinati writes, "In sum, modern history suggests that the genealogy of democratization began with the representative process. The democratization of state power and the unifying power of ideas and political movements brought about by representation were interconnected and self-reinforcing." Urbinati, "Continuity and Rupture, 196.
111 Brunkhorst, *Solidarity*, 73–74, 76.

5 The deliberative model of popular sovereignty: Jürgen Habermas

1 Jürgen Habermas, "Three Normative Models of Democracy," in Ciaran Cronin and Pablo De Grieff, eds., *The Inclusion of the Other* (Cambridge, MA: MIT Press, 1998), 248. Jürgen Habermas, *Between Facts and Norms*, trans. William Rehg (Cambridge, MA: MIT Press, 1996), 299–300.
2 Habermas, "Three Normative Models of Democracy," 241–44.
3 James Bohman remarks, "The main reason Habermas is not a Rousseauian is that complexity fundamentally changes the conditions for popular sovereignty, for the unified will of the people." James Bohman, "Complexity, Pluralism, and the Constitutional State: On Habermas's *Faktizität und Geltung*," *Law and Society Review* 28:4 (1994): 905.
4 Habermas, *Between Facts and Norms*, 486.
5 Bohman, "Complexity, Pluralism, and the Constitutional State." William E. Scheuerman, "Between Radicalism and Resignation: Democratic Theory in Habermas's *Between Facts and Norms*," in Peter Dews, ed., *Habermas: A Critical Reader* (Oxford: Blackwell, 1999). Kenneth Baynes, "Democracy and the *Rechtsstaat*: Habermas's *Faktizität und Geltung*," in Stephen K. White, ed., *The Cambridge Companion to Habermas* (Cambridge: Cambridge University Press, 1995).
6 Baynes, "Democracy and the *Rechtsstaat*," 214. The circularity of this structure should be apparent. However, as we will see, when discussed in terms of discourse theory the circularity is not "vicious," that is, it does not simply end where it began to begin anew in the same manner. Rather its circularity may be imagined as a widening spiral, beginning with the basic principles inherent to free and equal discourse and widening to include the potential participation of all affected parties.
7 Habermas, "Popular Sovereignty as Procedure" (1988), *Between Facts and Norms*, 463–90.

8 Jürgen Habermas, "Reply to Symposium Participants, Benjamin N. Cardozo School of Law," trans. William Rehg, in Michel Rosenfeld and Andrew Arato, eds., *Habermas on Law and Democracy: Critical Exchanges* (Berkeley: University of California Press, 1998), 408.
9 Baynes, "Democracy and the *Rechtsstaat*," 214. Rainer Forst, "The Rule of Reasons: Three Models of Deliberative Democracy," *Ratio Juris* 14:4 (December 2001). On process versus substance see Robert Dahl, *Democracy and its Critics* (New Haven, CT: Yale University Press, 1989), 163–75.
10 Habermas, *Between Facts and Norms*, 486.
11 Most notably, of course, see Habermas's landmark two-volume *The Theory of Communicative Action*, trans. Thomas McCarthy (Boston, MA: Beacon Press, Vol. I, 1984, Vol. II, 1987). Specifically, on universal pragmatics see "What is Universal Pragmatics?" *Communication and the Evolution of Society*, trans. Thomas McCarthy (Boston, MA: Beacon Press, 1979). Also, on discourse ethics, see Jürgen Habermas, *Moral Consciousness and Communicative Action*, trans. C. Lenhardt and S.W. Nicholsen (Cambridge, MA: MIT Press, 1990).
12 Habermas, *Between Facts and Norms*, 453.
13 Jürgen Habermas, *Justification and Application: Remarks on Discourse Ethics*, trans. Ciaran P. Cronin (Cambridge, MA: MIT Press, 1993), 50.
14 Jürgen Habermas, *The Theory of Communicative Action*, Vol. I, 284–88. See also Habermas, *Between Facts and Norms*, 17–19.
15 Habermas, *Moral Consciousness and Communicative Action*, 58.
16 Habermas, *Between Facts and Norms*, 4.
17 Specifically, Habermas argues, they make assertions regarding three dimensions: claims to objective truth, claims to normative rightness, and claims to sincerity or truthfulness. Habermas, *Moral Consciousness and Communicative Action*, 58–59.
18 Habermas, *Justification and Application*, 53.
19 Seyla Benhabib, "The Utopian Dimension in Communicative Ethics," in David Ingram and Julia Simon-Ingram, eds., *Critical Theory: The Essential Readings* (New York: Paragon House, 1991), 390.
20 Habermas, *Moral Consciousness and Communicative Action*, 88.
21 For example, Habermas argues that there are three categories of pragmatic presuppositions that *must* be made by the participants of an argumentative discourse oriented toward consensus. First, there are "logical" assumptions, for example that arguments will be consistent and lack contradiction. Second, there are "dialectical" assumptions: it is presupposed that assertions are sincere and that the goal is persuasion, not coercion. And finally, there are assumptions concerning comprehensiveness at the "level of processes": everyone with something at stake and the competence to take part must be allowed access. Habermas, *Moral Consciousness and Communicative Action*, 87–89.
22 Habermas, "What is Universal Pragmatics?" 1–68. Habermas, *The Theory of Communicative Action*, Vol. I, 273–337. Habermas, "Discourse Ethics: Notes on a Program of Philosophical Justification," *Moral Consciousness and Communicative Action*, 43–115.
23 Habermas, *Moral Consciousness and Communicative Action*, 86.
24 Habermas, *Moral Consciousness and Communicative Action*, 65.
25 Habermas, *Moral Consciousness and Communicative Action*, 92. Thus, as Nancy Fraser argues, the pragmatics view links the study of language to the study of society. It studies language as a social practice embedded in specific social contexts, allowing one to study how people "do things with words." And thus in linking discourse and society it opens the door to the study of power and inequality. See Nancy Fraser, *Justice Interruptus* (New York: Routledge, 1997), 160–61.

158 *Globalization and Popular Sovereignty*

26 On this point see Maeve Cooke, *Language and Reason: A Study of Habermas's Pragmatics* (Cambridge, MA: MIT Press, 1994), especially Chapter 1. In addition, this suggests that Dmitri Nikulin overstates the case when he claims "Consensus cancels the very possibility for a continuation of the unfinalizable polyphonic exchange…" On the contrary, the recognized fallibility of discourse means it must always be open to revision and thus also shares a degree of the "unfinalizable" Nikulin reserves for a concept of dialogue in opposition to Habermasian discourse. Dmitri Nikulin, "Dialogue versus Discourse: On the Possibility of Disagreement in Human Communication," *Graduate Faculty Philosophy Journal* 26:1 (2005): 98.
27 Habermas, *Moral Consciousness and Communicative Action*, 91.
28 Habermas, *Moral Consciousness and Communicative Action*, 88. Habermas, *The Theory of Communicative Action*, Vol. I, 42.
29 Habermas, "Reply to Symposium Participants, 418–19.
30 Michael K. Power, "Habermas and the Counterfactual Imagination," in Michel Rosenfeld and Andrew Arato, eds., *Habermas on Law and Democracy: Critical Exchanges* (Berkeley: University of California Press, 1998), 214–15.
31 Thus critics like Margaret Kohn who charge that Habermas assumes under ideal conditions language is totally transparent – a claim undermined by Wittgenstein, Baktin, Derrida, and Pierce, at the very least – miss the pragmatic foundation of Habermas's argument. It is not that language under ideal conditions would be totally transparent, but rather that in order to engage in earnest discourse we must, and do, assume that our speech acts are intelligible. Otherwise, they would be without purpose. See Margaret Kohn, "Language, Power, and Persuasion: Toward a Critique of Deliberative Democracy," *Constellations* 7:3 (September 2000). Nikulin, "Dialogue versus Discourse," 92–94.
32 These idealizations represent the pragmatic presuppositions of the practice of reaching understanding. As such they open up the possibility of critique. Habermas, *Between Facts and Norms*, 4–5. Maeve Cooke puts it succinctly: "strong idealizations… allow us to criticize actual processes of discussion on the basis of the tension between what is necessarily supposed by the participants and what actually happens in a given discusssion." Cooke, *Language and Reason*, 47.
33 Thomas McCarthy, "Legitimacy and Diversity: Dialectical Reflections on Analytic Distinctions," in Rosenfeld and Arato, *Habermas on Law and Democracy*, 150.
34 Habermas, *Between Facts and Norms*, 158.
35 Habermas, *Between Facts and Norms*, 128.
36 Habermas, *Between Facts and Norms*, 107–10. See Maeve Cooke, "The Weakness of Strong Intersubjectivism: Habermas's Conception of Justice," *European Journal of Political Theory* 2:3 (July 2003): 299.
37 Habermas, *Between Facts and Norms*, 121. On this point it is important to note that Habermas distances himself from the legal positivism of Weber, favoring a more Parsonian view of law that anchors legitimacy in civil society, the public sphere, and the development of modern citizenship rights. See Habermas, *Between Facts and Norms*, 72–73. And Habermas, *Theory of Communicative Action I*, 261–62.
38 Habermas, *Between Facts and Norms*, 459–60. Also, for this specific observation, see Cooke, "The Weakness of Strong Intersubjectivism", 299. And William Rehg, "Translator's Introduction," in Habermas, *Between Facts and Norms*, xxvi.
39 Habermas, *Between Facts and Norms*, 110.
40 Bohman, "Complexity, Pluralism, and the Constitutional State" See also William Rehg, "Against Subordination: Morality, Discourse, and Decision in the Legal Theory of Jürgen Habermas," in Rosenfeld and Arato, *Habermas on Law and Democracy*.

41 In Habermas's ideal process model each of these forms of discourse is taken in turn independently, starting with pragmatic considerations. However, in an endnote to the postscript of *Between Facts and Norms*, Habermas admits that in political discourse pragmatic, ethical, and moral questions are only *"analytically"* distinct, and thus must be regularly addressed simultaneously. Habermas, *Between Facts and Norms*, 565.
42 Habermas, *Between Facts and Norms*, 154.
43 Habermas, *Between Facts and Norms*, 165.
44 Habermas, *Between Facts and Norms*, 166.
45 Habermas, "Reply," 396.
46 Rehg, "Against Subordination," 267.
47 Bohman, "Complexity, Pluralism, and the Constitutional State," 921.
48 Habermas, "Reply," 396.
49 Habermas, "Reply," 397.
50 Bohman, "Complexity, Pluralism, and the Constitutional State," 921.
51 Habermas, *Between Facts and Norms*, 304–8. It should be noted that in large part the twin-track model is a response to the demands of the social complexity of modern capitalist society, and a proposed solution to the problem of how communicative power may affect the functionally differentiated subsystems of the economy and public administration without becoming more vulnerable to the further colonization of the lifeworld. In the interests of remaining focused, I have chosen to concentrate my discussion on the discourse theory of democracy, the *political* theory, rather than the *social* theory.
52 Habermas, *Between Facts and Norms*, 307.
53 Jürgen Habermas, *The Structural Transformation of the Public Sphere*, trans. Thomas Burger (Cambridge, MA: MIT Press, 1989).
54 Habermas, *Structural Transformation of the Public Sphere*, 27.
55 As is now well known, a long list of historians have taken issue with many of the specific claims of Habermas's historical narrative. For a good summary of some of these critiques, especially those concerning gender, see Fraser, *Justice Interruptus*, 72–77.
56 Jürgen Habermas, "Further Reflections on the Public Sphere," in Craig Calhoun, ed., *Habermas and the Public Sphere* (Cambridge, MA: MIT Press, 1992), 423.
57 Habermas, "Further Reflections on the Public Sphere," 425–30. Habermas, *Between Facts and Norms*, 307, 373–75. Jodi Dean, "Civil Society: Beyond the Public Sphere," in *The Handbook of Critical Theory*, ed. David Rasmussen (Oxford: Blackwell, 1996). Chantal Mouffe, *The Democratic Paradox* (London: Verso, 2000).
58 It should be noted that both models tend to be concerned with the "normal" functioning of communicative power in a stable society. In that sense, Nadia Urbinati is correct to observe that the model is perhaps insufficiently attentive to moments of "rupture" when the normal circulation patterns are disrupted. See Nadia Urbinati, "Continuity and Rupture: The Power of Judgment in Democratic Representation," *Constellations* 12:2 (June 2005): 198.
59 Fraser, *Justice Interruptus*, 89–92.
60 Habermas, *Between Facts and Norms*, 374.
61 Habermas, *Between Facts and Norms*, 307.
62 Fraser, *Justice Interruptus*, 90.
63 Habermas, *Between Facts and Norms*, 354–58.
64 Scheuerman, "Between Radicalism and Resignation," 164–68.
65 Habermas, *Between Facts and Norms*, 486. Habermas, "Further Reflections on the Public Sphere," 452.
66 Habermas, *Between Facts and Norms*, 486.
67 Habermas, *Between Facts and Norms*, 440.

160   *Globalization and Popular Sovereignty*

68 Habermas, *Between Facts and Norms*, 440–41.
69 Habermas, *Between Facts and Norms*, 385.
70 Habermas, *Between Facts and Norms*, 171.
71 Habermas, *Between Facts and Norms*, 104.
72 Habermas, *Between Facts and Norms*, 84–104, 463–90; Jürgen Habermas, *The Inclusion of the Other*, ed. C. Cronin and P. De Greiff (Cambridge, MA: MIT Press, 1998), 239–64, and Habermas, *Postnational Constellation*, 115–16.
73 Ingeborg Maus, "Liberties and Popular Sovereignty: On Jürgen Habermas's Reconstruction of the System of Rights," in René Von Schomberg and Kenneth Baynes, eds., *Discourse and Democracy: Essays on Habermas's Between Facts and Norms* (Albany: SUNY Press, 2002), 96.
74 Habermas, *Between Facts and Norms*, 104. Habermas, *Inclusion of the Other*, 260–64.
75 Baynes, "Democracy and the *Rechtsstaat*," 209.
76 Habermas, *Between Facts and Norms*, 110.
77 Habermas, *Between Facts and Norms*, 457.
78 Habermas, *Between Facts and Norms*, 39.
79 Jürgen Habermas, "Constitutional Democracy: A Paradoxical Union of Contradictory Principles?" *Political Theory* 29: 6 (December 2001): 774.
80 Habermas, *Postnational Constellation*, 110. Also see Habermas, *Inclusion of the Other*, 239–52.
81 Habermas, *Between Facts and Norms*, 300.
82 Habermas, *Between Facts and Norms*, 136.
83 For example see Rogers Brubaker, *Citizenship and Nationhood in France and Germany*, (Cambridge, MA: Harvard University Press, 1992).
84 Habermas, *Between Facts and Norms*, 494.
85 Habermas, *Between Facts and Norms*, 495. Habermas, *Inclusion of the Other*, 147.
86 Habermas, *Inclusion of the Other*, 111–12. Also see E.J. Hobsbawm, *Nations and Nationalism since 1780: Programme, Myth, Reality* (Cambridge: Cambridge University Press, 1990).
87 Habermas, *Inclusion of the Other*, 113.
88 Habermas, *Inclusion of the Other*, 113.
89 Carl Schmitt, *The Crisis of Parliamentary Democracy*, trans. Ellen Kennedy (Cambridge, MA: MIT Press, 1985), 9.
90 Schmitt writes, "The will of the people can be expressed just as well and perhaps better through acclamation, through something taken for granted, an obvious and unchallenged presence… [D]ictatorial and Caesaristic methods not only can produce the acclamation of the people but can also be a direct expression of democratic substance and power." Schmitt, *Crisis of Parliamentary Democracy*, 16–17.
91 Habermas, *Inclusion of the Other*, 117.
92 John Rawls, *Political Liberalism* (New York: Columbia University Press, 1993), 36.
93 Habermas, *Between Facts and Norms*, 23–27.
94 Habermas, *Inclusion of the Other*, 117–19.
95 Habermas, *Between Facts and Norms*, 122–27.
96 Habermas, *Inclusion of the Other*, 118, 225.
97 Richard J. Bernstein, "The Retrieval of the Democratic Ethos," in Rosenfeld and Arato, *Habermas on Law and Democracy*, 289–90.
98 Habermas, *Between Facts and Norms*, 302. And Habermas, "Reply," 384.
99 Habermas, "Reply," 385.
100 Habermas, "Reply," 389.
101 Frank Michelman, "Morality, Identity and 'Constitutional Patriotism'," *Ratio Juris* 14:3 (September 2001): 266.
102 Michelman, "Morality, Identity and 'Constitutional Patriotism'," 268.

103 Michelman, "Morality, Identity, and 'Constitutional Patriotism'," 269.
104 Habermas, *Between Facts and Norms*, 285. Here Habermas is specifically responding to Frank Michelman, "Law's Republic," *Yale Law Journal* 97:8 (July 1988).
105 Michelman, "Family Quarrel," in Rosenfeld and Arato, *Habermas on Law and Democracy*, 309–22. Habermas, "Reply," 389.
106 Habermas, *Inclusion of the Other*, 225.
107 Habermas, *Inclusion of the Other*, 225.
108 Habermas, *Inclusion of the Other*, 225.
109 Habermas, *Inclusion of the Other*, 225–26.
110 Habermas, "Further Reflections on the Public Sphere," 436, 443. Habermas, *Between Facts and Norms*, 80.
111 Habermas, *Between Facts and Norms*, 124.
112 Habermas, *Between Facts and Norms*, 298–301.
113 Habermas, *Between Facts and Norms*, 286.
114 John Dryzek, "Transnational Democracy," *Journal of Political Philosophy* 7:1 (1999). William E. Scheuerman, "Critical Theory beyond Habermas," in *The Oxford Handbook to Political Theory*, John Dryzek, Bonnie Honig and Anne Phillips, eds. (Oxford: Oxford University Press, 2006). .
115 James Bohman, "Reflexive Constitution Making and Transnational Governance," in Erik Oddvar Eriksen, ed., *Making the European Polity* (New York and London: Routledge, 2005), 39.
116 Anne-Marie Slaughter, *A New World Order* (Princeton, NJ: Princeton University Press, 2004).
117 Slaughter, *A New World Order*, 40.
118 Jürgen Habermas, "A Political Constitution for the Pluralist World Society?" Paper delivered as part of the "Twilight of Sovereignty" series, Program in Ethics, Politics and Economics, Yale Law School, November 17, 2005.
119 In fact, from the perspective of traditional public sphere theory, the very idea of a "transnational public sphere" is a contradiction in terms. Nancy Fraser has shown most recently how Habermas's original formulation of the concept of the public sphere presupposed the national framework, in assuming nation-state sovereignty, an independent national economy, defined national citizenship, a national language and literature, and a coherent national communication infrastructure. Nancy Fraser, "Transnationalizing the Public Sphere," in Max Pensky, ed., *Globalizing Critical Theory* (New York: Rowman & Littlefield, 2005).
120 Antonio Cassese, *International Law*, second edition (Oxford: Oxford University Press, 2005), 48–60, 201–03, 442–44.
121 On the responsibility to protect, see "2005 World Summit Outcome Document," UN Doc. A/60/L.1, September 15, 2005, paragraphs 138 and 139. See also Rachel Davis, Benjamin Majekodunmi, and Judy Smith-Höhn, rapporteurs, "Prevention of Genocide and Mass Atrocities and the Responsibility to Protect: Challenges for the UN and the International Community in the Twenty-first Century" (New York: International Peace Institute, June 2008).
122 Chris Brown, *Sovereignty, Rights and Justice: International Political Theory Today* (Oxford: Polity Press, 2002), 134.
123 Hauke Brunkhorst, *Solidarity: From Civic Friendship to a Global Legal Community*, trans. Jeffrey Flynn (Cambridge, MA: MIT Press, 2005), 74–76.
124 Habermas, *Postnational Constellation*, 119.
125 Brunkhorst, *Solidarity*, 119. Margaret Canovan, *The People* (Oxford: Polity Press, 2005), 65–90. Jean L. Cohen, "Whose Sovereignty? Empire versus International Law," *Ethics and International Affairs* (December 2004).
126 Brown, *Sovereignty, Rights and Justice*, 153–54.
127 Noam Chomsky, *The New Military Humanism* (London: Pluto Press, 1999).

162 Globalization and Popular Sovereignty

128 Jürgen Habermas, "Bestiality and Humanity: A War on the Border between Legality and Morality," *Constellations* 6:3 (September 1999). Cohen, "Whose Sovereignty? Empire versus International Law." Perry Anderson, "Arms and Rights: Rawls, Habermas and Bobbio in an Age of War," *New Left Review* 31 (January–February 2005): 27.
129 Habermas, "Bestiality and Humanity," 270. Habermas, "A Political Constitution for the Pluralist World Society?"
130 Habermas, *The Postnational Constellation*, 128.
131 Manfred B. Steger, *Globalism: Market Ideology meets Terrorism*, second edition (New York: Rowman & Littlefield, 2005), 37–43. Benjamin Barber, *Jihad vs. McWorld* (New York: Ballantine Books, 1996).
132 Ulf Hannerz, *Cultural Complexity: Studies in the Social Organization of Meaning* (New York: Columbia University Press, 1992).
133 Steger, *Globalism*, 40. Jan Nederveen Pieterse, "Globalization as Hybridization," in Mike Featherstone, Scott Lash, and Roland Robertson, eds., *Global Modernities* (London: Sage, 1995).
134 Roland Robertson, *Globalization: Social Theory and Global Culture* (London: Sage, 1992). Roland Robertson, "Glocalization: Time–Space and Homogeneity–Heterogeneity," in Featherstone et al., *Global Modernities*.
135 UNDP, "Globalization with a Human Face," *Human Development Report, 1999*. UNDP, "Human Rights and Human Development," *Human Development Report, 2000*. Steger, *Globalism*, 77.
136 International Labour Organization, *World of Work Report, 2008: Income Inequalities in the Age of Financial Globalization* (Geneva: International Institute of Labor Studies, 2008).
137 Nancy Birdsall, "Asymmetric Globalization: Global Markets require Good Global Politics," *Brookings Review*, 21: 2 (spring 2003).
138 A.T. Keaney Inc. and the Carnegie Endowment for International Peace, "Measuring Globalization: Economic Reversals, Forward Momentum," *Foreign Policy* (March–April 2004).
139 Saskia Sassen, *The Global City: New York, London, Tokyo*, second edition (Princeton, NJ: Princeton University Press, 2001), xviii.

6 Responses to globalization (I) Habermas's postnational constellation

1 David Held, *Democracy and the Global Order* (Stanford, CA: Stanford University Press, 1995). David Held, Anthony McGrew, David Goldblatt, and Jonathan Perraton, *Global Transformations* (Stanford, CA: Stanford University Press, 1999). Daniele Archibugi and David Held, *Cosmopolitan Democracy: An Agenda for a New World Order* (Cambridge: Polity Press, 1995). Daniele Archibugi, David Held, and Martin Koehler, eds., *Reimagining Political Community* (Stanford, CA: Stanford University Press, 1998). Daniele Archibugi, *The Global Commonwealth of Citizens: Toward Cosmopolitan Democracy* (Princeton, NJ: Princeton University Press, 2008).
2 Jürgen Habermas, *The Postnational Constellation* (Cambridge, MA: MIT Press, 2001). John Rawls, *The Law of Peoples* (Cambridge, MA: Harvard University Press, 1999).
3 Paul Hirst and Graham Thompson, *Globalization in Question*, second edition (Cambridge: Polity Press, 1999). Will Kymlicka, "Citizenship in an Era of Globalization: Commentary on Held", in Ian Shapiro and Casiano Hacker-Cordón, eds., *Democracy's Edges* (Cambridge: Cambridge University Press, 1999). Pierre Bourdieu, *Acts of Resistance*, trans. Richard Nice (New York: New Press, 1998).
4 Held, *Democracy and the Global Order*. While Held calls for a cosmopolitan system in which the nation-state would ultimately disappear, others argue that what

is needed is attention to reforming the political order of the states system to better constitute an international society to manage and address common problems. See Andrew Hurrell, *On Global Order: Power, Values, and the Constitution of International Society* (Oxford: Oxford University Press, 2007).
5 Manuel Castells, *The Information Age*, Vol. I, *The Rise of the Network Society* (Oxford: Blackwell, 1996). Kanishka Jayasuriya, "Globalization, Sovereignty, and the Rule of Law," *Constellations* 8 (December 2001). James Rosenau, *Turbulence in World Politics* (Brighton: Harvester Wheatsheaf, 1990).
6 Jürgen Habermas, *The Postnational Constellation*, trans. Max Pensky (Cambridge, MA: MIT Press, 2001). Hereafter cited parenthetically in the text as PC.
7 Held et al., *Global Transformations*, 2–10. David Held and Anthony McGrew, *Globalization/Anti-globalization* (Oxford: Polity Press, 2002).
8 Habermas, *Postnational Constellation*, 66.
9 Habermas, *Postnational Constellation*, 67.
10 Habermas, *Postnational Constellation*, 63.
11 Habermas, *Postnational Constellation*, 64.
12 Björn Hettne, András Inotai, and Osvaldo Sunkel, eds., *Globalism and the New Regionalism* (New York: St. Martin's Press, 1999). Björn Hettne, "Global Market versus Regionalism," in D. Held and A. McGrew, eds., *The Global Transformations Reader* (Cambridge: Polity Press, 2000).
13 Jürgen Habermas, *Between Facts and Norms*, trans. William Rehg (Cambridge, MA: MIT Press, 1996), 463–90.
14 The relationship between the informal or "weak" publics of civil society and the formal or "strong" publics of the administrative system has been identified as a major source of tension in Habermas's discourse theory of democracy. Habermas remains ambiguous on how communication may translate between the two. How the problems identified on the national level may become exacerbated at the regional level is an important question to pursue. See William E. Scheuerman, "Between Radicalism and Resignation: Democratic Theory in Habermas's *Between Facts and Norms*," in Peter Dews, ed., *Habermas: A Critical Reader* (Oxford: Blackwell, 1999).
15 "Draft Treaty establishing a Constitution for Europe" submitted by the President of the Convention to the European Council meeting in Thessaloniki on 20 June 2003, Doc. CONV 820/03. As a public intellectual Habermas has long advocated a constitution for Europe, as he has also been a vocal supporter of a common European foreign policy. See Jürgen Habermas, "Why Europe needs a Constitution," *New Left Review* 11 (September–October 2001). Habermas, *The Inclusion of the Other*, 155–61. Jürgen Habermas and Jacques Derrida, "February 15th, or, What Binds Europeans Together: A Plea for a Common Foreign Policy, Beginning in the Heart of Europe," *Constellations* 10:3 (September 2003).
16 Habermas, *Postnational Constellation*, 100–03. It remains to be seen whether the absence of a common language among Europeans may present an obstacle to the formation of a truly transnational public sphere. Habermas suggests that national education systems would in fact have to provide the basis for such a common language, most likely English (PC 103). However, the reliance on a second or third language raises the concern that postnational democratic politics would be dominated by an elite agenda. And this concern, some may say, lies at the root of the defeat of the Draft Constitution in France and the Netherlands as well as the subsequent Lisbon Treaty in Ireland. As Will Kymlicka has said, democracy is "politics in the vernacular." Will Kymlicka, *Politics in the Vernacular* (Oxford: Oxford University Press, 2001). Yet others have argued that multilingual debate can actually enhance the quality of deliberation. See William Scheuerman, "Globalization and Democratic Theory," *Polity* 33 (winter 2001): 339.
17 "Draft Treaty establishing a Constitution for Europe: Preamble," Doc. CONV 820/03, p. 4.

164 *Globalization and Popular Sovereignty*

18 Habermas, *Postnational Constellation*, 73.
19 Habermas, *Postnational Constellation*, 73.
20 Dudley Seers, *The Political Economy of Nationalism* (Oxford: Oxford University Press, 1983), 165.
21 For an account of Habermas's career as a public intellectual from the 1950s to the turn of the millennium see Martin Beck Matuštík, *Jürgen Habermas: A Philosophical-Political Profile* (Lanham, MD: Rowman & Littlefield, 2001).
22 Habermas, *The Inclusion of the Other*, Chapter 4.
23 Habermas, *The Inclusion of the Other*, 115.
24 Habermas, *The Inclusion of the Other*, 114–17.
25 Habermas, *The Inclusion of the Other*, 115.
26 Habermas, *The Inclusion of the Other*, 225. See also Jürgen Habermas, *The New Conservatism: Cultural Criticism and the Historians' Debate*, trans. S.W. Nicholsen (Cambridge, MA: MIT Press, 1989).
27 Habermas, *Between Facts and Norms*, 122.
28 Habermas, *Between Facts and Norms*, 499.
29 Jürgen Habermas, "Why Europe needs a Constitution," 8.
30 See for example, Jürgen Habermas, "The European Nation-State and the Pressures of Globalization," in Pablo De Grief and Ciaran Cronin, eds., *Global Justice and Transnational Politics* (Cambridge, MA: MIT Press, 2002). The "Washington Consensus" is no longer, if it ever was, an actual consensus. For example, see the scathing insider critique by Joseph E. Stiglitz in *Globalization and its Discontents* (New York: Norton, 2002) and also on the state of international economic institutions see Ngaire Woods, "Governing the Global Economy: Strengthening Multilateral Institutions" (New York: International Peace Institute, July 2008).
31 Eric Hobsbawm, *The Age of Extremes: A History of the World, 1914–1991* (New York: Vintage, 1994).
32 Habermas, *Postnational Constellation*, 103.
33 See, for example, Habermas and Derrida, "February 15th, or, What Binds Europeans Together."
34 Habermas, *Postnational Constellation*, 103.
35 Craig Calhoun, "The Class Consciousness of Frequent Travelers: Towards a Critique of Actually Existing Cosmopolitanism," *South Atlantic Quarterly* 101 (fall 2002).
36 Dudley Seers in discussing the political economy of the European Union discusses the future of Europe in these terms. Seers, *The Political Economy of Nationalism*. See also Hettne, "Global Market versus Regionalism."
37 Calhoun, "The Class Consciousness of Frequent Travelers". See also Craig Calhoun, "Constitutional Patriotism and the Public Sphere: Interests, Identity, and Solidarity in the Integration of Europe," in De Grief and Cronin, *Global Justice and Transnational Politics*, 279.
38 Emmanuel Joseph Sieyès, *What is the Third Estate?* trans. M. Blondel, ed. S.E. Finer (New York: Praeger, 1964 [1789]), 58. Also see Ulrich Preuss, "Constitutional Powermaking for the New Polity: Some Deliberations on the Relations between Constituent Power and the Constitution," *Cardozo Law Review* 14 (January 1993): 645.
39 In this sense it is important to note that I do not equate the ethnic–civic nationalism divide to be one between culture and reason, or between inheritance and choice, such as in Michael Ignatieff's *Blood and Belonging* (New York: Farrar Straus & Giroux, 1993). Rather, as stated, I understand the distinction as one between prepolitical identity and identity inseparable from political and legal institutions. Habermas is clear that "constitutional patriotism" includes a dimension of culture or shared way of life. See also Kymlicka, *Politics in the Vernacular*, 41 n. 3.

40 Habermas, *Postnational Constellation*, 88–89.
41 Hettne, "Global Market versus Regionalism," 164.
42 Habermas, *Postnational Constellation*, 104.
43 Held et al., *Global Transformations*, 168. See also Castells, *The Rise of the Network Society*, 110–16.
44 Castells, *The Rise of the Network Society*.
45 Habermas, *Postnational Constellation*, 109–10.
46 Habermas, *Postnational Constellation*, 103, emphasis added.
47 Deborah J. Yashar, "Contesting Citizenship: Indigenous Movements and Democracy in Latin America," *Comparative Politics* 31 (October 1998): 25.
48 Yashar, "Contesting Citizenship." See also Deborah J. Yashar, "Democracy, Indigenous Movements, and the Postliberal Challenge in Latin America," *World Politics* 52 (October 1999).
49 Peter J. Katzenstein, *A World of Regions: Asia and Europe in the American Imperium* (Ithaca, NY: Cornell University Press, 2005). Ellen Frost, *Asia's New Regionalism* (Boulder, CO: Lynne Rienner, 2008).
50 Katzenstein, *A World of Regions*, Chapters 2 and 4. Frost, *Asia's New Regionalism*.
51 Frost, *Asia's New Regionalism*.
52 Katzenstein, *A World of Regions*. Also, for more on the network economy of Asia, see Peter Katzenstein and Takashi Shiraishi, eds., *Network Power: Japan and Asia* (Ithaca, NY: Cornell University Press, 1997).
53 Frost, *Asia's New Regionalism*, p. 11.
54 Max Weber, *The Theory of Social and Economic Organization*, trans. A.M. Henderson and Talcott Parsons, ed. Talcott Parsons (New York: Oxford University Press, 1947), 154.
55 Weber, *Social and Economic Organization*, 156.
56 Joel S. Migdal, *Strong Societies and Weak States* (Princeton, NJ: Princeton University Press, 1988), and Joel S. Migdal, *State in Society* (Cambridge: Cambridge University Press, 2001).
57 Migdal, *State in Society*, 15–16, 22.
58 Most notably Immanuel Kant, "Toward Perpetual Peace: A Philosophical Sketch" (1796).
59 Held, *Democracy and the Global Order*.
60 Jürgen Habermas, "The European Nation-State and the Pressures of Globalization," 232.
61 Habermas, *Postnational Constellation*, 108.
62 Habermas, *The Inclusion of the Other*, 179.
63 Habermas, *The Inclusion of the Other*, 181.
64 Habermas, *The Inclusion of the Other*, 183.
65 Habermas, *Postnational Constellation*, 108.
66 See Robert Fine and Will Smith, "Jürgen Habermas's Theory of Cosmopolitanism," *Constellations* 10:4 (December 2003).
67 William Scheuerman, "Global Governance without Global Government? Habermas on Postnational Democracy," *Political Theory* 36:1 (February 2008).
68 Habermas, "Why Europe needs a Constitution."

7 Responding to globalization (II) David Held's cosmopolitan democracy

1 David Held, *Democracy and the Global Order* (Stanford, CA: Stanford University Press, 1995).
2 Held, *Democracy and the Global Order*, 99–136.

166 *Globalization and Popular Sovereignty*

3 Stephen D. Krasner, *Sovereignty: Organized Hypocrisy* (Princeton, NJ: Princeton University Press, 1999). On the proliferation of centers of authority, Anne-Marie Slaughter, *A New World Order* (Princeton, NJ: Princeton University Press, 2004).
4 David Held, *Global Covenant* (Cambridge: Polity Press, 2004), 119–23.
5 Hedley Bull, *The Anarchical Society: A Study of Order in World Politics* (London: Macmillan, 1977). David Held, "Cosmopolitanism: Ideas, Realities and Deficits," in David Held and Anthony McGrew, eds., *Governing Globalization* (Cambridge: Polity Press, 2002). Held, *Global Covenant*, 123.
6 Held, *Democracy and the Global Order*. Held, "Cosmopolitanism," 313–14.
7 United Nations General Assembly, "2005 World Summit Outcome Document," paras. 138–39. Rachel Davis, Benjamin Majekodunmi, and Judith Smith Höhn, rapporteurs, "Prevention of Genocide and Mass Atrocities and the Responsibility to Protect: Challenges for the UN and the International Community in the Twenty-first Century" (New York: International Peace Institute, June 2008). Gareth Evans, *The Responsibility to Protect* (Washington, DC: Brookings Institution Press, 2008).
8 Held, *Democracy and the Global Order*, 233.
9 Held, *Democracy and the Global Order*, 219–86. Held, *Global Covenant*.
10 Held, *Democracy and the Global Order*.
11 Held *Democracy and the Global Order*, 279.
12 Held, *Democracy and the Global Order*, 233.
13 Held, *Global Covenant*.
14 Held, *Global Covenant*, 157.
15 Held, *Democracy and the Global Order*, 145.
16 On multiculturalist concerns with cosmopolitan democracy see Will Kymlicka, *Politics in the Vernacular* (Oxford: Oxford University Press, 2001), and Craig Calhoun, "The Class Consciousness of Frequent Travelers: Towards a Critique of Actually Existing Cosmopolitanism," *South Atlantic Quarterly* 101 (fall 2002). On the communitarian critique see Daniele Archibugi, David Held, and Martin Köhler, eds., *Reimagining Political Community* (Cambridge: Polity Press, 1998).
17 Held, *Democracy and the Global Order*, 147.
18 Held *Democracy and the Global Order*, 156.
19 Held, *Democracy and the Global Order*, 125. Held, *Global Covenant*, 172.
20 Held, *Democracy and the Global Order*, 235, 278.
21 Held, *Democracy and the Global Order*, 137.
22 In fact some have argued that this would put extraordinary power into the hands of cosmopolitan judges, risking a form of global "judicial imperialism." See William E. Scheuerman, "Cosmopolitan Democracy and the Rule of Law," *Ratio Juris* 15 (2002). Danilo Zolo, "The Lords of Peace: From the Holy Alliance to the New International Criminal Tribunals," in B. Holden, ed., *Global Democracy* (New York: Routledge, 2000), 79–80.
23 Held, *Democracy and the Global Order*, 140.
24 Held, *Democracy and the Global Order*, 233.
25 James H. Mittelman, "Globalization, Cosmopolitanism, and the Kantian Revival: Commentary on David Held's 'At the Global Crossroads'," *Globalizations* 2:1 (May 2005).
26 Held, *Democracy and the Global Order*, 149.
27 Held et al., *Global Transformations*, 28.
28 Held, *Global Covenant*, 145–46.
29 Alexander Wendt, "A Comment on Held's Cosmopolitanism," in Ian Shapiro and Casiano Hacker-Cordón, eds., *Democracy's Edges* (Cambridge: Cambridge University Press, 1999).
30 Andreas Hasenclever, Peter Mayer, and Volker Rittberger, *Theories of International Regimes* (Cambridge: Cambridge University Press, 1997).

Notes 167

31 Hasenclever et al., *International Regimes*.
32 Jean L. Cohen, "Whose Sovereignty? Empire versus International Law," *Ethics and International Affairs* (December 2004). Furthermore, William Scheuerman argues that Held does not follow traditional notions of the rule of law that demand norms be clear, general, prospective and stable, which invites dangerous forms of executive authority. "From the perspective of traditional liberal jurisprudence, the potential danger with Archibugi's and Held's conceptual lacuna on this matter is that it may leave cosmopolitan democracy ill-equipped to ward off problematic forms of discretionary state authority." Scheuerman, "Cosmopolitan Democracy and the Rule of Law."
33 David Held, *Global Covenant*.
34 Jean L. Cohen, "Changing Paradigms of Citizenship and the Exclusiveness of the Demos," *International Sociology* 14:3 (September 1999). See also Jean L. Cohen, "Rights, Citizenship, and the Modern Form of the Social: Dilemmas of Arendtian Republicanism," *Constellations* 3:2 (October 1996).
35 See Peter C. Caldwell on the legal theory of Hans Kelsen in *Popular Sovereignty and the Crisis of German Constitutional Law* (Durham, NC: Duke University Press, 1997), Chapters 2, 4.
36 Cohen, "Rights, Citizenship, and the Modern Form of the Social," 184.
37 Molly Cochran, "A Democratic Critique of Cosmopolitan Democracy: Pragmatism from the Bottom Up," *European Journal of International Relations*, 8:4 (2002).
38 See David Held and Anthony McGrew, eds., *Governing Globalization* (Oxford: Polity Press, 2002).
39 Ngaire Woods, "Global Governance and the Role of Institutions," in Held and McGrew, *Governing Globalization*, 31.
40 James N. Rosenau, "Governance in a New Global Order," in Held and McGrew, *Governing Globalization*, 77.
41 Manuel Castells, *The Rise of the Network Society*, second edition (Oxford: Blackwell, 2000), 501.
42 I borrow the idea of "chains of equivalence" from the political theory of Ernesto Laclau.
43 Woods, "Global Governance and the Role of Institutions," 34.
44 Held and McGrew, *Governing Globalization*, 13.
45 Jean Cohen and Andrew Arato, *Civil Society and Political Theory* (Cambridge, MA: MIT Press, 1992). Mary Kaldor, ed., *Global Civil Society: An Answer to War* (Oxford: Polity Press, 2003).
46 Marlies Glasius and Mary Kaldor, "The State of Global Civil Society: Before and After September 11," in Kaldor, *Global Civil Society*.
47 Kenneth Anderson, "The Ottawa Convention Banning Landmines, the Role of International Non-governmental Organizations and the Idea of International Civil Society," *European Journal of International Law* 11:1 (2000).
48 James Rosenau, "Governance and Democracy in a Globalizing World," in D. Archibugi, D. Held, and M. Köhler, eds., *Reimagining Political Community* (Cambridge: Polity Press, 1998).
49 John S. Dryzek, "Transnational Democracy," *Journal of Political Philosophy* 7:1 (1999): 48.
50 Neera Chandhoke, "The Limits of Global Civil Society," in Kaldor, *Global Civil Society*.
51 Kaldor, *Global Civil Society*, 6 table 1.1.
52 Simone Chambers and Jeffrey Kopstein, "Bad Civil Society," *Political Theory* 29:6 (December 2001).
53 Kaldor, *Global Civil Society*, 131–32.
54 Margaret E. Keck and Kathryn Sikkink, *Activists Beyond Borders* (Ithaca, NY: Cornell University Press, 1998), 12–28.
55 Keck and Sikkink, *Activists Beyond Borders*, 7–9.

8 Conclusion: Toward a transnational politics of popular sovereignty

1 Connie Koch, *2/15: The Day the World said No to War* (Oakland, CA: AK Press, 2003).
2 Jürgen Habermas, "The Kantian Project of the Constitutionalization of International Law: Does it Still have a Chance?" in Omid Payrow Shabani, ed. *Multiculturalism and Law: a Critical Debate* (Chicago: University of Chicago Press, 2007). Robert Kagan, "The Benevolent Empire," *Foreign Policy* 111 (spring 1998). See also, for a review of the Bush administration's attacks on international law, Brian Urquhart, "The Outlaw World," *New York Review of Books* 53:8 (May 11, 2006).
3 Francis Fukuyama, *The End of History and the Last Man* (New York: Free Press, 1992). Fukuyama has himself reflected on how the current context differs in his much publicized break with the neoconservatives: Francis Fukuyama, *America at the Crossroads: Democracy, Power, and the Neoconservative Legacy* (New Haven, CT: Yale University Press, 2006).
4 On this notion of "hybrid" regimes see John Gray, "The Global Delusion," *New York Review of Books* 53:7 (April 27, 2006). For a damning critique of US militarism and its threat to democracy see Chalmers Johnson, *The Sorrows of Empire: Militarism, Secrecy, and the End of the Republic* (New York: Holt, 2004).
5 Etienne Balibar, *We, the People of Europe? Reflections on Transnational Citizenship*, trans. James Swenson (Princeton, NJ: Princeton University Press, 2002), 184–85.
6 Ngaire Woods, *Governing the Global Economy: Strengthening Multilateral Institutions*, (New York: International Peace Institute, July 2008), p. 7.
7 Brad W. Setser, "Sovereign Wealth and Sovereign Power: The Strategic Consequences of American Indebtedness," Council Special Report No. 37 (Washington, DC: Council on Foreign Relations, September 2008). Richard N. Hass, "The Age of Nonpolarity: What will Follow US Dominance?" *Foreign Affairs*, May–June 2008.
8 Mark Lander, "Global Fears of a Recession Grow Stronger," *New York Times*, October 7, 2008, late edition.
9 Edmond Morgan, *Inventing the People: The Rise of Popular Sovereignty in England and America* (New York: Norton, 1988), 153.
10 Anne-Marie Slaughter, *A New World Order* (Princeton, NJ: Princeton University Press, 2004). Seyla Benhabib, "Borders, Boundaries, and Citizenship," *PS: Political Science and Politics* 38:4 (October 2005).
11 Benhabib, "Borders, Boundaries, and Citizenship," 676.
12 Nancy Fraser, *Reframing Justice* (Amsterdam: Van Gorcum, 2005). Nancy Fraser, "Reframing Global Justice," *New Left Review* 36 (November–December, 2005). Sidney Tarrow, *The New Transnational Activism* (Cambridge: Cambridge University Press, 2005).
13 In fact, early responsibility to protect language can be found in the Constitutive Act of the African Union. Such issues were the topic of discussion at a seminar, "Regional Perspectives on the Responsibility to Protect," at the International Peace Institute in New York on May 12, 2008.
14 Charles E. Merriam, Jr., *History of the Theory of Sovereignty since Rousseau* (New York: Garland Publishing, 1972 [1900]), 11–12. F.H. Hinsley, *Sovereignty*, second edition (Cambridge: Cambridge University Press, 1986), 36–41. See also Andreas Kalyvas, "Popular Sovereignty, Democracy, and the Constituent Power," *Constellations* 12:2 (June 2005).
15 Ingeborg Maus, "Liberties and Popular Sovereignty: On Jürgen Habermas's Reconstruction of the System of Rights," in René Von Schomberg and Kenneth

Baynes, eds., *Discourse and Democracy: Essays on Habermas's Between Facts and Norms* (Albany, NY: SUNY Press, 2002), 114–17.
16 James Fishkin, *The Voice of the People: Public Opinion: and Democracy* (New Haven, CT: Yale University Press, 1995).
17 In the eighteenth century the notion of "the people" meant precisely those outside government, the common people. Thus in the context of aristocratic society it was understood as an implicitly radical term. Maus, "Liberties and Popular Sovereignty," 117. Shklar, *Men and Citizens*, 168. During the English Civil War, once the gentry evoked popular sovereignty to pressure the King as the natural representative of the people, the Levellers seized upon the principle to claim political rights for the excluded masses. Canovan, *The People*, 68–69.
18 Jürgen Habermas, *Between Facts and Norms*, trans. William Rehg (Cambridge, MA: MIT Press, 1996), 104.
19 Tarrow, *The New Transnational Activism*. Doug McAdam, Sidney Tarrow, and Charles Tilly, *Dynamics of Contention* (Cambridge: Cambridge University Press, 2001).
20 Tarrow also discusses three other related processes: *internalization*, "a response to foreign or international pressures within domestic politics"; *diffusion*, "the transfer of claims or forms of contention from one site to another;" and *externalization*, "the vertical projection of domestic claims on to international institutions or foreign actors." Tarrow, *The New Transnational Activism*, 32–34
21 For a series of essays on the legitimacy of this process and the potential constitutionalization of international law see the articles collected in *Constellations* 15:4 (December 2008).
22 Jürgen Habermas, "Constitutional Democracy: A Paradoxical Union of Contradictory Principles?" *Political Theory* 29:6 (December 2001): 768.
23 See Alessandro Ferrara, "Of Boats and Principles: Reflections on Habermas's 'Constitutional Democracy'," *Political Theory* 29:6 (December 2001).
24 See, for example, Morgan's excellent historical account: Edmund S. Morgan, *Inventing the People: The Rise of Popular Sovereignty in England and America* (New York: Norton, 1988).

Bibliography

Ackerman, Bruce. *We the People: Foundations.* Cambridge, MA: Harvard University Press, 1991.
Acton, Lord. "Nationality," in *Mapping the Nation*, ed. Gopal Balakrishnan. London: Verso, 1996 [1862].
Anderson, Kenneth. "The Ottawa Convention Banning Landmines: The Role of International Non-governmental Organizations and the Idea of International Civil Society," *European Journal of International Law* 11:1 (2000): 91–120.
Anderson, Perry. "Arms and Rights: Rawls, Habermas and Bobbio in an Age of War," *New Left Review* 31 (January–February 2005): 5–40.
Appadurai, Arjun. *Modernity at Large: Cultural Dimensions of Globalization.* Minneapolis: University of Minnesota Press, 1996.
APSA Task Force on Inequality and American Democracy. "American Democracy in an Age of Rising Inequality." Washington, DC: American Political Science Association, 2004. Available at www.apsanet.org/imgtest/taskforcereport.pdf.
Arato, Andrew. "Sistani v. Bush: Constitutional Politics in Iraq," *Constellations* 11:2 (June 2004): 174–92.
——*Civil Society, Constitution, and Legitimacy.* New York: Rowman & Littlefield, 2000.
——"Good-bye to Dictatorships?" *Social Research* 67:4 (winter 2000): 925–55.
Archibugi, Daniele. *"The Global Commonwealth of Citizens: Toward Cosmopolitan Democracy.* Princeton, NJ: Princeton University Press, 2008.
Archibugi, Daniele, David Held, and Martin Koehler, eds. *Reimagining Political Community.* Stanford, CA: Stanford University Press, 1998.
Archibugi, Daniele, and David Held *Cosmopolitan Democracy: An Agenda for a New World Order.* Cambridge: Polity Press, 1995.
Arendt, Hannah. *On Violence.* New York: Harcourt Brace, 1969.
——*On Revolution.* New York: Penguin, 1963.
Aristotle. *The Politics of Aristotle*, ed. and trans. Ernest Barker. Oxford: Oxford University Press, 1958.
A.T. Keaney Inc. and Carnegie Endowment for International Peace. "Measuring Globalization: Economic Reversals, Forward Momentum," *Foreign Policy* (March–April 2004): 54–70.
Austin, John. *The Province of Jurisprudence Determined, etc.* London: Weidenfeld & Nicolson, 1954 [1832].
Baker, Keith Michael. *Inventing the French Revolution.* Cambridge: Cambridge University Press, 1990.

Balibar, Etienne. *We, the People of Europe? Reflections on Transnational Citizenship*, trans. James Swenson. Princeton, NJ: Princeton University Press, 2002.
Balibar, Etienne, and Immanuel Wallerstein. *Race, Nation, Class*. London: Verso, 1991.
Barber, Benjamin. *Jihad vs. McWorld*. New York: Ballantine Books, 1996.
Baynes, Kenneth. "Democracy and the *Rechtsstaat:* Habermas's *Faktizität und Geltung*," in *The Cambridge Companion to Habermas*, ed. Stephen K. White. Cambridge: Cambridge University Press, 1995.
Beck, Ulrich. *What is Globalization?* trans. Patrick Camiller. Cambridge: Polity Press, 2000.
Beitz, Charles R. *Political Theory and International Relations*. Princeton, NJ: Princeton University Press, 1979.
Bellamy, Richard, and Dario Castiglione. "The Uses of Democracy: Reflections on the European Democratic Deficit," in *Democracy in the European Union: Integration through Deliberation?* ed. E. O. Eriksen and J. E. Fossum. London: Routledge, 2000.
Benhabib, Seyla. "Borders, Boundaries, and Citizenship," *PS: Political Science and Politics* 38:4 (October 2005): 673–77.
——— *The Claims of Culture: Equality and Diversity in the Global Era*. Princeton, NJ: Princeton University Press, 2002.
——— "The Utopian Dimension in Communicative Ethics," in *Critical Theory: The Essential Readings*, ed. David Ingram and Julia Simon-Ingram. New York: Paragon House, 1991.
Bernstein, Richard J. "The Retrieval of the Democratic Ethos," in *Habermas on Law and Democracy: Critical Exchanges*, ed. Michel Rosenfeld and Andrew Arato. Berkeley: University of California Press, 1998.
Bernstein, Robert. "Coming to America: A Profile of the Nation's Foreign Born (2000 update)," in *Census Brief: Current Population Survey*, CENBR/01–1. Washington, DC: US Census Bureau, 2002.
Birdsall, Nancy. "Asymmetric Globalization: Global Markets Require Good Global Politics," *Brookings Review*, 21:2 (spring 2003): 22–27.
Bobbio, Norberto. *The Future of Democracy*. Minneapolis: University of Minnesota Press, 1987.
Bodin, Jean. *On Sovereignty: Four Chapters from the Six Books of the Commonwealth*, ed. and trans. Julian H. Franklin. Cambridge: Cambridge University Press, 1992.
Bohman, James. "Complexity, Pluralism, and the Constitutional State: On Habermas's *Faktizität und Geltung*," *Law and Society Review* 28:4 (1994): 801–34.
——— "Reflexive Constitution Making and Transnational Governance," in *Making the European Polity*, ed. Erik Oddvar Eriksen. New York and London: Routledge, 2005.
Bourdieu, Pierre. *Acts of Resistance*, trans. Richard Nice. New York: New Press, 1998.
Brandolini, Andrea, and Timothy M. Smeeding. "Patterns of Economic Inequality in Western Democracies: Some Facts on Levels and Trends," *Political Science and Politics* 39:1 (January 2006): 21–26.
Brown, Chris. *Sovereignty, Rights and Justice: International Political Theory Today*. Oxford: Polity Press, 2002.
Brubaker, Rogers. *Citizenship and Nationhood in France and Germany*. Cambridge, MA: Harvard University Press, 1992.
Brunkhorst, Hauke. *Solidarity: From Civic Friendship to a Global Legal Community*, trans. Jeff Flynn. Cambridge, MA: MIT Press, 2005.

Bull, Hedley. *The Anarchical Society: A Study of Order in World Politics*. London: Macmillan, 1977.
Caldwell, Peter C. *Popular Sovereignty and the Crisis of German Constitutional Law*. Durham, NC: Duke University Press, 1997.
Calhoun, Craig. "The Class Consciousness of Frequent Travelers: Towards a Critique of Actually Existing Cosmopolitanism," *South Atlantic Quarterly* 101 (fall 2002): 869–97.
Canovan, Margaret. *The People*. Oxford: Polity Press, 2005.
Cassese, Antonio. *International Law*, second edition. Oxford: Oxford University Press, 2005.
Castañeda, Jorge G. "Latin America's Left Turn," *Foreign Affairs* 85:3 (May–June 2006): 28–43.
Castells, Manuel. *The Information Age*, Vol. I, *The Rise of the Network Society*. Oxford: Blackwell, 1996.
Chambers, Simone, and Jeffrey Kopstein. "Bad Civil Society," *Political Theory* 29:6 (December 2001): 837–65.
Chandhoke, Neera. "The Limits of Global Civil Society," in *Global Civil Society 2002*. Oxford: Oxford University Press, 2002.
Chapman, John W. *Rousseau: Totalitarian or Liberal?* New York: Columbia University Press, 1956.
Charvet, John. *The Social Problem in the Philosophy of Rousseau*. Cambridge: Cambridge University Press, 1974.
——"Rousseau, the Problem of Sovereignty and the Limits of Political Obligation," *Rousseau and Liberty*, ed. Robert Wokler. New York: St. Martin's Press, 1995.
Chomsky, Noam. *The New Military Humanism*. London: Pluto Press, 1999.
Cochran, Molly. "A Democratic Critique of Cosmopolitan Democracy: Pragmatism from the Bottom Up," *European Journal of International Relations*, 8:4 (2002): 517–48.
Cohen, Jean L. "Whose Sovereignty? Empire versus International Law," *Ethics and International Affairs* (December 2004): 1–24.
——"Changing Paradigms of Citizenship and the Exclusiveness of the Demos," *International Sociology* 14:3 (September 1999): 245–68.
——"Rights, Citizenship, and the Modern Form of the Social: Dilemmas of Arendtian Republicanism," *Constellations* 3:2 (October 1996): 164–89.
Cohen, Jean L., and Andrew Arato. *Civil Society and Political Theory*. Cambridge, MA: MIT Press, 1992.
Cooke, Maeve. "The Weakness of Strong Intersubjectivism: Habermas's Conception of Justice," *European Journal of Political Theory* 2:3 (July 2003): 281–305.
——*Language and Reason: A Study of Habermas's Pragmatics*. Cambridge, MA: MIT Press, 1994.
Cox, Robert. "Democracy in Hard Times: Economic Globalization and the Limits to Liberal Democracy," in *The Transformation of Democracy?* ed. Anthony McGrew, Cambridge: Polity Press, 1997.
Cutler, A. Claire. "Globalization, the Rule of Law, and the Modern Law Merchant: Medieval or Late Capitalist Associations?" *Constellations* 8:4 (December 2001): 480–502.
Cutler, A. Claire, Virginia Haufler, and Tony Porter, eds. *Private Authority and International Affairs*. New York: SUNY Press, 1999.
Dahl, Robert. *Democracy and its Critics*. New Haven, CT: Yale University Press, 1989.

Dean, Jodi. "Civil Society: Beyond the Public Sphere," in *The Handbook of Critical Theory*, ed. David Rasmussen. Oxford: Blackwell, 1996.
Decker, Frank. "Governance beyond the Nation State: Reflections on the Democratic Deficit of the European Union," *Journal of European Public Policy* 9:2 (April 2002): 256–72.
Dicey, A. V. *Introduction to the Study of the Law of the Constitution*. New York: St. Martin's Press, 1961 [1885].
Diderot, Denis. "Droit naturel," *Article de l'Encyclopédie*, Paris, 1755. See Diderot, *Political Writings*, ed. John Hope Mason and Robert Wokler (Cambridge: Cambridge University Press, 1992).
Dryzek, John. "Transnational Democracy," *Journal of Political Philosophy* 7:1 (1999): 30–51.
Dunn, John. *The Political Thought of John Locke*. Cambridge: Cambridge University Press, 1969.
——"Consent in the Political Theory of John Locke," in *Political Obligation in its Historical Context*. Cambridge: Cambridge University Press, 2002.
Dunn, Richard S. *The Age of Religious Wars, 1559–1715*, second edition. New York: Norton, 1979.
Ellenburg, Stephen. *Rousseau's Political Philosophy: An Interpretation from Within*. Ithaca, NY: Cornell University Press, 1976.
Evans, Gareth. *The Responsibility to Protect: Ending Mass Atrocity Crimes Once and For All*. Washington, DC: Brookings Institution Press, 2008.
Faux, Jeff. *The Global Class War*. New York: Wiley Press, 2006.
Ferrara, Alessandro. "Of Boats and Principles: Reflections on Habermas's *Constitutional Democracy*," *Political Theory* 29:6 (December 2001): 782–91.
Fine, Robert, and Will Smith. "Jürgen Habermas's Theory of Cosmopolitanism," *Constellations* 10:4 (December 2003): 467–87.
Fisher, William F., and Thomas Ponniah, eds. *Another World is Possible: Popular Alternatives to Globalization at the World Social Forum*. New York: Zed Books, 2003.
Fishkin, James. *The Voice of the People: Public Opinion: and Democracy*. New Haven, CT: Yale University Press, 1995.
Forst, Rainer. "The Rule of Reasons: Three Models of Deliberative Democracy," *Ratio Juris* 14:4 (December 2001): 489–500.
Franklin, Julian. *John Locke and the Theory of Sovereignty*. Cambridge: Cambridge University Press, 1978.
Fraser, Nancy. *Reframing Justice*. Amsterdam: Van Gorcum, 2005.
——"Reframing Justice in a Globalizing World," *New Left Review* 36 (November–December, 2005): 69–88.
——"Transnationalizing the Public Sphere," in *Globalizing Critical Theory*, ed. Max Pensky. New York: Rowman & Littlefield, 2005.
——*Justice Interruptus*. New York: Routledge, 1997.
Friedman, Thomas. *The Lexus and the Olive Tree: Understanding Globalization*. New York: Anchor Books, 2000.
Fukuyama, Francis. *America at the Crossroads: Democracy, Power, and the Neoconservative Legacy*. New Haven, CT: Yale University Press, 2006.
——*The End of History and the Last Man*. New York: Free Press, 1992.
Giddens, Anthony. *The Consequences of Modernity*. Cambridge: Polity Press, 1990.
——*Runaway World: How Globalization is Reshaping our Lives*. New York: Routledge, 2003.

Gilpin, Robert. "A Realist Perspective on International Governance," in *Governing Globalization*, ed. David Held and Anthony McGrew. Cambridge: Polity Press, 2002.
——*The Challenge of Global Capitalism*. Princeton, NJ: Princeton University Press, 2000.
Glasius, Marlies, and Mary Kaldor. "The State of Global Civil Society: Before and after September 11," in *Global Civil Society 2002*. Oxford: Oxford University Press, 2002.
Gray, John. "The Global Delusion," *New York Review of Books* 53:7 (April 27, 2006): 20–23.
——*Two Faces of Liberalism*. New York: New Press, 2000.
——*Liberalism*. Minneapolis: University of Minnesota Press, 1986.
Guidry, John A., Michael D. Kennedy, and Mayer N. Zald, eds. *Globalizations and Social Movements*. Ann Arbor: University of Michigan Press, 2000.
Habermas, Jürgen. "The Kantian Project of the Constitutionalization of International Law: Does it Still have a Chance?" in *Multiculturalism and Law: A Critical Debate*, ed. Omid Payrow Shabani. Chicago: University of Chicago Press, 2007.
——"A Political Constitution for the Pluralist World Society?" Paper delivered as part of the "Twilight of Sovereignty" series, Program in Ethics, Politics and Economics, Yale Law School, November 17, 2005.
——"The European Nation State and the Pressures of Globalization," in *Global Justice and Transnational Politics*, ed. Pablo De Grief and Ciaran Cronin. Cambridge, MA: MIT Press, 2002.
——*The Postnational Constellation*, trans. Max Pensky. Cambridge, MA: MIT Press, 2001.
——"Constitutional Democracy: A Paradoxical Union of Contradictory Principles?" *Political Theory* 29:6 (December 2001): 766–81.
——"Why Europe needs a Constitution," *New Left Review* 11 (September–October 2001): 5–26.
——"Bestiality and Humanity: A War on the Border between Legality and Morality," *Constellations* 6:3 (September 1999): 263–72.
——*The Inclusion of the Other*. Cambridge, MA: MIT Press, 1998.
——"Reply to Symposium Participants, Benjamin N. Cardozo School of Law," trans. William Rehg, in *Habermas on Law and Democracy: Critical Exchanges*, ed. Michel Rosenfeld and Andrew Arato. Berkeley: University of California Press, 1998.
——*Between Facts and Norms*, trans. William Rehg. Cambridge, MA: MIT Press, 1996.
——*Justification and Application: Remarks on Discourse Ethics*, trans. Ciaran P. Cronin. Cambridge, MA: MIT Press, 1993.
——*Moral Consciousness and Communicative Action*, trans. C. Lenhardt and S.W. Nicholsen. Cambridge, MA: MIT Press, 1990.
——*The New Conservatism: Cultural Criticism and the Historians' Debate*, trans. S.W. Nicholsen. Cambridge, MA: MIT Press, 1989.
——*The Theory of Communicative Action*, trans. Thomas McCarthy. Boston, MA: Beacon Press, Vol. I, 1984, Vol. II, 1987.
——*Communication and the Evolution of Society*, trans. Thomas McCarthy. Boston, MA: Beacon Press, 1979.

Habermas, Jürgen, and Jacques Derrida, "February 15th, or, What Binds Europeans Together: A Plea for a Common Foreign Policy, Beginning in the Heart of Europe," *Constellations* 10:3 (September 2003): 291–97.
Hannerz, Ulf. *Cultural Complexity: Studies in the Social Organization of Meaning*. New York: Columbia University Press, 1992.
Hart, H. L. A. *The Concept of Law*, second edition. Oxford: Clarendon Press, 1994.
Harvey, David. *The New Imperialism*. Oxford: Oxford University Press, 2003.
Hasenclever, Andreas, Peter Mayer, and Volker Rittberger. *Theories of International Regimes*. Cambridge: Cambridge University Press, 1997.
Held, David. *Global Covenant: The Social Democratic Alternative to the Washington Consensus*. Cambridge: Polity Press, 2004.
——*Models of Democracy*, second edition. Stanford, CA: Stanford University Press, 1996.
——*Democracy and the Global Order*. Stanford, CA: Stanford University Press, 1995.
Held, David, and Anthony McGrew, eds. *The Global Transformations Reader*, second edition. Cambridge: Polity Press, 2003.
——*Governing Globalization: Power Authority and Global Governance*. Cambridge: Polity Press, 2002.
Held, David, and Anthony McGrew. *Globalization/Anti-globalization*. Oxford: Polity Press, 2002.
Held, David, Anthony McGrew, David Goldblatt, and Jonathan Perraton, *Global Transformations: Politics, Economics and Culture*. Stanford, CA: Stanford University Press, 1999.
Herder, Johann Gottfried von. "Reflections on the Philosophy of the History of Mankind," in *The Nationalism Reader*, ed. Omar Dahbour and Micheline R Ishey. New York: Humanities Press, 1995 [1791].
Hettne, Björn. "Global Market versus Regionalism," in *The Global Transformations Reader*, ed. David Held and Anthony McGrew. Cambridge: Polity Press, 2000.
Hettne, Björn, András Inotai, and Osvaldo Sunkel, eds. *Globalism and the New Regionalism*. New York: St. Martin's Press, 1999.
Hewson, Martin, and Timothy J. Sinclair, eds. *Approaches to Global Governance Theory*. Albany: SUNY Press, 1999.
Hinsley, F. H. *Sovereignty*, second edition. Cambridge: Cambridge University Press, 1986.
Hirst, Paul, and Graham Thompson. *Globalization in Question*, second edition. Cambridge: Polity Press, 1999.
Hobbes, Thomas. *Leviathan*, ed. Richard Tuck. Cambridge: Cambridge University Press, 1996.
Hobsbawm, Eric J. *The Age of Extremes: A History of the World, 1914–1991*. New York: Vintage, 1994.
——*Nations and Nationalism since 1780: Programme, Myth, Reality*. Cambridge: Cambridge University Press, 1990.
Ignatieff, Michael. *Blood and Belonging*. New York: Farrar Straus & Giroux, 1993.
Jardin, Xeni. "Exporting Censorship," Op-Ed, *New York Times*, March 9, 2006, p. A23.
Jayasuriya, Kanishka. "Globalization, Sovereignty, and the Rule of Law: From Political to Economic Constitutionalism?" *Constellations* 8:4 (December 2001): 442–60.
Johnson, Chalmers. *The Sorrows of Empire: Militarism, Secrecy and the End of the Republic*. New York: Holt, 2004.

Kagan, Robert. "The Benevolent Empire," *Foreign Policy* 111 (spring 1998): 24–35.
Kaldor, Mary. *Global Civil Society: An Answer to War.* Oxford: Polity Press, 2003.
Kalyvas, Andreas. "Popular Sovereignty, Democracy, and the Constituent Power," *Constellations* 12:2 (June 2005): 223–44.
——"Carl Schmitt and the Three Moments of Democracy," *Cardozo Law Review* 21 (2000): 1525–65.
Kant, Immanuel. *The Metaphysics of Morals*, trans. Mary Gregor. Cambridge: Cambridge University Press, 1996 [1797].
——"To Perpetual Peace: A Philosophical Sketch," in *Perpetual Peace and other Essays*, trans. Ted Humphrey. Cambridge: Hackett, 1983 [1795].
Karavas, Vaios, and Gunther Teubner. "http://www.CompanyNameSucks.com: The Horizontal Effect of Fundamental Rights on 'Private Parties' within Autonomous Internet Law," *German Law Journal*, 4:12: 1335–58.
Katzenstein, Peter, and Takashi Shiraishi, eds. *Network Power: Japan and Asia.* Ithaca, NY: Cornell University Press, 1997.
Keck, Margaret E., and Kathryn Sikkink. *Activists Beyond Borders.* Ithaca, NY: Cornell University Press, 1998.
Keohane, Robert O. "Sovereignty in International Society," in *The Global Transformations Reader*, second edition, ed. David Held and Anthony McGrew. Oxford: Polity Press, 2003.
Keohane, Robert O., and Joseph S. Nye, eds. *Power and Interdependence: World Politics in Transition*, revised edition. New York: Addison-Wesley, 2001.
Koch, Connie. *2/15: The Day the World said No to War.* Oakland, CA: AK Press, 2003.
Koenig-Archibugi, Mathias. "Mapping Global Governance," in *Governing Globalization*, ed. David Held and Anthony McGrew. Cambridge: Polity Press, 2002.
Kohn, Margaret. "Language, Power, and Persuasion: Toward a Critique of Deliberative Democracy," *Constellations* 7:3 (September 2000): 408–29.
Krasner, Stephen D. *Sovereignty: Organized Hypocrisy.* Princeton, NJ: Princeton University Press, 1999.
Kymlicka, Will. *Politics in the Vernacular.* Oxford: Oxford University Press, 2001.
——"Citizenship in an Era of Globalization: Commentary on Held," in *Democracy's Edges*, ed. Ian Shapiro and Casiano Hacker-Cordón. Cambridge: Cambridge University Press, 1999.
——*Multicultural Citizenship.* Oxford: Oxford University Press, 1995.
Larsen, Luke J. "The Foreign-born Population in the United States, 2003," *Current Population Reports*, P20–551. Washington, DC: US Census Bureau, 2004.
Locke, John. *Two Treatises*, ed. Peter Laslett. Cambridge: Cambridge University Press, 1988.
——*A Letter Concerning Toleration.* New York: Prometheus Books, 1990 [1689].
McAdam, Doug, Sidney Tarrow, and Charles Tilly. *Dynamics of Contention.* Cambridge: Cambridge University Press, 2001.
McCarthy, Thomas. "Legitimacy and Diversity: Dialectical Reflections on Analytic Distinctions," *Habermas on Law and Democracy: Critical Exchanges*, ed. Michel Rosenfeld and Andrew Arato. Berkeley: University of California Press, 1998.
Madison, James. *"Federalist* No. 40," in *The Federalist Papers*, ed. Clinton Rossiter. New York: Penguin, 1961.
Maus, Ingeborg. "Liberties and Popular Sovereignty: On Jürgen Habermas's Reconstruction of the System of Rights," in *Discourse and Democracy: Essays on*

Habermas's Between Facts and Norms, ed. René Von Schomberg and Kenneth-Baynes. Albany, NY: SUNY University Press, 2002.

Merriam, Charles, Jr. *History of the Theory of Sovereignty since Rousseau.* New York: Garland Publishing, 1972 [1900].

——"Family Quarrel," in *Habermas on Law and Democracy,* ed. Michel Rosenfeld and Andrew Arato. Berkeley: University of California Press, 1998.

——"Law's *Republic,*" *Yale Law Journal* 97:8 (July 1988): 1493–537.

Michelman, Frank. "Morality, Identity and 'Constitutional Patriotism'." *Ratio Juris* 14:3 (September 2001): 253–71.

Migdal, Joel S. *State in Society.* Cambridge: Cambridge University Press, 2001.

——*Strong Societies and Weak States.* Princeton, NJ: Princeton University Press, 1988.

Milanovic, Branko. "Global Income Inequality: What it is and Why it Matters," DESA Working Paper No. 26, August 2006. UN Doc. ST/ESA/2006/DWP/26.

Mittelman, James H. "Globalization, Cosmopolitanism, and the Kantian Revival: Commentary on David Held's 'At the Global Crossroads'," *Globalizations* 2:1 (May 2005): 114–16.

Morgan, Edmund S. *Inventing the People: The Rise of Popular Sovereignty in England and America.* New York: Norton, 1988.

Mouffe, Chantal. *The Democratic Paradox.* London: Verso, 2000.

Muthu, Sankar. *Enlightenment against Empire.* Princeton, NJ: Princeton University Press, 2003.

Mydans, Seth. "A Burst of Raw Democracy: Anything Wrong with That?" *New York Times,* Wednesday, January 7, 2004.

Nikulin, Dmitri. "Dialogue versus Discourse: On the Possibility of Disagreement in Human Communication," *Graduate Faculty Philosophy Journal* 26:1 (2005): 89–106.

Ohmae, Kenichi. *The End of the Nation State: The Rise of Regional Economies.* New York: Free Press, 1995.

Pettit, Philip. *Republicanism: A Theory of Freedom and Government.* Oxford: Oxford University Press, 2000.

Pieterse, Jan Nederveen. "Globalization as Hybridization," in *Global Modernities,* ed. Mike Featherstone, Scott Lash, and Roland Robertson. London: Sage, 1995.

Pogge, Thomas W. "Creating Supranational Institutions Democratically: Reflections on the European Union's 'Democratic Deficit'," *Journal of Political Philosophy* 5:2 (June 1997): 163–82.

Power, Michael K. "Habermas and the Counterfactual Imagination," *Habermas on Law and Democracy: Critical Exchanges,* ed. Michel Rosenfeld and Andrew Arato. Berkeley: University of California Press, 1998.

Preuss, Ulrich. "Constitutional Powermaking for the New Polity: Some Deliberations on the Relations between Constituent Power and the Constitution," *Cardozo Law Review* 14 (January 1993): 639–60.

Rahe, Paul. *Republics Ancient and Modern.* Chapel Hill: University of North Carolina Press, 1992.

Rawls, John. *The Law of Peoples.* Cambridge, MA: Harvard University Press, 1999.

——*Political Liberalism.* New York: Columbia University Press, 1993.

Rehg, William. "Against Subordination: Morality, Discourse, and Decision in the Legal Theory of Jürgen Habermas," in *Habermas on Law and Democracy: Critical*

178 *Globalization and Popular Sovereignty*

    Exchanges, ed. Michel Rosenfeld and Andrew Arato. Berkeley and Los Angeles: University of California Press, 1998.

Reinicke, Wolfgang H. *Global Public Policy: Governing without Government?* Washington, DC: Brookings Institution, 1989.

Riley, Patrick. *Will and Political Legitimacy*. Cambridge, MA: Harvard University Press, 1982.

Roberts, Sam. "Whites to be Minority in New York Area Soon, Data Show," *New York Times*, March 7, 2006, p. B1.

Robertson, Roland. *Globalization: Social Theory and Global Culture*. London: Sage, 1992.

——"Glocalization: Time–Space and Homogeneity–Heterogeneity," in *Global Modernities*, ed. Mike Featherstone, Scott Lash, and Roland Robertson. London: Sage, 1995.

Robinson, William I. *Transnational Conflicts*. London: Verso, 2003.

Rosenau, James N. *Distant Proximities*. Princeton, NJ: Princeton University Press, 2003.

——"Governance in a New Global Order," in *Governing Globalization*, ed. David Held and Anthony McGrew. Cambridge: Polity Press, 2002.

——"Governance and Democracy in a Globalizing World," in *Reimagining Political Community*, ed. Daniele Archibugi, David Held, and Martin Köhler. Stanford, CA: Stanford University Press, 1998.

——"Governance in the Twenty-first Century," *Global Governance* 1 (1995).

——*Along the Domestic–Foreign Frontier*. Cambridge: Cambridge University Press, 1997.

——*Turbulence in World Politics*. Brighton: Harvester Wheatsheaf, 1990.

Rosenau, James, and Ernst-Otto Czempiel. *Governance without Government: Order and Change in World Politics*. Cambridge: Cambridge University Press, 1992.

Rousseau, Jean-Jacques. *The* Discourses *and other early Political Writings*, ed. Victor Gourevitch, ed. Cambridge: Cambridge University Press, 1997.

——*The Social Contract and other later Political Writings*, ed. Victor Gourevitch. Cambridge: Cambridge University Press, 1997.

——"Lettre a Malesherbes," 1249, January 12, 1762. *Correspondance Générale de Jean-Jacques Rousseau*, ed. Dufour and Plan, twenty volumes. Paris, 1924–34. Vol. VII, p. 5051.

——*Emile, or, On Education*, trans. Alan Bloom. New York: Basic Books, 1979.

——"Extrait du projet de paix perpétuelle de Monsieur l'abbé de Saint-Pierre," *Oeuvres Complètes*. Paris: Gallimard, 1964.

Sassen, Saskia. *The Global City: New York, London, Tokyo*, second edition. Princeton, NJ: Princeton University Press, 2001.

——*Losing Control? Sovereignty in an Age of Globalization*. New York: Columbia University Press, 1996.

Scheuerman, William E. "Critical Theory beyond Habermas," *The Oxford Handbook to Political Theory*. Oxford: Oxford University Press, 2006.

——"Cosmopolitan Democracy and the Rule of Law," *Ratio Juris* 15 (2002): 439–57.

——"Globalization and Democratic Theory," *Polity* 33 (winter 2001): 331–42.

——"Between Radicalism and Resignation: Democratic Theory in Habermas's *Between Facts and Norms*," in *Habermas: A Critical Reader*, ed. Peter Dews. Oxford: Blackwell, 1999.

Schmitt, Carl. *Political Theology: Four Chapters on the Concept of Sovereignty*, trans. George Schwab. Cambridge, MA: MIT Press, 1985 [German revised edition, 1934].
——*The Crisis of Parliamentary Democracy*, trans. Ellen Kennedy. Cambridge, MA: MIT Press, 1985).
——*Teoría de la constitución*, trans. Francisco Ayala. Madrid: Alianza, 1982.
——*Die Diktatur.* Leipzig: Duncker & Humblot, 1922.
Scholte, Jan Aart. "Global Capitalism and the State," *International Affairs* 73:3 (July 1997): 427–52.
——"The WTO and Civil Society," *Journal of World Trade* 33:1 (February 1999): 107–24.
Scott, John T. "Rousseau's Anti-agenda-setting Agenda and Contemporary Democratic Theory," *American Political Science Review* 99:1 (February 2005): 137–44.
Sen, Amartya. *Development as Freedom.* New York: Anchor Books, 1999.
Seers, Dudley. *The Political Economy of Nationalism.* Oxford: Oxford University Press, 1983.
Sewell, William H., Jr. *A Rhetoric of Bourgeois Revolution: The Abbé Sieyés and What is the Third Estate?* Durham, NC: Duke University Press, 1994.
Shapiro, Ian. *The Moral Foundation of Politics.* New Haven, CT: Yale University Press, 2003.
——*Democratic Justice.* New Haven, CT: Yale University Press, 1999.
Shklar, Judith. *Men and Citizens: A Study of Rousseau's Social Theory.* Cambridge: Cambridge University Press, 1969.
Sieyés, Emmanuel Joseph. *What is the Third Estate?* ed. S. E. Finer. New York: Praeger, 1964.
Skinner, Quentin. *The Foundations of Modern Political Thought.* Cambridge: Cambridge University Press, 1978.
Slaughter, Anne-Marie. *A New World Order.* Princeton, NJ: Princeton University Press, 2004.
——"The Real New World Order," *Foreign Affairs* 76:5 (September–October 1997): 183–97.
Starobinski, Jean. *Jean-Jacques Rousseau: Transparency and Obstruction*, trans. Arthur Goldhammer. Chicago: Unversity of Chicago Press, 1988.
Steger, Manfred B. *Globalism: Market Ideology meets Terrorism*, second edition. New York: Rowman & Littlefield, 2005.
Stiglitz, Joseph E. *Globalization and its Discontents.* New York: Norton, 2003.
Strange, Susan. *The Retreat of the State.* Cambridge: Cambridge University Press, 1996.
Tarrow, Sidney. *The New Transnational Activism.* Cambridge: Cambridge University Press, 2005.
Teubner, Gunther, ed. *Global Law without a State.* Aldershot: Dartmouth, 1997.
Touraine, Alain. "Meaningless Politics," *Constellations* 10:3 (September 2003): 298–311.
Tully, James. "On Law, Democracy and Imperialism." Twenty-first annual public lecture, Centre for Law and Society, University of Edinburgh, March 10–11, 2005.
——*An Approach to Political Philosophy: Locke in Contexts.* Cambridge: Cambridge University Press, 1993.
United Nations Development Programme (UNDP). "Democracy in Latin America: Towards a Citizens' Democracy," Geneva: UNDP, 2004.
——*Human Development Report.* New York: Oxford University Press, 1999.

Urbinati, Nadia. "Continuity and Rupture: The Power of Judgment in Democratic Representation," *Constellations* 12:2 (June 2005): 194–222.
Urquhart, Brian. "The Outlaw World," *New York Review of Books* 53:8 (May 11, 2006): 25–28.
Vargas Llosa, Álvaro. "The Return of Latin America's Left," Op-Ed, *New York Times*, March 22, 2005, p. A23.
Wallerstein, Immanuel. "States? Sovereignty?" in *States and Sovereignty in the Global Economy*, ed. D. A. Smith, D. J. Solinger, and S. C. Topik. New York: Routledge,1999.
Weber, Max. *The Theory of Social and Economic Organization*, trans. A. M. Henderson and Talcott Parsons, ed. Talcott Parsons. London: Oxford University Press, 1947.
Weinstein, Fred, and Gerald M. Platt. "Rousseau: the Ambivalent Democrat," in *The Wish to be Free*. Los Angeles: University of California Press, 1969.
Wendt, Alexander. "A Comment on Held's Cosmopolitanism," in *Democracy's Edges*, ed. Ian Shapiro and Casiano Hacker-Cordón. Cambridge: Cambridge University Press, 1999.
Williams, Howard. "Rousseau: The Impossibility of International Harmony," in *International Relations in Political Theory*. Philadelphia: Open University Press, 1992.
Wood, Gordon. *The Creation of the American Republic, 1776–1787.* New York: Norton, 1998.
Woods, Ngaire. "Global Governance and the Role of Institutions," in *Governing Globalization*, ed. David Held and Anthony McGrew. Oxford, Polity Press, 2002.
———"Governing the Global Economy: Strengthening Multilateral Institutions." New York: International Peace Institute, 2008.
Yack, Bernard. "Popular Sovereignty and Nationalism," *Political Theory* 29:4 (August 2001): 517–36.
Yashar, Deborah J. "Contesting Citizenship: Indigenous Movements and Democracy in Latin America," *Comparative Politics* 31 (October 1998): 23–42.
———"Democracy, Indigenous Movements, and the Postliberal Challenge in Latin America," *World Politics* 52 (October 1999): 76–104.
Zolo, Danilo. "The Lords of Peace: From the Holy Alliance to the New International Criminal Tribunals," in *Global Democracy*, ed. B. Holden. New York: Routledge, 2000.

Index

absolute sovereignty 9–15, 18–20
abuse of power 34, 40, 67, 91, 113, 138
accounting standards 37, 121
Acton, Lord 50–51
advocacy *see* transnational advocacy networks
African Union 106
Algeria 62
alienation of power 29
Althusius, Johannes 34
Andean Community 105
arbitration, international 39
Archibugi, Daniele 94
Arendt, Hannah 10
Aristotle 10
Association of South-East Asian Nations (ASEAN) 105
Austin, John 30
authoritarian leadership 81
autonomy, democratic 114–17

Balibar, Etienne 130
Barber, Benjamin 92
Beck, Ulrich 40
Benhabib, Seyla 63–64, 70
Bergsten, C. Fred 135
Bernstein, Richard 83
Bobbio, Norberto 39
Bodin, Jean 11–15, 24, 29, 44, 46
Bohman, James 73–74, 77
Bolivia 41, 105
"boundary court" proposal 113
Brazil 40–41
Brunkhorst, Hauke 65
Bush, George W. (and Bush doctrine) x, 6, 118, 128–29

Castells, Manuel 104, 121–22
censorship 57

center-periphery divide 75–77
Chambers, Simone 124
Chavez, Hugo 21
China 2, 57, 60, 96, 129–30
Chomsky, Noam 90
citizenship: categories of 64; democratic xi, 82; disaggregated 119–21; legal definition of 100; liberal 67; and nation 80–82; postnational 99
civic-republicanism 99
"civil religion" (Rousseau) 54–55
civil society 12–15, 24–35, 45–47, 51–52, 56, 107; global 42, 112, 121–28, 134, 141; transnational 120, 140
civil war 29
climate change 125
Cohen, Jean 119–20
collective self-determination 44–45, 49, 57–59, 67, 77–83, 87, 114–15, 132–33
Colombia 62, 105
communicative action 69–70
consensus, rules of 72–73
consent, theory of 26–27, 31–34
constitution drafting 53–54
constitutionalism 19–20
constitutive authority 79, 133–35; challenge to 36–38; of the people 31–33, 133–34; sovereignty as 24–26
co-optation of sovereignty 49
cosmopolitan democracy 8, 91, 94, 99–100, 111–20, 126, 133–35; and regionalism 107–10
cosmopolitan founding, problem of 3, 8–9, 93, 112, 117–21, 126–27, 137, 140; and popular sovereignty 133–35
Cox, Robert 38
credit crunch (2008) x, 1–2
cultural diversity 91, 132
cultural homogeneity 82

182 Index

culture industry 92
Cutler, A. Claire 36, 38

Dean, Jodi 75
democracy, attitudes to 1
democratic deficit 2, 123, 130
democratic ethos 83
democratic principle of consensus 72–73, 78
demos 51
developing countries 60
Dicey, A.V. 14, 28
Diderot, Denis 48
discourse ethics 70–72
discourse principle 72–73, 77–79
discourse theory of democracy 87–88, 98
Dryzek, John 124

Ecuador 105
environmentalism 112, 125
equality: legal 51, 100; material 51
ethnic cleansing 81, 90
ethnonationalism 99–102
European Convention on Human Rights 90
European Parliament 98
European political integration 100–102
European Union 2, 63–64, 95–109, 134, 137; proposed constitution for 89, 98–101, 117, 130, 139
Faux, Jeff 60

Fishkin, James 138
Foreign Policy (magazine) 23
"fragmegration" (Rosenau) 42
France and the French Revolution 16–20, 43, 63, 80, 102
Fraser, Nancy 75–76
free trade 60
Friedman, Thomas 57
Friends of the Earth 125
Fukuyama, Francis 130

Gaitán, Jorge Eliécer 21
Garrett, Geoffrey 60
Gazprom 2
general will, the, concept of 45–51, 54, 57–59, 67, 81
genocide 81, 89–90
Georgia 41
Germany 61, 80
Giddens, Anthony 5

global governance 8, 21–22, 36–40, 94, 108, 110–13, 121, 123, 126, 129, 135–36, 139–41
"globality" (Beck) 40
globalization 106, 109, 111–20, 126, 129–36; alternative perspectives on 6; challenges of 35–38, 55–66, 87–96, 102; of consent, right and legitimacy 38–40; criticisms of 92; definitions of 4–5; differential impact of 92–93; and regionalism 95–99; and resistance 40–42
"glocalisation" 92
Google 57
governmental authority 45–46, 79
Gray, John 33
Greenpeace 125
Grotius, Hugo 32
"guaranteed autonomy of public spheres" 77

Habermas, Jürgen 1, 7–8, 20–21, 25, 42, 65–109, 120–21, 132, 134, 138–41
Haider, Jörg 63
Held, David 6–8, 65, 94–95, 110–23, 134
Herder, Johann Gottfried 81
Hettne, Björn 97
Hinsley, F.H. 9, 19
Hobbes, Thomas 11–15, 20, 24–25, 29–32, 35, 43, 54
Holy Roman Empire 57
human rights 4, 89–91, 108, 112–15, 120, 123, 132, 136
humanitarian intervention 90
hyperglobalist perspective 6

ideal speech situation 71
immigration and immigrant communities 61–64
imperialism 58, 90–91, 129
imperium 10–15, 138
India 196
inequality 59–61, 132
International Accounting Standards Committee 37, 121
International Chamber of Commerce 37
international community, the 7, 112–13, 137
International Criminal Court 90, 125, 128
International Labour Organization 92
international law 58, 89–91, 112, 118, 128–29
International Monetary Fund (IMF) 44, 133

internet access 92
Iraq and the Iraq War (2003) 1, 23, 90, 128

Kant, Immanuel (and Kantianism) 19, 139
Kearney, A.T. 23
Keck, Margaret 41, 125
Keohane, Robert 58
Keynesian policies 40
Kopstein, Jeff 124
Kosovo campaign (1999) 90
Krasner, Stephen 112

landmines campaign 123, 125
Latin America 1, 21, 44, 105, 130, 137
lawgivers 53–55
Lawson, George 34–35
legal validity as distinct from power 10
legitimacy, democratic 72–74, 78, 108–10, 119–21, 126, 130, 134, 137, 140
Le Pen, Jean Marie 63
lex digitalis 36–37
lex mercatoria 36–38, 131
Lisbon Treaty 89, 99
Locke, John 13–15, 23–24, 31–35, 46, 50, 52, 77–81, 87–88, 131–32, 138
Lula da Silva, Luiz Ignácio 40–41

McAdam, Doug 139
McCarthy, Thomas 71, 73
McGrew, Anthony 6, 95
Madison, James 19
Marxism 117
Maus, Ingeborg 78
"metadiscourse" (Rehg) 73
Mexico 62
Michelman, Frank 84–85
Migdal, Joel 106
Milanovic, Bruno 60
military force 108, 113, 134
Milosevic, Slobodan 41
Mittelman, James 116
monarchomach literature 34–35
Morales, Eva 41
Mouffe, Chantal 75
multiculturalism 63, 82, 85–86, 114
multilayered governance 39, 108

nation-states: capacities of 95–97; defining characteristics of 95; role of 111–13, 116, 132–35
national culture 81

national identity and nationhood 53, 62–63, 96
national sovereignty 16–19
nationalism 80, 83; civic 84, 99; ethnic *see* ethnonationalism; extended 99, 102–3, 109
nationality, concept of 50
natural law 25–26
nébuleuse, the (Cox) 38
neoliberal ideology and policies 44, 60, 101, 117
network governance 121–26, 133–34
non-governmental organizations (NGOs) 41, 125
North Atlantic Treaty Organization (NATO) 133

Obama, Barack 130
Olympic Games, Beijing x
Organization for Economic Cooperation and Development (OECD) 124

parliamentary principle 77
participatory democracy 57
patriotism 55–56; constitutional 83–87, 91–92, 100, 102, 108, 132; and the democratic ethos 82–83
people, the: as the agent of revolution 34–35; concept of 94; constitutive authority of 31–33, 133–34; definition of 80; as a political category 39; postnational 99–102; sovereignty of 138; as the subject of consent 33
Peters, Bernhard 75
Poland 55
polis 16
political culture 100, 109, 118–21, 134
political discourses 73
popular sovereignty xi, 2–3, 12–15, 98, 120–21, 127; challenges to 7, 131–33; and collective self-ordering of society 45; concept of 129–30, 133; definition of 3; deliberative model of 67–93, 124, 132; development of theory of 20; effectiveness of 21; and global governance 8; and globalization 6, 10, 21; history of 10; instability of 35; in the international domain 128; liberal model of 23–42, 77; mediated form of 16; and norm-guided legal procedures 6, 19–20; participatory aspect of 51; as a principle of right 26; and the problem of cosmopolitan founding 133–35; as procedure 20–21,

68–69, 74; as protection against tyranny 64; and public consent 24; and the public sphere 74–77; rationalization of 15–16; in relation to state sovereignty 9; republican model of 43–66, 74–77; and rights 78–80, 89–91; transnational politics of 135–41; transnational 3, 8–9; utility of concept of 9; voluntaristic model of 20–21
population movements 61–62
populism 21, 90, 130
populus 10–15
positive law 17
"postnational constellation" 7–8, 94, 109
postnational democracy 97–103
poverty 61
Power, Michael 71
power, political 10, 20, 23; alienation of 29; definition of 32–35; *see also* abuse of power
private sphere 67
protectionism 103
public opinion 128
public sphere 67, 87, 91, 98, 138; and popular sovereignty 74–77; *strong* and *weak* 75–77, 88–89, 124, 132, 134
Pufendorf, Samuel von 32

radical individualism 13
ratio concept 10, 15–16, 19–20
Rawls, John 25, 82, 94
realism in international relations 112, 118, 129, 139
regime theory 117
regionalism 97–110, 120–21, 126, 133–34; alternative paths to 104–6; and cosmopolitan democracy 107–10; and globalization 95–99
Rehg, William 73
representation, principle of 16–18
resistance movements 40–42
"responsibility to protect" 137
revolution, right to engage in 29–30, 34–35, 138
rights 78, 96; categories of 82–83; without popular sovereignty 89–91
Riley, Patrick 47–48
Robertson, Roland 92
Robespierre, Maximilien 18
Roman Catholic Church 57
Roman Empire 10–11
Rosenau, James 42, 121–24

Rousseau, Jean-Jacques 14–18, 42–66, 69, 79, 81, 87–88, 113, 117, 129–32, 138, 141
rule of law 68, 79, 115, 136, 141
Russia 129–30

Saint-Pierre, Abbé 56
Sarkozy, Nicholas 63
Sassen, Saskia 93
Scheuerman, William 108
Schmitt, Carl 17, 20–21, 26, 30, 81
self-determination *see* collective self-determination
Sen, Amartya 61
separation of powers 20, 136
September 10th 2001 attacks x, 5–6, 23
Serbia 41
Shevardnadze, Eduard 41
Shklar, Judith 56
Sieyès, Emmanuel-Joseph 16–19, 26, 102, 138
Sikkink, Kathryn 41, 125
al-Sistani, Ali, Grand Ayatollah 1
skeptic perspective on globalization 6
Slaughter, Anne-Marie 88
social contract theory 12–15, 24–25, 31–32, 38, 43–44, 47–53
social democracy 118, 134
social justice 108, 113, 117, 123, 134
social norms 82
socialization 47, 50, 52, 87
solidarity, civic 108–10
South East Asia Treaty Organization (SEATO) 97
sovereign states 117, 133; *see also* state sovereignty
sovereignty: cosmopolitan 112–18; concept and theory of 11–12, 94; as constitutive authority 24–26; definitions of 45–46; Lockean 24–30, 35–44, 67, 69, 77, 87–88, 131, 138; as distinct from government 45–47, 138; *political* and *legal* 28; Rousseauian 44–50, 56–69, 77, 87–88, 131–32, 138; *see also* absolute sovereignty; national sovereignty; popular sovereignty; state sovereignty
Sparta 55–56
"standard-setting" arrangements 37
Starobinksi, Jean 44
state of nature 12–19, 24–33, 47, 52–53, 69
state sovereignty 58, 96, 137–40; challenges to 4; definition of 3–4; in

relation to popular sovereignty 9; *see also* sovereign states
states, role of 2–6, 33; *see also* nation-states
Strange, Susan 39
strategic action 69
supranational regimes 104, 112
Sweden 61

tacit consent 27
Tarrow, Sidney 139
territoriality 96
Teubner, Gunther 36–37
Tilly, Charles 139
time–space distanciation 5
totalitarian rule 46–48
transformationalism 6, 95
transnational advocacy networks 41, 125
transnational governance 8, 10; *see also* global governance
Tully, James 28, 30, 32, 34
tyranny 48, 64, 129

Ukraine 41
United Nations 37, 58, 89–90, 108; General Assembly 112–13, 135; *Human Development Reports* 92; Security Council 113, 128, 133, 140
United States 61, 118, 128–29, 133, 135; Constitution of 19
Universal Declaration of Human Rights 90, 113, 128
universalization principle 70–73

validity basis of speech 70
Venezuela 40
voluntas 10, 15–16, 19–20

War on Terror 23, 118
warfare 23, 56
"Washington consensus" 101
Weber, Max 106
welfare state provision 101
Westphalian state system 3–4, 108, 112, 118
Woods, Ngaire 37, 122
World Bank 2, 44, 133
World Economic Forum 38
World Social Forum 44, 61, 123
World Trade Organization x, 2, 4, 7, 139
world wide web 122

Yack, Bernard 31

eBooks – at www.eBookstore.tandf.co.uk

A library at your fingertips!

eBooks are electronic versions of printed books. You can store them on your PC/laptop or browse them online.

They have advantages for anyone needing rapid access to a wide variety of published, copyright information.

eBooks can help your research by enabling you to bookmark chapters, annotate text and use instant searches to find specific words or phrases. Several eBook files would fit on even a small laptop or PDA.

NEW: Save money by eSubscribing: cheap, online access to any eBook for as long as you need it.

Annual subscription packages

We now offer special low-cost bulk subscriptions to packages of eBooks in certain subject areas. These are available to libraries or to individuals.

For more information please contact webmaster.ebooks@tandf.co.uk

We're continually developing the eBook concept, so keep up to date by visiting the website.

www.eBookstore.tandf.co.uk